Dark City : The Film Noir

DARK CITY

The Film Noir

by
Spencer Selby

St-J
St James Press
Chicago and London

**Frontispiece: Burt Lancaster, playing "the Swede,"
awaits *The Killers* (Universal, 1956).**

Published in the United Kingdom by
St. James Press
3 Percy Street
London W1P 9FA
England

Originally published in the United States by
McFarland & Company, Inc., Publishers,
Jefferson, North Carolina

ISBN 1-55862-099-0

For "the girls," my parents,
and Kirk's collection

Acknowledgments

I would like to thank Richard Dyer MacCann, professor of film at the University of Iowa, for reading an early draft of the manuscript and giving encouragement at a time when I had almost given up hope of finding a publisher, Martha Wilson for translating portions of *Panorama du Film Noir Americain*, and Charles Scribner's Sons for permission to reprint part of Hemingway's "The Killers." I would also like to thank my brother, Kirk Selby, and Bill Hesson, whose friendship and general interest in movies was a source of early inspiration. Lastly and ultimately, I would like to extend very special thanks to the three most important people in my life: Biff O'Meara, Colleen Lookingbill and Sara O'Meara. Without their love and support, this project would surely never have been realized.

Table of Contents

Introduction

Film noir is a historical, stylistic and thematic trend that took place primarily, but not exclusively, within the generic complex of the American crime film* of the forties and fifties. The term was first introduced by French *cinéaste* Nino Frank in 1946. For many years it was known only to the French, who seemed to be the only ones equipped (critically or otherwise) to grapple with its definition and/or historical implications. The high water mark of this period of film criticism came with the publication of Borde and Chaumeton's *Panorama du Film Noir Americain* in 1955. After that not much was heard about film noir from the French or anyone else. Then in the late sixties, the term began cropping up in English and American criticism. Higham and Greenberg's *Hollywood in the Forties*, published in 1968, was the first book in English to devote an entire chapter to "black cinema." This landmark was followed by Raymond Durgnat's "The Family Tree of Film Noir," published in 1970. And while Durgnat's description of eleven film noir themes represented the first important attempt in English criticism to define noir, the article actually created almost as many confusions as it resolved about the subject.

Some of these confusions (or, perhaps, controversies) were all but cleared up in 1972 by Paul Schrader. In "Notes on Film Noir," he points out that Durgnat's most helpful contribution was the notion that film noir is not a genre: "It is not definded, as are the western and gangster genres, by conventions of setting and conflict, but rather by the more subtle qualities of tone and mood." Schrader goes on to describe the main components of noir style, things like visual chiaroscuro, voice-over narration and frequent flashback structures. In addition, he concisely elucidates both the artistic roots (German Expressionism, French "poetic realism,"

This includes the various and often overlapping generic headings of crime drama, gangster film, mystery, suspense thriller and psychological melodrama. Under these headings come a large array of subgenres, such as policier, detective, prison, heist, fight and newspaper films, as well as the frequent overlapping of crossbred genres like "the woman's picture" and the gothic and Victorian melodrama.

and the hard-boiled tradition in American literature) and the historical trends (postwar disillusionment and realism) that helped to produce the noir movement.

Though many of his ideas were not entirely original, Schrader's article was the first to approach noir from virtually every relevant perspective in a way that made it impossible not to have a fairly good (introductory, at least) feel for the term. In so doing, he came closer to resolving certain previous disagreements about film noir than anyone has since. For example, Borde and Chaumeton believed that realistic *policiers* like *Call Northside 777* (Hathaway, 1948) and *Boomerang* (Kazan, 1947) were not film noir. This was based upon defining the term too narrowly, and upon jumping too quickly to unwarranted conclusions about the philosophical and stylistic viewpoints of these films. Durgnat, on the other hand, had been guilty of defining the term too broadly, whereby certain famous gangster films of the thirties were wrongly classed as noir. By convincingly arguing that film noir is primarily a historical and stylistic trend of the forties and fifties, Schrader makes it clear that *Boomerang* definitely is a noir and *Scarface* (Hawks, 1932) is not.

A great deal has been written about film noir in the years since Schrader's article appeared. It is not within the scope of this study to cover or evaluate this published material. I will say that only two significant articles on the general subject of film noir have come to my attention in that time ("Some Visual Motifs of Film Noir," by Place and Peterson, 1974, and Robert G. Porfirio's "Existential Motifs in the Film Noir," published in 1976). As for books, a number have appeared in this country since 1976 (for a list, see "Works Cited," page 220), each taking a somewhat different approach and presenting different opinions on the subject. The most important of these books, by far, was Silver and Ward's *Film Noir*, a formidable encyclopedic reference work (actually written by twenty people) which describes and analyzes some 300 films. Even this book, however, leaves sizable gaps and confusions in our understanding of this great cycle of films.

The present work is divided into two main sections. The first comprises a detailed, film-by-film analysis of twenty-five notable films noirs. Each of these twenty-five articles is in two parts, a detailed plot synopsis and an interpretive essay. Though the essays are mainly concerned with thematic discussion, stylistic or structural aspects are dealt with when they relate closely to a film's primary themes. In addition, particular attention is often paid to certain sophisticated or deeper levels of meaning, which are then related back to an overall interpretation of the film. The goal is to demonstrate that these meanings do exist, by developing a method through which the reader can restructure them within a complete narrative context.

It should be stressed that no attempt was made to fit the films to any preconceived or accepted notions of noir thematics. This tendency has been a major problem with previous material on film noir. In writing this book, I have approached each film as a unique, creative entity, with its own special thematic content and view of life. Resulting connections between films or overall noir images were thus limited to their actual occurrence rather than attempts by a zealous critic to derive them.

Readers who are more interested in such connections or in overall noir definitions will perhaps be attracted to the second section of this book, an exhaustive filmography of nearly 500 films noirs. This filmography, the largest ever compiled, includes the basic credits of each film and a sentence or two of description, noting the basic story line and giving further significant information whenever appropriate.

It is the position of this book that the film noir represented an outburst of artistic maturity, style and meaning which is still unappreciated and, in some ways, unsurpassed today. I believe that film noir must be and shall always remain something of an enigma. The classification of films has always been a tenuous business, and with film noir, which is perhaps the most slippery of all film categories, complications of this type reach a level of almost baffling complexity. Still, there is something very important about the idea of film noir, whether or not we are able to completely pin it down. With this firm conviction in mind, I have written and now offer *Dark City*.

Twenty-Five Films Noirs

The Maltese Falcon (1941)

Director: John Huston. *Screenplay*: John Huston, from the novel by Dashiell Hammett. *Photography*: Arthur Edeson. *Music*: Adolph Deutsch. *Art Director*: Robert Haas. *Film Editor*: Thomas Richards. *Producer*: Hal B. Wallis. *Production/release*: Warner Brothers, October, 1941. 100 minutes. **Cast**: Humphrey Bogart (playing Sam Spade), Mary Astor (Brigid O'Shaughnessy), Gladys George (Iva Archer), Peter Lorre (Joel Cairo), Barton MacLane (Lt. Detective Dundy), Lee Patrick (Effie Perine), Sydney Greenstreet (Kasper Gutman), Ward Bond (Detective Tom Polhaus), Jerome Cowan (Miles Archer), Elisha Cook, Jr. (Wilmer Cook), Walter Huston (Captain Jacobi), James Burke, Murray Alper, John Hamilton, Emory Parnell.

Brigid O'Shaughnessy comes to private detective Sam Spade and hires him to follow Floyd Thursby, who she says has run away with her sister. Spade's partner, Miles Archer, agrees to tail Thursby when he meets her that night. Spade gets a call late that evening informing him that Archer has been murdered. Spade seems unaffected by his partner's death and refuses to tell the police much about the case he was working on. The police become very suspicious of Spade when Thursby is shot hours after Archer's body has been discovered. Archer's wife visits Spade at his office the next day and asks him if he killed his partner to be with her. Despite their obvious past, Spade is now sickened by this woman and quickly gets rid of her. Spade goes to see Brigid at her apartment. He knew she was lying from the start and now he demands the truth about her and Thursby. She lies some more, and Spade is obviously attracted to her. For all of her money, he promises to conceal her existence from the police and look after her interests, even though he doesn't know much about them. Joel Cairo visits Spade at his office and offers him $5,000 for a statuette known as the Maltese Falcon. Cairo intends to search Spade's office but is easily disarmed and knocked out cold when he tries to pull a gun on the slick detective. Spade eventually agrees to look for the falcon and laughingly lets Cairo search his office. Spade then returns to Brigid and tries to fish more information out of her, with little success. When Brigid asks him what she can offer besides money, Spade brutally embraces

her. The two of them meet with Cairo that evening. Brigid tells Cairo that she will have the falcon in less than a week, and they guardedly discuss their past dealings with "the fat man" in Istanbul. The police show up, and Spade stops them at the door. When Cairo starts fighting with Brigid, Spade is forced to let the cops in. They demand an explanation, and Spade gives them a false story consistent with their somewhat limited knowledge. After the cops and Cairo leave, Spade tries again to get more information out of Brigid, but she puts him off by seducing him. The next day Spade meets "the fat man," Kasper Gutman. Neither party is willing to divulge what he knows first, and Spade leaves in an apparently false act of rage. The police pull Spade in, and he tells them off, confident that they have nothing on him. Spade then returns to Gutman, who tells him the exotic story of the falcon and its origin. Gutman had hired Brigid and Thursby to steal the falcon away from a Russian general in Istanbul, and they betrayed him. While discussing the falcon's value, Spade passes out (having been drugged by Gutman and Cairo). When he wakes up, Spade searches Gutman's apartment and finds a newspaper with the arrival of a ship from Hong Kong underlined. Spade gets to the dock just in time to see the abandoned ship burn down. Spade goes back to his office and a dying man staggers in with the falcon. Brigid phones the office, saying she is in trouble. Spade mails the falcon to himself and tries to find Brigid, but the address she gave over the phone was false. Spade arrives at his home to find Cairo, Brigid, Gutman and Wilmer ("the fat man's" trusty gunsel) waiting for him. Spade agrees to turn over the falcon for $10,000 if they can find a "fall guy" for the murders that the police are hounding him about. Spade relishes picking Wilmer as the logical choice, since he feels sure that the gunsel probably did commit several of the murders. Gutman first refuses but later agrees to sell out Wilmer when Spade analyzes the delicacy and danger of his alternatives. Gutman then gives Spade the part of the plot that he and the viewers had missed: Gutman had Wilmer kill Thursby to scare Brigid into returning the falcon. Cairo guessed that the captain of the La Paloma was bringing the falcon to Brigid, since he knew the two were friends. Cairo, Gutman and Wilmer found Captain Jacoby with Brigid on the ship. Wilmer shot him but could not stop him. Brigid was persuaded to try and draw Spade away from his office before Jacoby arrived there, but the call came too late. Having learned as much as Gutman knows, Spade has his secretary bring them the falcon. To everyone's disappointment, the statuette turns out to be a fake. As the group tries to recompose themselves, they realize that Wilmer has escaped. Gutman quickly accepts another failure and vows to continue his pursuit of the real bird along with Cairo. As soon as they leave, Spade phones the police and turns them in. That leaves one final loose end. Spade forces Brigid to confess to Archer's murder. She appeals to their love and begs him not to turn her in. Spade admits that he might love Brigid, but says there's too many other reasons for turning her in, the main one being that he can't bring himself to trust her. Having captured the others, the police arrive at Spade's. He turns Brigid over to them, and the case is closed.

Sam Spade cleverly pretends to share the evil which motivates the other contestants in the fight for the Maltese Falcon, so as to trap them and bring them to justice. While the film may superficially accommodate such a view (which sees Spade as a traditional hero nobly battling the forces of evil), close scrutiny yields a much more ambiguous interpretation of Spade's character. To begin with, he is quite unmoved by Archer's death. One could almost say that he treats it as an unextraordinary occurrence. Several scenes later, we learn that he has been having an affair with Archer's wife. We also learn that he never really liked her much, and that he now wants nothing more to do with her. This may be because Archer has been killed or it may be because she has been replaced by someone who interests Spade more, namely Brigid O'Shaughnessy. One cannot really say, nor can one say what Spade's motives are toward Brigid. As with his pretense of evil, it is not clear how much Spade is putting on an act.

The first scene with Gutman is quite illustrative of the kind of ambiguity we are dealing with here. When Gutman refuses to give him information about the falcon, Spade blows up, as if to indicate his own impatient greed. Spade then leaves Gutman's apartment and laughs about the role he has just played. Spade's motivation would be clear if it were left at that, but it isn't. In the midst of laughing off the act, Spade glances down at his hands, which are visibly trembling. This little touch has an importance which is well out of proportion with its minor emphasis, for it would seem to imply that Spade wasn't in such total control after all and that his rage wasn't entirely an act.

This ambiguity is further developed in Spade's final confrontation with the four criminals who quest for the falcon. One can never really say that Spade is not tempted to accept Gutman's $10,000 offer for the bird. Sacrificing Wilmer to the police seems the perfect arrangement, since the gunsel actually is guilty of two of the three murders in the case. On the other hand, one can argue that this fall guy demand is just a clever way of getting at the truth, and that Spade never intends to make such a deal. Since Wilmer escapes and the falcon turns out to be a fake, we can never know for sure which view is correct. All we can do is focus in on Spade's own declaration to Brigid in the last scene:

> *Brigid*: Would you have done this to me if the falcon had been real, and you'd got your money?
>
> *Spade*: Don't be too sure I'm as crooked as I'm supposed to be. That sort of reputation might be good business—bringing high priced jobs and making it easier to deal with the enemy, but a lot more money would have been one more item on your side of the ledger.

Spade can't quite bring himself to say for sure that he wouldn't have given in to temptation. In admitting that a lot more money would have been an undeniable factor, he leaves open the possibility that $10,000 could have tipped the scales in Brigid's favor. For this reason, we cannot use this declaration to resolve the doubt about Spade's pretense of evil. Spade refuses to maintain complete assurance regarding his "act," and the viewer must share his doubt.

The importance of this climactic confrontation cannot be over-stressed. Any conclusions that we are to make about Spade must be based primarily upon the things he says to Brigid in those tense minutes before the police arrive. Spade's overriding self-protective motives are evident from the start. As he tries to get Brigid to confess to her crime, Spade says, "We're both of us sitting under the gallows." Spade acts as if Brigid must confess for their mutual protection, but this is obviously not so. What he really means is that *he's* sitting under the gallows until *she* confesses. By the time she does admit her crime, Spade seems to relish her fear: "Yes, Angel, I'm gonna send you over. The chances are you'll get off with life. That means if you're a good girl, you'll be out in twenty years. I'll be waiting for you. If they hang you, I'll always remember you." The ruthless irony with which Spade delivers these lines indicates anything but real sympathy for Brigid's plight. He truly seems to hate her at this point, and she responds with an accusation charged with its own kind of irony: "You've been playing with me; just pretending you cared, to trap me like this. You don't care at all! You don't love me!" This comment could represent Spade's distrust as well as Brigid's. He replies that he won't "play the sap" for her, and she desperately tries to argue the existence of their mutual love. Spade refuses to completely deny the love but maintains that other factors make it untenable. The hatred seems to have gone out of Spade at this point, and he makes one last attempt to explain to Brigid why he must turn her in:

> Listen, This won't do any good. You'll never understand me, but I'll try once, and then give it up. When a man's partner's killed, he's supposed to do something about it. It doesn't make any difference what you thought of him. He was your partner and you're supposed to do something about it. And it happens we're in the detective business. Well, when one of your organization gets killed, it's bad for business to let the killer get away with it; bad all around, bad for every detective everywhere.

Spade's attempt to invoke some sort of committment to his profession as a factor in his decision only serves to reinforce one's feelings about his selfish motivation. It is obvious that he cares about his partner and other detectives mainly because it is to his own advantage. He must help them discourage murdering detectives to protect his own life and business. At any rate, the viewer tends to agree with Brigid when she replies, "You don't expect me to think that these things you're saying are sufficient reasons to send me to the ..." Spade interrupts her saying, "Wait'll I'm through. Then you can talk. I've no earthly reason to think I can trust you. And if I do this and get away with it, you'll have something on me that you can use whenever you want to. Since I've got something on you, I couldn't be sure that you wouldn't put a hole in me some day." Spade coldly analyzes his decision by weighing the benefits against the risks of both alternatives. He admits that some of the reasons for turning Brigid in may be unimportant, but still maintains that the risks of letting her go outweigh the possibility of mutual love. It seems fairly certain that Spade has a strong emotional feeling for her. The question is whether it could be called real love. Brigid maintains that love could never be outweighed by the factors Spade has outlined, and Spade has no reply for that one. The viewer is forced to agree with Brigid and admit that Spade refuses to let himself really love her because it is too dangerous.

Turning Brigid in may very well be the "right" thing to do, but Spade does it for the wrong reasons. He cares nothing about the immorality or illegality of her act. Nor does he really care much about avenging her victim. He denies the feelings he has for her and sends her to prison by following the same self-protective instincts that motivate all of his actions. One comes to feel that Spade is on the right side of the law because it is safe and still lucrative, and because he would rather be the hunter than the hunted. This is the ultimate irony of the film. Hammett's detective hero is motivated by the same basic selfishness that leads the criminals he captures into evil. Psychologically speaking, he is little better than them. He will never kill anyone, but Hammett makes it clear that this is not because he has any real moral convictions. Spade is morally superior to the film's villains only because it is to his advantage to be. He won't kill anyone for the same reason that he refuses to love Brigid—it's too risky.

The audience's fascination with Bogart's Spade is largely due to his great skill at manipulating the other characters in the film. Rather than triumphing over evil, he beats the evil at their own game and then slickly extracts himself from their web at the last moment. He is a cold-hearted businessman who prefers to satisfy his twisted needs on the right side of the law. He probably knew Brigid murdered Archer all along and was still strongly attracted to her. One is almost tempted to say that he was attracted to her evil, but he could never go all the way and admit the nature of his attraction because he was afraid of the consequences. Such a fear may be healthy morally, but nothing we learn about Spade indicates that morality prompted it. While the film's other characters may have been bold or desperate or stupid enough to challenge the law, Spade is simply too deft at protecting his own position to take such a chance. Being a good gambler, he knows that the odds are always in favor of the house.

Double Indemnity (1944)

Director: Billy Wilder. *Screenplay*: Billy Wilder and Raymond Chandler from the novel by James M. Cain. *Photographer*: John F. Seitz. *Music*: Miklos Rozsa. *Art Director*: Hal Pereira. *Film Editor*: Doane Harrison. *Producer*: Joseph Sistrom. *Production/release*: Paramount, May, 1944. 106 minutes. **Cast**: Fred MacMurray (playing Walter Neff), Barbara Stanwyck (Phyllis Dietrichson), Edward G. Robinson (Barton Keyes), Jean Heather (Lola Dietrichson), Tom Powers (Mr. Dietrichson), Porter Hall (Mr. Jackson), Byron Barr (Nino Zachetti), Richard Gaines, Fortunio Bonaova, John Philliber.

Self-confident insurance salesman Walter Neff becomes romantically involved with the seductive Phyllis Dietrichson while trying to sell her husband a routine automobile policy. It doesn't take long for Phyllis to reveal thoughts of murdering her husband. After a futile attempt to walk out on her, Neff agrees to plan the perfect crime. By switching contracts, he sells the husband a fifty thousand dollar life insurance policy with double indemnity provisions. The next step involves waiting for the right set of circumstances to arise. The perfect opportunity finally comes when Mr. Dietrichson plans a business trip on the train. After meticulously establishing an alibi, Neff hides in the Dietrichson's car and murders Mr. Dietrichson on the way to the train station. Neff then boards the train, masquerading as Dietrichson. At a prearranged point, he jumps off the train and meets Phyllis. Together they dump Dietrichson's body on the tracks, so that it looks like he was killed falling off the train. Having pulled off the crime without a hitch, Neff and Phyllis now must sweat out the resulting investigation of Dietrichson's death. The police suspect no foul play, but they aren't the only ones investigating the case. Barton Keyes, Neff's close friend and the insurance company's crack claims manager, isn't satisfied with the authorities' conclusion. This is when all the trouble starts for Neff. First, Keyes visits him at his apartment and nearly runs into Phyllis. Then Phyllis' young stepsister comes to Neff and discloses some dangerous suspicions that she harbors. Lola Dietrichson tells Neff of the mysterious circumstances surrounding her mother's death years before, and how she had always suspected Phyllis (who had been the mother's nurse) of foul play. Having seen Phyllis trying on mourning attire before her husband's "accidental" death, Lola again suspects that she is responsible. Neff listens sympathetically to Lola but carefully cautions her against taking any action. The next bad break comes when Keyes introduces Neff to the one man who saw him on the train. Though the witness doesn't recognize Neff, he does swear that the man on the train was not Dietrichson, and Keyes now seems positive that murder is involved. By this time, things are becoming strained between Neff and Phyllis. She is anxious to sue for the insurance claim, but he warns her to hold off because of Keyes. In addition, she has become suspicious of his meetings with Lola, and they argue about this. That evening, Lola meets Neff and tells him that her boyfriend has been seeing Phyllis. Lola believes that the two of them killed her father together. Quickly realizing that Lola's accusation would probably bring out the truth, Neff persuades her to keep quiet for a few more days. The next morning, Keyes tells Neff that he's cracked the case wide open. The desperate Neff sneaks into Keyes' office while he is out and listens to his dictaphone to find out what has been concluded. It turns out that Keyes thinks the same thing as Lola. On the dictaphone is a letter advising the immediate arrest of Phyllis and Nino Zachetti, Lola's boyfriend. Neff races to Phyllis' house with the intention of killing her and framing Zachetti for both murders. When Neff tells Phyllis of his plan, she shoots *him* first. The wounded Neff dares Phyllis to finish the job, but she can't bring herself to do it. Phyllis breaks down in a genuine display of emotion, but Neff isn't buying it. He grimly

Top: Barbara Stanwyck (playing Phyllis Dietrichson) and Fred MacMurray (Walter Neff) execute the murder plan; bottom: Edward G. Robinson (left, as Barton Keyes) confronts MacMurray at the conclusion. *Double Indemnity* (Paramount, 1944).

shoots her and takes a taxi to the insurance office, where he dictates a letter to Keyes confessing the whole story. The film actually begins when Neff arrives to dictate his confession. This dictation serves as the first-person narration which accompanies the flashbacks that make up the bulk of the film. When Neff's story is done, he looks up to see Keyes standing in the door of the office. He makes a feeble effort to escape, but gets no farther than that same door before collapsing. Keyes calls an ambulance, and together they wait for the authorities to arrive.

Identification with a murderer and his murder plot made *Double Indemnity* a groundbreaker in American film history. Consistent with this radical structure, the film displays a central theme which delves beyond the obvious treatment of an all-pervasive evil. Though the narrative seems focused upon the protagonist and his *femme fatale* accomplice, they are really no more important than their notorious nemesis, Barton Keyes. He is the self-appointed guardian of society's rules that Neff loves (like a father?) but must defeat. Keyes represents morality while Neff is seemingly motivated by ambition, desire and greed.

Wilder's emphasis on Neff's evil is carefully balanced by the crucial flaws of Keyes' guardian of the law. He is intolerant, inflexible, self-righteous and incapable of sympathy or forgiveness. This personality is stressed through his early encounter with a dumb truck driver guilty of petty insurance fraud. Keyes treats the man with haughty disgust and is only interested in obtaining his written confession nullifying the fraudulent claim. When the trucker makes a feeble attempt to explain his circumstances, Keys insultingly throws him out.

According to his own description, Keyes has a "little man" inside him who suspects everyone of wrongdoing. Whenever his intuitive stomach acts up, he knows that there is evil at hand which must be caught and punished. This "little man" has determined the course of Keyes' entire life. When he was young, Keyes planned to marry a beautiful girl who he thought he loved. The "little man" started acting up, and Keyes promptly had his fiancée investigated. When he discovered her sordid past, Keyes broke the engagement and never became seriously involved with a woman again. This story, which Keyes tells Neff, further underscores the stringent, heartless intolerance which results from Keyes' obsessive absolutist morality.

Neff's motivation is directly linked to his relationship with Keyes in the important roulette wheel speech. Here Neff admits that it wasn't just desire and greed that prompted his decision to attempt the perfect murder. Like the man who runs the roulette wheel, Neff has learned the mechanics of the system to a degree impossible for the average gambler. Since the wheel itself is right under his hand, Neff feels that he has the power to beat the system, and the urge to do just that has been building in him for a long time.

In stark contrast to Keyes, Neff has no moral compunctions whatsoever. All his life he has followed the rules only due to fear of taking the criminal's risks. Keyes' emphasis on integrity means absolutely nothing to Neff. To him, you get whatever you have the guts to take, and that's all there is to it. Crime is just a dangerous game that you play with the social authority that Keyes represents.

Neff and Keyes symbolize Wilder's cynical view of good and evil in a society dominated by moral absolutism. Their extreme moral polarization is the direct result of that absolutism, and that is where Keyes' harsh, inflexible intolerance comes in. Keyes' absolutism forces him to deny the humanity of his victims. He refuses to try to understand them because such understanding would undercut his simplistic characterization of evil. Neff, on the other hand, understands Keyes perhaps too well. His attempt at the perfect crime is an act of irreverent rebellion. Since Keyes' harsh piety makes honest communication impossible, Neff is stimulated to challenge his friend's power.

Hopelessly trapped by their inflexible feelings about good and evil, the two men are doomed to play out that age-old game of concealment and detection. The irony is that they are still the closest of friends. Neff loves Keyes despite (or maybe because of) his moral stringency, and Keyes loves Neff even though he doesn't really know him. The climactic question if whether Keyes' love is dependent upon Neff's superficial veneer of morality. The final answer to this question must be a qualified no. Though Keyes is not about to relinquish his social role, it is still evident from his reactions in the last scene that he feels more sympathy than he has ever felt before for a criminal he has just caught. This, in itself, is a step forward for a man whose obsessive moral commitment turned people evil.

The structure of *Double Indemnity* is carefully calculated to get the viewer to take a similar step. One is encouraged to understand and even sympathize with Neff, without condoning his acts of murder. The result is a complex, deterministic attitude toward evil which places a great deal of blame on a hypocritical society that encourages immorality while still harshly punishing criminals.

The Woman in the Window (1944)

Director: Fritz Lang. *Screenplay*: Nunnally Johnson, from the novel *Once Off*

Guard by J.H. Wallis. *Photography*: Milton Krasner. *Special Effects*: Vernon Walder. *Music*: Arthur Lange. *Art Director*: Duncan Cramer. *Film Editor*: Paul Weatherwax. *Producer*: Nunnally Johnson. *Production*: International Pictures. *Release*: RKO, October 11, 1944. **Cast**: Edward G. Robinson (playing Richard Wanley), Joan Bennett (Alice Reed), Raymond Massey (D.A. Frank Lalor), Dan Duryea (Heidt), Edmond Breon (Dr. Barkstone), Arthur Loft (Mazard), Thomas E. Jackson, Dorothy Peterson, Frank Dawson, Bobby Blake.

Professor Richard Wanley is a middle-aged instructor of psychology at a small urban college. While his family is away on vacation, Wanley spends much of his time socializing at a men's club with his two good friends, District Attorney Frank Lalor and Dr. Barkstone. On his way to the club, Wanley stops to admire the portrait of a beautiful woman in a shop window. His two friends spot his gaze and joke about their mutual appreciation of the portrait. At the club, the three men complacently discuss their reserved bourgeois lives. They continue to joke about the woman in the window and the lure of amorous adventures which she seems to represent. Wanley admits his yearning for the excitement and freedom of youth, but agrees with the others that he would be well-advised to stay in his place. After a quiet night of reading, Wanley leaves the club and stops again to admire the portrait. He sees the reflection of a beautiful woman in the window and turns around to find himself face to face with the girl who posed for the painting. Her name is Ann Reed, and after introducing herself, she tactfully invites Wanley to her apartment. Unable to decline the offer, Wanley spends a gay evening drinking and talking with the beautiful stranger. Suddenly, the girl's jealous lover appears out of nowhere and attacks Wanley. Before the professor knows it, he has killed the man in self-defense. He starts to phone the police but stops himself at the last moment, realizing that his respectable life will be shattered even if he is found innocent. Wanley plans with Reed to dispose of the body. He tries to cover up all the evidence but gets careless and leaves a mass of clues before dumping the body in the country. The next day Lalor tells Wanley about a prominent financier that is missing, and Wanley deduces that this must be his victim. When the body is found by a Boy Scout, Lalor heads the murder investigation and keeps Wanley up to date on all the developments. Wanley's paranoia grows by the day and he nearly gives himself away to Lalor several times. The clever D.A. deduces most of the circumstances of the killing from the evidence but can't find the woman he knows must be involved. Wanley accompanies Lalor on the investigation one day and thinks he's lost when a woman is produced. He avoids meeting her by feigning sickness but later finds out that she was not Ann Reed. Lalor tells Wanley that the key witness is the victim's bodyguard, who must have

Top: Edward G. Robinson (playing Professor Wanley) and two friends stop to admire *The Woman in the Window* **(RKO, 1944); bottom: a fearful Robinson.**

tailed him the night of the killing. The man has disappeared because he is wanted in connection with another crime, and Lalor is content to wait until the police track him down. The bodyguard, whose name is Heidt, shows up at Ann Reed's and promptly blackmails her. Reed tries to deny knowing the financier, but Heidt is too clever for her. Reed contacts Wanley, who decides that they must kill Heidt because he will never leave them alone if they pay. Wanley gives Reed some poison. She tries to put it into Heidt's drink, but he catches her. Heidt takes all her money and promises to return for more. Reed calls Wanley and tells him of her failure. Wanley has been deteriorating from the strain and his spirit is crushed by the news. As he prepares to commit suicide, the film abruptly cuts to a gun battle near Reed's apartment. The police have spotted Heidt, who starts shooting when they try to stop him. Heidt is killed in the ensuing fight, and the police conclude that he must have been the financier's murderer. Reed then happens by and sees Heidt lying dead in the street. She tries to phone Wanley to give him the good news, but there is no answer. Wanley sits in his chair dying as the phone rings in his ear. A man taps Wanley on the shoulder and he wakes up. Wanley then realizes that it has all been a dream and that he never left the club that first night. With a feeling of great relief, Wanley leaves the club and stops to admire the portrait. But when a woman comes up to him and asks for a light, Wanley runs away in fear.

Only after the film is over does the viewer realize the importance of that first conversation between Wanley and his two middle-aged friends. Wanley's dream is the direct result of their discussion regarding the dangers and risks of succumbing to temptation. Reed may not be a full-fledged *femme fatale*, but to Wanley she is still a symbol of his forbidden desire. Once he has accepted her invitation, Wanley's fate is sealed. He is doomed to confront the deep-seated evil supposedly locked within everyone. This is a gradual process which begins with the most justifiable homicide possible. It really does seem like the financier intends to kill Wanley, whose fatal retaliation deserves to be characterized as pure self-defense. From that point on, every decision Wanley makes is both understandable and exposes more evil. He doesn't want his respectable life to be destroyed, so he decides not to phone the police. This decision is significant because Wanley has switched from protecting the existence of his life to protecting the circumstances of that life. Such a switch is crucial morally because it sets Wanley on a path from which there is no escape. It means that he is willing to become a criminal in order to protect his reputation and position. Reed goes along with him for the same reasons and perpetuates the shared guilt which she initiated when she helped him kill the financier. Wanley sets about trying to conceal the evidence, and this forces him to act just like a premeditated criminal. When he learns from Lalor how much evidence he left behind, Wanley becomes desperate and paranoid, but he just has to sweat it out.

Heidt's appearance is the final link in the alarming chain of events which foster Wanley's descent. Heidt is the type of two-bit extortionist who never stops blackmailing his victims until he has gotten all of their money. Wanley knows this, and his analysis of the situation is based upon that knowledge. He reasons that if they agree to pay Heidt, their lives will be destroyed as surely as if they are caught by the police. This is why they must kill him.

One can now see how the need for self-protection can be taken to the point of desperation which results in premeditated murder. It is again emphasized that Wanley and Reed share the guilt. He makes the actual decision to murder Heidt, and she agrees to carry it out. When her attempt fails, Wanley can no longer go on. A probable combination of fear and extreme guilt result in his suicide.

The dream's ironic climax puts a final decisive accent on the all-important fate theme. The inevitability of Wanley's doom is cleverly underscored through a parallel sequence which emphasizes the simultaneity of his suicide and the circumstances which would have freed him from danger. Viewed in retrospect, Wanley's attempt to protect his life appears to have been hopeless from the start; his doom was apparently sealed the moment he accepted Reed's invitation. From that point on, fate produced a series of circumstances which gradually revealed the potential evil within him, and which necessarily led to eventual self-destruction. This inevitable doom is the whole point of the dream, which is the narrative working out of the fears that control Wanley's existence. When his family leaves on vacation, the reserved professor is suddenly free to pursue the suppressed desires that he constantly harbors. The dream is the reason why he is afraid to pursue those desires. It is a warning of the possible results of giving in to the temptation represented by Reed.

The psychological key to the whole film is Wanley's true feelings about the type of liaison he dreams of having with Reed. His Victorian outlook renders him incapable of seeing the encounter as a relatively harmless urge for the freedom of youth. He cannot respond to the most minor temptation for fear of releasing the evil forces of the id imprisoned within him. His respectable bourgeois life is based upon suppression of the uncivilized evil which he believes is in everyone. The dream reinforces these fears by demonstrating how it only takes a series of unlucky circumstances to turn anyone into a murderer. Those circumstances must occur when Wanley gives in to Reed's temptation because he sees this minor evil as inseparable from the greater potential evil within him. His inevitable fate is actually the working out of the guilt that he has regarding this liaison. If he could believe that there was nothing wrong with it, that it was perfectly civilized and moral, no fateful circumstances would occur. Instead, he is doomed by his bourgeois Puritanism to assume that any urge he has for freedom from the narrow moral boundaries of his life must be the evil rumblings of his id.

The Woman in the Window can be seen as a profound and cynical attack upon its own generic underpinnings. The film's thematic drift constitutes a clever exposé of the type of subjective thriller which was so successfully pioneered by Lang and Hitchcock. Such films always involve a normal protagonist being cast adrift in a chaotic world of danger and evil. The dream structure and fate theme of The Woman in the Window serve as a penetrating analysis of that generic format. The psychological function which Wanley's dream performs is symbolic of mass functions that all subjective thrillers perform. When the film is revealed as Wanley's nightmare, the viewer realizes that fate was really just a contrived manifestation of the protagonists' neurotic fears. One can no longer accept such fate as valid once the psychological function is understood. Wanley simply dreamed up the whole thing to justify his conservative fear of freedom. He responds to the dream as proof of his fears when it is really just a contrived manifestation of them.

The same type of circular reasoning traps the viewer of most subjective thrillers. Being afraid to experience real, adventurous freedom, the viewer does so vicariously in Hitchcock-type movies. These films always involve verification of the audience's neurotic fears, in the form of extreme danger and evil. The viewer comes out of the film with his urge for adventure and his neutrotic fears satisfied. He will continue to be afraid of real freedom because his fears have been reinforced by the movie. This is a totally unreliable reinforcement, since these films are virtually contrived to capitalize upon such fears. The movie, like the dream, cannot be trusted because of the deceptive psychological function it performs. This is the subversive truth which is implied by Wanley's dream and which gives The Woman in the Window some very meaningful structural irony.

Laura (1944)

Director and Producer: Otto Preminger. *Screenplay*: Jay Dratler, Samuel Hoffenstein and Betty Reinhardt, from the novel by Vera Caspary. *Photography*:

Joseph La Shelle. *Special Effects*: Fred Sersen. *Music*: David Raksin. *Art Directors*: Lyle Wheeler, Leland Fuller. *Film Editor*: Louis Loeffler. *Production/ release*: 20th Century–Fox, October 11, 1944. 88 minutes. **Cast**: Gene Tierney (playing Laura Hunt), Dana Andrews (Mark McPherson), Clifton Webb (Waldo Lydecker), Vincent Price (Shelby Carpenter), Judith Anderson (Ann Treadwell), Dorothy Adams (Bessie Clary), James Flavin, Clyde Fillmore, Ralph Dunn, Grant Mitchell, Kathleen Howard.

A woman's body, with the face destroyed by a shotgun blast, is found in the apartment of Laura Hunt, and the police assume that it is hers. On Sunday morning, two days after the murder, detective Mark McPherson is called in to conduct the investigation. The first person on McPherson's list of suspects is a well-known art critic named Waldo Lydecker. Though Waldo claims to be the only man who really knew Laura, he is unable to shed much light on the murder. Waldo accompanies McPherson to the home of Anne Treadwell, Laura's wealthy aunt. She admits to having an affair with Shelby Carpenter, even though he had been engaged to Laura. Shelby then appears and offers an alibi which turns out to be just as questionable as Waldo's and Anne's. After visiting the scene of the crime, McPherson finally gets Waldo to open up a little. His story of Laura's past is portrayed in an economical flashback sequence which begins with their meeting five years earlier. As an enterprising young saleswoman for an advertising firm, Laura approaches Waldo in a restaurant and requests that he endorse her fountain pen ad. After rejecting the request and harshly ridiculing her, Waldo has a sudden change of heart. By way of apology for his behavior at the restaurant, he offers to endorse the pen and then asks Laura out for dinner. This proves to be the beginning of a happy and mutually fulfilling relationship between Waldo and Laura. With Waldo's aid and encouragement, Laura soon becomes a top level executive in her field. Though she eventually begins to see other men, none of them mean anything until she meets Shelby Carpenter at a cocktail party. Playing upon her sympathetic nature, Shelby gets a job under Laura, and they soon become romantically involved. Only a few days before the murder, Laura announces her engagement to Shelby. In a desperate attempt to prevent the marriage, Waldo tells Laura that Shelby is also involved with Anne Treadwell and a model named Diane Redfern. After verifying this charge, Laura decides that she must go to the country to think things out. On the night of the murder, she calls Waldo and tells him of her plans. Having learned a great deal from this story, McPherson parts company with Waldo. The next evening, he returns to Laura's apartment to think things out. Stumped by the case and haunted by the "memory" of Laura, McPerson has several stiff drinks and falls asleep in a chair. A few minutes later, he is awakened by someone entering the apartment. To his astonishment, it is Laura in

Top: Dana Andrews (playing detective Mark McPherson) gazes at portrait of *Laura* (20th Century-Fox, 1944); bottom: Vincent Price (as Shelby Carpenter) levels shotgun at Andrews, in Laura's cabin in the country.

the flesh. She claims to have been in the country the whole time, unaware that she was believed to be murdered. When Diane Redfern's dress is found in the closet, McPherson realizes that it was the model who was found with her head blown apart. His elation at Laura's return to life is quickly dampened by the sobering fact that she is now one of the murder suspects. Before he leaves for the night, McPherson orders Laura not to use the phone or let anyone in the apartment. Ignoring these directions, Laura phones Shelby and arranges to meet him as soon as possible. McPherson follows Laura to this secret meeting, then follows Shelby to Laura's cabin in the country. Though he won't admit it, Shelby thinks that Laura murdered Diane Redfern with a shotgun she keeps at the cabin. McPherson catches Shelby with the gun in his hands and forces him to tell the truth about his actions on the night of the murder. After Laura left town, Shelby had snuck into her place with Diane, supposedly with the intention of breaking off their affair. When the doorbell rang, Shelby sent Diane to answer it, and it was then that she was murdered. Fearing for himself and Laura, Shelby had remained quiet until now. Unfortunately for McPherson, Shelby's story doesn't shed much light on the murderer's identity. Refusing to give up, McPherson arranges a party for Laura and her friends. At the height of the festivities, McPherson announces that he's arresting Laura for the murder of Diane Redfern. McPherson then escorts Laura to police headquarters, where it soon becomes clear that he just needs to erase the last bit of doubt he was regarding her innocence. After forcing her to admit that she never loved Shelby Carpenter, McPherson takes Laura home. From there he goes to see Waldo, who has now become the number one suspect. Waldo is out, and McPherson takes the opportunity to search his place for clues. On a hunch, he breaks into an antique clock whose duplicate Waldo had given to Laura. Finding nothing, McPherson returns to Laura's apartment. Waldo is there, making a desperate effort to talk Laura out of her new relationship with McPherson. Finally fed up with Waldo's devious possessiveness, Laura breaks off their relationship. Waldo pretends to leave, but actually waits in the hallway while McPherson discovers the murder weapon inside of Laura's antique clock. When McPherson finally leaves, Waldo sneaks back into Laura's with the intention of murdering the right person this time. Before he can pull the trigger, McPherson returns with several other policemen to rescue Laura. Waldo is mortally wounded in the exchange of gunfire, and Laura goes to his side as he dies.

What starts out as just another murder case soon becomes an obsession for Mark McPherson. This situation would be perfectly consistent with the classic detective tradition but for one twist: The obsession is with the victim instead of the murderer. It takes McPherson approximately one day to realize that Laura is the exact opposite of "just another dame." The job is still to catch the murderer, but the investigation gives McPherson (and the viewer) a haunting image of Laura which captures his personal feelings. This image comes primarily from Waldo Lydecker, the supercilious art critic who is a self-appointed authority on beauty. No one was ever more aware or more appreciative of Laura's perfection than Waldo. He says that he made Laura, but what he really did was help her attain success and sophistication. When it became obvious that she could never love him, Waldo tried to destroy his creation. Before he makes his second attempt on her life, Waldo tries to explain: "When a man has everything he wants except what he wants most, he loses his self-respect. He becomes bitter and wants to hurt someone like he's been hurt."

To Waldo, Laura is much more than just a beautiful woman — she is an enigmatic dream come true. As affected by his influence and filtered through his perceptions, she becomes an almost abstract personification of his refined aesthetic ideals. This image of Laura is so important because it is about all that McPherson and the viewer have to go on in the first half of the film. As it turns out, it is this dream which captures McPherson's heart, and which dominates the film's elegant romanticism. Instead of falling in love with the real Laura, McPherson falls in love with a narrative portrait of her, "painted" by the artist-villain Lydecker.

Though he did not create the real Laura, Waldo is, indeed, largely responsible for the romantic dream that she comes to represent. It may even be said that he tries to turn Laura into a work of art, by giving her an aesthetic sensibility and the money to afford it. But he can never win Laura's love because she isn't a person to him. He wants to possess her, like you would possess a painting, and he learns the hard way that such a dream is inevitably unattainable.

McPherson learns the same thing, but in a very different way. When he believes she is dead, McPherson is tormented because he knows that he has fallen in love with a phantom. By sharing Waldo's dream when Laura is believed dead, McPherson unwittingly demonstrates that Laura need not even be alive to be loved. This is perhaps the crucial thematic point of the film because it reveals the most significant distinction between Laura, the woman, and Laura, the dream. One is encouraged to question the meaning and value of an aesthetic love which does not require its human object to be alive. The dream of Laura ultimately comes true for McPherson only because he is capable of disregarding her romantic portrait in favor of her. Waldo, on the other hand, must be rejected because he can only love the dream (which he thinks he owns anyway).

Waldo epitomizes the cultural decadence of an entire upper class milieu actually being attacked by the film. Anne Treadwell and Shelby

Carpenter are just as incapable of love as he. Though they are both innocent this time, Anne thinks that they are certainly evil enough to murder under the right (Waldo's?) circumstances. The attitude of all three characters to life is basically selfish and acquisitive. Their love for art is entirely consistent with a snobbish egotism which cleverly rationalizes their selfishness and greed. In Waldo's case, a total commitment to art becomes a complete hypocrisy which reinforces the self-centered mode that perpetuates his evil. To put it simply, because he is a successful authority on art, Waldo thinks he's better than everyone else.

Built into the structure of *Laura* is a self-consciousness about its own artistic nature (a major signpost of the noir movement it helped to usher in) which makes its anti-art theme quite ironic. The painting of Laura which opens and closes the film has an implicit symbolic meaning which refers directly to the "dream-portrait" of Laura that is drawn by Waldo for McPherson and the viewer. In the first half of the film, this painting looms ominously over McPherson because he is under the spell of this dream. But when Laura comes alive, the painting recedes into the background. This transition is most evident in the pivotal scene of Laura's return. For several tense minutes, the painting stands between McPherson and Laura in the frame, as if he is being offered a choice between dream and reality. Near the end of the scene, when Laura tells him that she has decided not to marry Shelby Carpenter, McPherson finally makes this choice. At that very moment, he takes a step forward, completely blotting out the painting.

In the second half of the film, the viewer himself is forced to confront the full implications of his relationship to Laura. The viewer wants to feel total identification with McPherson as he wins Laura's love, but the subversive art theme keeps breaking the illusion by constantly reminding him that Laura cannot become any more real to him than she was to McPherson in the first half of the film. Tierney's performance serves to encourage this phenomena by making Laura seem even more enigmatic after she "comes alive." And so, while McPherson is replacing a dream with reality, the viewer is falling deeper into the dream. Perhaps, one is led to speculate, Laura's most alluring quality is her unattainability, and perhaps the viewer has a lot more in common with Waldo than he would like to admit.

Detour (1945)

Director: Edgar G. Ulmer. *Screenplay*: Martin Goldsmith. *Photography*: Benjamin H. Kline. *Music*: Leo Erdody. *Art Director*: Edward C. Jewell. *Film Editor*: George McGuire. *Producer*: Leon Fromkess. *Production/release*: Producers Releasing Corporation, November 30, 1945. 68 minutes. **Cast**: Tom Neal (playing Al Roberts), Ann Savage (Vera) Claudia Drake (Sue), Edmund MacDonald (Charles Haskell, Jr.), Tim Ryan (Diner Proprietor), Roger Clark, Pat Gleason, Esther Howard.

Al Roberts tells, in several lengthy flashbacks, the story of how his normal life turned into a nightmare from which there was no escape. Roberts is a talented pianist who just never got the breaks to make it as a serious performer. Instead he plays in a two-bit bar in New York City. Sue, his girlfriend, sings at the same bar. She's ambitious and leaves him to try her luck in Hollywood. After awhile, Roberts decides to join her in L.A. He is broke and is forced to hitchhike across the country. He is picked up by a fast-talking bookie named Charles Haskell, Jr. He takes the wheel of the car so Haskell can get some sleep, and it begins to rain. When he stops to put the convertible top up, Roberts is unable to wake Haskell. He opens the door of the car and Haskell falls out, hitting his head on a rock. Realizing that Haskell is dead, Roberts panics. Since the incident is so incriminating, he decides to hide the corpse and drive the car into L.A. under Haskell's name. Everything goes fine until Roberts picks up a hitchhiker named Vera. By a fateful coincidence. Vera just happens to have ridden with Haskell earlier. Roberts tries to assure her that he is innocent of Haskell's death, but she refuses to believe him. Roberts then becomes Vera's prisoner, since she will turn him in if he doesn't obey her. They agree to stay together until the car is sold in L.A. Just as Roberts is trying to sell the car, Vera stops him. She has read in the paper that Haskell's rich father is dying and looking for his son. She wants Roberts to pose as the long-lost son, so as to inherit the father's fortune. Roberts knows the plan is crazy. He and Vera argue violently about it. Finally, she grabs the phone and runs into the bedroom of their apartment. She is drunk and intends to phone the police. Roberts is frantic. He grabs the phone cord, pulling with all his might in a desperate effort to break it. He gives up, breaks the bedroom door down and finds Vera's corpse lying across the bed. Fate has dealt its final blow, as Roberts has accidentally strangled her with the phone cord. He escapes but can't return to L.A. or New York for fear of getting caught. There is too much evidence that would link him to Vera's and/or Haskell's death. The film ends as Roberts imagines his eventual capture by the police.

Ann Savage (playing Vera) and Tom Neal (as Al Roberts) in *Detour* **(PRC, 1945).**

The crucial turning point in *Detour* occurs when Roberts discovers that Haskell is dead. It is his fear that the authorities would never believe the truth that begins his paranoid nightmare. From that point on, Roberts becomes increasingly enclosed in a chain of events which reinforce and increase his fear. Things get really sticky when he picks up the only person in the world who could deduce that Haskell is dead. Vera is a horrifying *femme fatale* who represents the worst kind of merciless distrust that Roberts has imagined his social accusers would have. With ruthless cunning, Vera takes complete control of Roberts, and in so doing, she becomes the literal personification of his paranoid fear. Roberts soon realizes that fearing her will destroy him as surely as capture by the police. He makes a desperate effort to stand up to her, which ends in an even more freakish replay of the bizarre accident that started his nightmare. Though he's free of Vera, his fear is greater than ever because he is now implicated in two incredible incidents that the authorities would never believe. Under such circumstances, it would be easy for anyone to believe that fate had put the finger on them.

One could argue endlessly about how "realistic" or "reasonable" Roberts' fear was in connection with Haskell's death, but it isn't really necessary to resolve such a controversy. The film's main issue comes into perspective only if one accepts the validity of Roberts' lack of faith in society. Once the viewer accepts this, he can examine the more powerful force which tyrannizes the protagonist. Social justice or no social justice, Roberts still had to be a victim of fantastic circumstances to get deeper and deeper into trouble (and after all, it is these incredible circumstances which lead the social authorities astray). Roberts believes that fate controls these circumstances, and that is why he is so afraid. No matter what he does to try to escape his predicament, fate reaches out and produces another fantastic turn of events that makes things even worse.

The existential answer to this mythic dilemma is a realization that one is not simply a pawn in the hands of mysterious, evil forces. Ulmer subtly implies that Roberts ironically controls his own fate by emphasizing the close relationship between his fear and the freakish chain of events that reinforces it. He expects the worst and the worst occurs. Roberts maintains that he only expects the worst because he knows some exterior fate has "put the finger on me," but how does he know this? It seems just as reasonable to assume that this is just his way of tyrannizing himself.

Such speculations are certainly being encouraged by the film's ending, where Roberts only imagines his final capture. Through this clever twist, Ulmer forces the viewer to make his own judgment about Roberts' real fate, which in turn forces him to admit how great his identification has become. What had seemed so incredible at first now seems almost like a foregone conclusion. In fact, Roberts' capture and eventual conviction now seem so believable that it's easy to forget that the ending is just in his mind.

This distinction, however, is very important, and we must not forget or pass over it if we are to understand the full meaning of Roberts' story. In making the protagonist's fears so believable, Ulmer is pointing directly to the root of all the trouble (in him as well as the viewer). By getting most viewers to accept Roberts' fear as his probable fate, Ulmer is clearly implying that this fear has been the source of his ongoing fate all along. To overcome that fear Roberts would not have had to pretend an unreasonable faith in society. His fear of society and his fear of fate were (or should have been) two different things. In other words, Roberts did not have to turn himself in after Haskell's death to avoid the fateful chain of events which followed. If he had realized that the incident's meaning resulted largely from his pessimistic attitude toward it, he would have had a good chance to escape further trouble. Since he could not do this, Roberts was doomed to prove to himself that he was doomed.

Scarlet Street (1945)

Director and Producer: Fritz Lang. *Screenplay*: Dudley Nichols, from the novel and play *La Chienne* by Georges de la Fouchardiere. *Photography*: Milton Krasner. *Special Photography*: John P. Fulton. *Music*: Hans J. Salter. *Art Director*: Alexander Golitzen. *Film Editor*: Arthur Hilton. *Production*: Diana Productions. *Release*: Universal, December 28, 1945. 102 minutes. **Cast**: Edward G. Robinson (playing Christopher Cross), Joan Bennett (Kitty March), Dan Duryea (Johnny Prince), Margaret Lindsay (Millie), Rosalind Ivan (Adele Cross), Samuel S. Hinds (Charles Pringle), Arthur Loft (Dellarowe), Vladimir Sokoloff (Pop Lejon), Russell Hicks (Hogarth), Charles Kemper, Anita Bolster, Cyrus W. Kendall, Fred Essler.

Meek, bourgeois bank clerk Christopher Cross is honored at a dinner for twenty-five years of faithful service. On the way home, Cross sees a beautiful woman being beaten up by a man. In an uncharacteristic moment of boldness, Cross strikes the man with his umbrella and knocks him out. Cross then runs down the block to fetch a policeman. When he returns, the man is gone and the woman asks him to walk her home. Her name is Kitty March, and she easily captivates Cross with her seductive charms. She tells him that she's an actress, which is a lie, and he tells her that he's a painter, which is only half a lie. Cross really does paint as a hobby, while Kitty is a former underwear model, now unemployed. After their encounter, Kitty meets the man who was beating her up earlier. Johnny often treats Kitty like that, but Kitty takes it because she loves him. When Kitty tells Johnny that Cross is a successful painter, he calls it the perfect set-up. Johnny encourages Kitty to keep the fish on the hook so they can squeeze all they can out of him. At their next meeting, Kitty gives Cross a sob story about being broke and needing a place to live. Kitty easily persuades Cross to give her the money to rent a studio apartment, where she says he can visit her and paint. Cross confesses that he is married, but assures Kitty that he loves her and not his mean, ugly wife. Cross steals money for Kitty from his wife's savings, but she asks for more. To grant Kitty's demands, Cross resorts to embezzling twelve hundred dollars from the bank. Laughing at what a sucker he is, Kitty and Johnny spend Cross' money as fast as he can raise it. Then one day, Cross brings all his paintings to the studio to prevent his wife from throwing them out. Johnny takes a couple of the paintings and tries to sell them. To his surprise, he is only able to peddle them for twenty-five dollars to an obscure street painter. Johnny is upset, but not for long. A famous art critic discovers Cross' two paintings and decides they're the work of a modern genius. The critic and an exclusive art dealer come to Kitty's studio looking for the painter they have just discovered. Johnny forces Kitty to say that she is the artist they are looking for. The art dealer buys all of Cross' paintings and displays them as the work of Katherine March. Cross' wife sees her husband's painting in the art dealer's window and immediately assumes that he has copied all of his stuff from the famous Katherine March. Realizing what has happened, Cross tells Kitty that he is not upset by her scheme. Because of his great love, he wants her to get all the fame and riches from his paintings. As proof of his feelings, Cross paints a "self-portrait" for Kitty. The humble Cross is now even more desperate for a miracle to free him from his hateful wife. The miracle occurs when the wife's first husband, who was supposed to be dead, confronts Cross at work. Thinking that Cross wants to stay married, the "dead husband" demands blackmail to remain dead. Cross pretends to go along with the "dead husband" just long enough to trick him into meeting his wife. Thinking he is now free to marry Kitty, Cross goes to the studio and finds her making love to Johnny. When Cross later confronts Kitty with her deception, she proudly admits her love for Johnny and laughs in his face. Cross explodes and stabs Kitty to death. The police challenge Cross at the bank, but it's only for his embezzlement. The bank refuses to press charges but does have him fired. Cross keeps silent while Johnny is wrongly convicted for the murder of Kitty. He becomes crazed with guilt and is plagued with the mocking voice of Kitty, laughingly declaring her love for Johnny. Cross attempts suicide but is

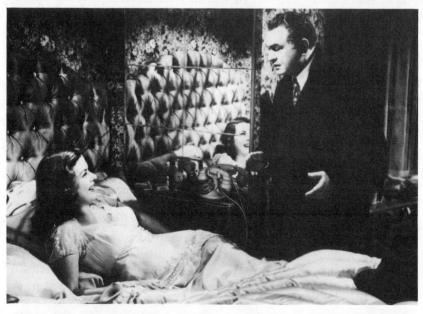

Top: Edward G. Robinson (left, playing Christopher Cross) and Dan Duryea (as Johnny Prince); bottom: Joan Bennett (as Kitty Marsh) coldly laughs at Robinson. *Scarlet Street* (Universal, 1945).

saved to continue his nightmare existence. Five years later, Cross wanders the streets as a well-known bum. He has confessed repeatedly to Kitty's murder, but the police think he's crazy. As the film ends, Cross deliriously walks the streets, oblivious to anyone and anything but the endless voice of Kitty, torturing him with her hatred and his guilt.

Cross and a friend sneak out of his testimonial dinner and carry on a short conversation while waiting for the bus. The dinner had ended in a burst of employee gossip when the married bank president was seen meeting his beautiful mistress by the entire group. Cross admits that he too dreams of having an affair with a beautiful woman, and they talk further about dreams of one sort or another. Cross says that when he was young he used to dream of nothing but painting. He invites the friend over to see his work, and they part company. Minutes later Cross meets his "beautiful woman" when he "saves" Kitty March from an unknown assailant. Unknown, that is, only to him. Kitty slyly goes along with Cross' misunderstanding of the encounter because she's always on the lookout for a sucker. Johnny has taught her that, and he agrees that Cross is a prime target. What he doesn't know is that Kitty fell victim to her own selfish dream when she quickly jumped to the conclusion that Cross was a famous painter.

Kitty and Cross knowingly deceive each other to satisfy the reciprocal but different wish-fulfillment dreams that they try to turn each other into. To Kitty, Cross becomes the meal ticket that Johnny demands, and to Cross, Kitty becomes the love he yearns for. Actually, both deceptions are for reasons of "love," but not of each other. Kitty is just following Johnny's orders because of her love for him. It is really Johnny who wants so badly for Cross to be a gold mine. At any rate, each character is trying to turn one of the other characters into his or her own selfish conception, while pretending to satisfy another's wishful expectations through a clever act. Johnny pretends to love Kitty so he can use her to get his dream of riches. Cross pretends to satisfy Kitty's expectations so he can win his dream of her love. And Kitty pretends to satisfy Cross' expectations so that she can preserve her dream, which is her love for Johnny.

The idea of wishful dreams, around which *Scarlet Street* is built, becomes strongly linked with the idea of art. Cross' standing as Johnny and Kitty's key to riches is totally dependent upon his identity as an artist. To Johnny, great art is a "dream come true" solely because it is worth a lot of money. With Cross, the association of art, wishful dreams and glamorous love was first established in that early dialogue with the friend. The link is extended and further clarified when he compares his love for Kitty to his love for art. Though more genuinely aesthetic than Johnny's, this association is really just as selfish and subjective. For both characters, art represents a dreamlike escape from the problems and frustrations that plague their mundane existence. Johnny's dream takes a beating when he pierces the illusion of Cross' artistic fame by selling two of his paintings. However, in doing this he has set the stage for real success and a new illusion. As the work of Katherine March, Cross' paintings become instantly popular and valuable. Johnny engineers this deception solely for his own profit, but thematically his action further reinforces the important link between art and illusion.

The film's accelerating accumulation of illusions reaches a peak with the "dead husband" character. We first see him looming over the Cross home in a large painting (which is an illusion in itself because the picture is really a photograph that just looks like a painting). Then, as soon as his death has been firmly established, the character turns up completely alive at Cross' bank. He engineered the illusion of his death to get the same thing that Cross now wants — freedom from Adele. He now exposes himself to Cross in a greedy attempt to blackmail him. Wrongly assuming that Cross is happily married, the "dead husband" threatens to take his wife back unless paid. Cross immediately realizes that he now has the liberating illusion on his side. He pretends to fear the "dead husband's" threats so that he can make sure that they are carried out. The complete shattering of the husband's death in Adele's eyes automatically frees Cross from her. As it turns out, Cross escapes from his wife by pulling off one illusion and destroying another. Unfortunately, the dream of love to which he is escaping is also a definite illusion. When he learns this, Cross is cast into the deepest pit of *Scarlet Street's* hellish reality. Instead of happiness and love, Cross finds only the evil which he shares with Kitty by brutally killing her.

This brings us to Johnny's mistaken conviction for Kitty's murder, a turn of events which serves a convenient and extremely fateful dual purpose. Poetic justice is satisfied (even though technical legal justice isn't) because Johnny actually did bear a lot of responsibility for Kitty's death, through his manipulation of her and Cross. But more importantly, Johnny's conviction forces Cross to face the harsher punishment of continuing to live in his hellish subjective reality. Kitty's last words constantly echo in his mind as an endless reminder of his and the world's selfish ugliness. He can never escape this mental torment because everyone thinks he's a deluded bum. Actually, he was a lot more deluded when he was a respectable, bourgeois bank clerk. At that time he still had the naive, innocent dreams that sustain the masses in their dismal lives.

In an important sense, Cross' fate was sealed from the moment he met and fell for Kitty. Cross got into trouble because he tried to turn all of his escapist ideals of beauty and love into some kind of perfect reality. Before he met Kitty, Cross was content to channel his yearnings into his art. She represented his attempt to make the perfect beauty of his creative urge into a love that would satisfy all of his desires in life. This was asking far too much of his humble existence. This represented the psychological melding of the feelings associated with aesthetic illusion and the emotional desires of real life.

Scarlet Street defines contemporary life within society as basically ugly. It sees the hope for perfect beauty and love as a dangerous illusion. Perhaps even more important, it associates this hope with the omnipresent, selfish desires that make the "real world" such an ugly place. Cross' love for Kitty is metaphorically linked to her and Johnny's selfish motivation through the illusion theme. All three wrongly believed that one of the others would make their desire for escape a reality. All three correctly saw art as the only escape, but they didn't respect its inevitable illusion. They wanted to make the illusions real, and in wanting this, they fell victim to the biggest illusion of all.

Scarlet Street is so obsessed with this idea of dreams and illusion because it is an aspect of all art that films seem to intensify. Hollywood films are being defined by Lang and Nichols as the wish-fulfillment fantasies of the American bourgeoisie, who escape by satisfying all their desires through idealized heros that live fairy tale lives. *Scarlet Street* attempts to throw these expectations back in the face of the viewer by giving him a protagonist that mirrors his desperate needs and a parable that comments perceptively about them. Through Cross, *Scarlet Street* attacks the hopes and desires that underly its audiences' imaginary expectations. The need for escape is inevitable because life in the mainstream of society is so bleak and frustrating. But escape must only be through art. Once one attempts to make the vicarious desires that art satisfies a reality, one is doomed. This is being taken in by an illusion that can only destroy life, and this is what happened to all three main characters in *Scarlet Street*. Cross' doom is the greatest because he remains alive. In a very ironic way, he gets his wish to turn his life into a dream. There's just one small catch. Instead of the best kind of fantasy, Cross' life becomes the worst kind of nightmare. In the dark world of *Scarlet Street*, this is the only kind of dream that ever comes true.

Gilda (1946)

Director: Charles Vidor. *Screenplay*: Marion Parsonnet, adapted by Jo Eisinger, from a story by E.A. Ellington. *Photography*: Rudolph Maté. *Music Score*: Hugo Friedhofer. *Songs*: "Put the Blame on Mame" and "Amado Mio" by Doris Fisher and Allan Roberts. *Art Directors*: Stephen Goosson, Van Nest Polglase. *Film Editor*: Charles Nelson. *Producer*: Virginia Van Upp. *Production/release*: Columbia, April 25, 1946. 110 minutes. **Cast**: Rita Hayworth (playing Gilda), Glenn Ford (Johnny Farrell), George Macready (Ballin Mundsen), Joseph Calleia (Obregon), Steven Geray (Uncle Pio), Joe Sawyer (Casey), Gerald Mohr (Capt. Delgado), Robert Scott, Ludwig Donath, Don Douglas, Lionel Royce, S.Z. Martel.

A crooked American gambler named Johnny Farrell leaves a waterfront dice game in Buenos Aires with large winnings. When a man tries to rob Johnny, Ballin Mundsen rescues him and invites him to his lush gambling casino. Johnny foils the crooked blackjack dealers with tricks of his own and wins big. Mundsen hires Johnny as a dealer, and he quickly rises to second in command of the casino. Mundsen returns from a trip with a sultry new wife named Gilda. Johnny is visibly shaken by Mundsen's new "possession." The vibrations between he and Gilda crackle with unclear tension. Mundsen suspects that Gilda had known Johnny in the States, but he can't get Gilda to admit it. When an attempt is made on his life by a mysterious gambler, Mundsen decides to confide in Johnny. He tells him of his dealings with former Nazis, involving an international monopoly in tungsten and strategic power of unlimited proportions. Johnny accepts Mundsen's trust and agrees to carry on in his place if anything happens. Gilda begins to act like a tramp and goes out with other men whenever she can. Johnny follows Gilda around, supposedly to prevent Mundsen from learning of her infidelity. When he brings Gilda home on carnival night, Johnny breaks down and embraces her. Mundsen sees them and races out before Johnny can stop him. Johnny and the police follow Mundsen to a private airstrip. They watch in awe as he takes off and crashes into the sea, in an apparent suicide. Johnny thinks that he and Gilda are responsible, but actually Mundsen's suicide was fake. Having been implicated in the killing of one of his Nazi associates, Mundsen staged the crash to get the police off his neck. Johnny marries Gilda and continues in Mundsen's place, both at the casino and as head of the crooked cartel. He distrusts Gilda completely and tries to keep her trapped in Buenos Aires. Gilda escapes to Rio, but Johnny catches her and tricks her into returning to Buenos Aires for a divorce he will never grant. Police Inspector Obregon demands that Johnny turn over vital information regarding the illegal cartel, but

George MaCready (as Ballin Mundsen) presents Rita Hayworth (playing *Gilda* — Columbia, 1946) with a gift.

Johnny refuses. Obregon closes the casino to force Johnny's hand and informs him that Gilda is leaving for America. Johnny meets Gilda at the casino and they are finally reconciled. Gilda says, "Isn't it nice. No one has to apologize since we were both stinkers." Just then, Mundsen returns "from the dead," intent on killing them both for betraying him. The colorful servent, Uncle Pio, saves the couple's lives by stabbing Mundsen just as he is about to make good his threat. Inspector Obregon terms the killing "justifiable homicide," and Johnny leaves with Gilda.

When Ballin Mundsen and Johnny Farrell first meet, they agree on the advantages of not knowing anything about each other's past. Johnny says to Mundsen, "It's as if I was born again when you met me, and that's the way I like it." This dialogue serves nicely as a reference to the viewer's situation in watching *Gilda*. The film embodies that classic thriller structure, whereby the viewer is tantalized with his ignorance about the characters' past, information that is crucial to a total understanding of their behavior. The viewer's ignorance is counterpointed by the protagonist's first person narration, in which Johnny repeatedly alludes to his knowledge of both the past and the future outcome of the story.

The central question of the past regards Johnny's relationship with Gilda. For a long time the viewer is not even sure if they had known each other before. Once this is assured, we're still left in the dark about the circumstances of their falling out. Eventually we find out that Johnny walked out on Gilda, but we never learn exactly why. It seems a good guess that he thought she was playing around with other men. She offers to defend herself of this apparent accusation, but Johnny refuses to listen, and we never learn any more.

Johnny's cynical quest for money and power seems to be his reaction to Gilda's alleged unfaithfulness in the past. He loved her so much that her breach of commitment transformed his whole perception of life. The same can be said of Gilda, whose promiscuity is her way of expressing a bitter despair. Since Johnny thought she was "no good," she decided to act the part. They both became involved with Ballin Mundsen because he represents the ultimate result of this cynical, bitter approach to life. Through most of the film, Johnny and Gilda reinforce each other's hatred. When Johnny sees Gilda going out on Mundsen, he believes that this proves his suspicions from the past. Actually, it is nothing more than her reaction to his hatred. She never cared much about Mundsen in the first place. For Gilda, marrying Mundsen and going out on him were similar responses to her loss of Johnny's love.

Johnny becomes devoted to Mundsen and tries to protect him from Gilda's faithlessness. Despite all his efforts, he is still drawn to her. In the famous seduction scene, Johnny succombs to Gilda's advances as she ironically comments on the excitement of their mutual hatred. Johnny thinks that Mundsen commits suicide after seeing he and Gilda together. This guilt further reinforces his belief that he and Gilda are both "no good." He punishes Gilda by marrying her and then turning that marriage into an oppressive trap. He easily replaces Mundsen as the head of the monopolistic cartel, since this power quest is a perfect expression of his hatred of life. Like Mundsen, Johnny's ruthless approach to life is clearly a result of his emotional bad faith. Mundsen apparently invested what little faith and trust he did have in Johnny, who feels that he betrayed it. For this reason, Johnny thinks that he is worse than Mundsen ever was.

The film's positive resolution, which seems to come out of nowhere, actually has as its basis Johnny's desperate emotional need for Gilda. Only when he thinks he is losing her for good does he miraculously wake up and admit his love. Then, just as they become reconciled, Mundsen appears. Having finally rid themselves of the Mundsen within their minds, Johnny and Gilda are now confronted with the villain himself. Johnny immediately realizes that he had been wrong about his betrayal of Mundsen. He now knows that the evil within himself had "come from" Mundsen all along and not Gilda.

Uncle Pio had been trying to tell Johnny the truth about Mundsen for some time, but with little success. In the last scene, when Mundsen appears out of nowhere with murder in his heart, Uncle Pio finally gets his chance to help Johnny. In saving him from Mundsen's attack at the end, the old servant underscores the inseparability of the "real" Mundsen and the evil influence which had taken control of Johnny's mind throughout the film. Since they were inseparable, both of these Mundsens had to be destroyed before Johnny (and Gilda) could be free, and it was Uncle Pio who made this destruction complete.

This thematic implication of two Mundsens brings us full circle, back to the film's subjective narrative structure. In a sense, Mundsen has no reality apart from his relationship to Johnny, simply because *Gilda's* narrative is a subjective representation of Johnny's stream of consciousness. At least, that is how the film works once we know enough about Johnny's past to understand his behavior. Since this information isn't fully complete until the last reel, the viewer spends most of the film caught in the mind of a character whose actions are largely unpredictable. Such a situation is, in fact, the primary key to suspense in many a noir thriller. The life of the film, just like the life of the protagonist, exists in that film's ongoing experience of now, while the meaning only arises later, after all of the past is revealed.

The Killers (1946)

Director: Robert Siodmak. *Screenplay*: Anthony Veiller, from the short story by Ernest Hemingway. *Photography*: Woody Bredell. *Special Photography*: David S. Horsley. *Music*: Miklos Rozsa. *Art Directors*: Jack Otterson, Martin Obzina. *Film Editor*: Athur Hilton. *Producer*: Mark Hellinger. *Production*: Mark Hellinger Productions. *Release*: Universal, August 30, 1946. 105 minutes. **Cast:** Burt Lancaster (playing "Swede" — Ole Andreson), Edmond O'Brien (Jim Riordan), Ava Gardner (Kitty Collins), Albert Dekker (Colfax), Jeff Corey (Blinky), Virginia Christine (Lilly), Vince Barnett (Charleston), Charles D. Brown (Packy), Charles McGraw and William Conrad (The Killers), Phil Brown (Nick Adams), Jack Lambert (Dum Dum), John Miljan, Donald MacBride, Queenie Smith, Harry Hayden, Garry Owen, Bill Walker, Wally Scott.

Two hired killers arrive in the small midwestern town of Brentwood and enter a local diner. After playfully terrorizing the establishment's three occupants for several minutes, the two men reveal their intention to kill "the Swede" when he comes in for dinner. When they realize that he isn't coming, the killers leave to find the Swede's home. By taking a shortcut through backyards, Nick Adams gets there well ahead of them. The Swede, however, is both unsurprised and unalarmed by Nick's warning of impending doom. He tells Nick there's nothing he can do about it, and then makes him leave. Minutes later, the killers arrive and deliver their message of death to the passive victim. Several days later, insurance detective Jim Riordan arrives in Brentwood to investigate the case because of a small life insurance policy held by the dead man. The remainder of the film chronicles Riordan's meticulous investigation into the life of the Swede named Ole Andreson. Riordan systematically tracks down all of the important people in Ole's life over the past ten years and conducts a series of interviews from which he is able to reconstruct Ole's past. These interviews are depicted as an intricate maze of flashbacks which, when reassembled, tell the following story:

Ole is a young fighter in Chicago, whose injured hand has just forced him to retire from the ring. At a party given by some underworld figures, Ole meets and falls instantly in love with the beautiful and sexy Kitty Collins. To save her from being arrested for wearing stolen jewelry, Ole goes to prison for a robbery he never committed. He then serves two long years with nothing to do but dream of her, though she never even visits him. When Ole gets out, needless to say, Kitty's not waiting at the gate or anywhere else for him. He finally does see her, but only under the most deadly of circumstances. Racketeer Jim Colfax has invited Ole and several other small time criminals to participate in a big heist he's planning. Kitty, it turns out, is Colfax's girl, but this doesn't stop Ole from again falling prey to her alluring advances. Kitty pretends to fall in love with Ole and then cruelly double-crosses him on the night before the big robbery. She tells him that the rest of the gang is planning a betrayal and induces him to get revenge by stealing all the money for himself. She then lures him to Atlantic City, where she steals back the money and rejoins Colfax. As Riordan says at the end of the film, "It's the double-cross to end all double-crosses!" The rest of the gang members are left thinking that Ole has all the money, which allows Colfax and Kitty to establish a new life without fear of detection or reprisal. Kitty's vicious stab in the back leaves Ole a broken man, and he retires to a life of quiet obscurity in Brentwood. Six years later, Colfax stumbles across Ole's secretive existence while driving through the small town. As a result of this encounter, Colfax decides that Ole must be eliminated to protect his position, and he hires the killers to do the job.

Top: Burt Lancaster (playing Ole Andreson, or "Swede") waits in the shadows for Ava Gardner (as Kitty Collins); bottom: Jack Lambert (as Dum Dum) is cornered by the police. *The Killers* (Universal, 1946).

Once assembled, the flashbacks which comprise Ole's story represent roughly half of the film. The rest, which is interwoven between the flashbacks, involves Riordan's adventures in the film's present. The early part of this "present plot" centers around Riordan's relationship with his boss at the insurance company. After he has been on the Andreson case for several days, Riordan's superior tries to get him to switch to something "more important." Riordan is so obsessed with the case that he puts his job on the line in order to buy more time to continue the investigation. When he learns that the unsolved robbery at the Prentiss Hat Factory is involved, Riordan finally has extra reasons for pursuing the case further. Two hundred and fifty thousand dollars is now at stake, and Riordan isn't the only one interested in that. Another big break comes when a former member of the heist team is found mortally wounded. After getting all the information out of Blinky that he can, Riordan deduces that he was shot by another criminal from the heist who is also trying to track down the loot. Riordan then returns to Brentwood and catches Dum Dum searching Ole's room for the money he thinks Ole got away with years earlier. While they are questioning each other, both men realize that Ole never got his hands on the money, and that Kitty Collins is the person they should be looking for. Riordan discovers both Kitty and Jim Colfax in Pittsburgh. Now a respectable contractor, Colfax disclaims all knowledge of Ole and the Prentiss Hat Factory job. Kitty is seemingly more cooperative. In fact, she supplies the final bit of information that complete's Ole' story by relating how she set him up. But Kitty's confession has the usual deadly catch. Colfax (who is now actually married to Kitty) has sent the killers who murdered Ole to eliminate Riordan. This time, however, they are themselves killed in a violent gun battle with Riordan and Lieutenant Lubinsky (the policeman who grew up with Ole). Kitty escapes in the confusion, but Riordan knows where to find her. He leads police to Colfax's house, where they walk right in on the result of a gun battle between Dum Dum and Colfax. Just as they are huddling around the mortally wounded Colfax, Kitty shows up, and, in a final stunning expression of her heartless selfishness, begs Colfax to lie to the police to save her from prison. This time, however, Kitty's luck has run out, as Colfax dies in the midst of her desperate pleas.

Hemingway's famous short story is portrayed almost in its entirety in the first ten minutes of the film. Rather than showing Ole being killed, the last page of the story follows Nick Adams back to the diner, after he has delivered his warning about the killers. The story then concludes with a short conversation between Nick and the owner of the diner regarding Ole's fate:

"Did you tell him about it?" George asked.

"Sure. I told him but he knows what it's all about."

"What's he going to do?"

"Nothing."

"They'll kill him."

"I guess they will."

"He must have gotten mixed up in something in Chicago."

"I guess so," said Nick.

"It's a hell of a thing."

"It's an awful thing," Nick said.

They did not say anything. George reached down for a towel and wiped the counter.

"I wonder what he did?" Nick said.

"Double-crossed somebody. That's what they kill them for..."*

In a sense, the rest of the film is an elaboration on the speculation contained within this conversation. Though we learn very little about Ole's past in the short story, that past still looms as the mysterious cause of his predicament, and the killers are definitely seen as deadly symbols of that past finally destroying him. The film then produces Riordan to answer the questions that the viewer must have about this story. Riordan's insurance investigation supplies a credible reason for uncovering Ole's past, while the flashback structure of the film carefully preserves Hemingway's idea of the deterministic tyranny of that past.

The entire thematic content of *The Killers* grows out of the scrambled and disconnected story within a story that is told through these flashbacks. Since he identifies with Riordan, the viewer is forced to discover this story in the same piecemeal way that he does. Though this structure seems to recall *Citizen Kane*, its meaning is less metaphysical and more formalistic. There is really no question of inconsistent versions or relative truths, as in Kane. Each friend (or enemy) of Ole's simply relates different pieces of the puzzle which is his life. The overall effect of this convoluted flashback structure thus resides mainly in the temporal realm. When discovered within a narrative context, the past lacks the normal temporal chronology of the film's present. That chronology must be reconstructed by the viewer, once he has received all the parts of the puzzle. The overall impact of the film is due largely to the demands that this structure makes of the viewer. Because of the effort involved in narrative reconstruction, one is never allowed to forget that Ole's story is in the past and that its meaning has a lot to do with time.

*From Ernest Hemingway's "The Killers," in Men Without Women, copyright 1927 Charles Scribner's Sons; copyright renewed 1955 Ernest Hemingway. Reprinted with permission.

In all, there are eleven flashbacks which combine to make up the story which Riordan's investigation uncovers. The following chart is an attempt to offset the misleading effect of reducing this film to plot and theme. The chart lists each flashback in reconstructed temporal order, along with each source.

1. Ole's last fight in 1935 (told by Lubinsky).
2. Ole meets Kitty and her underworld friends (told by Lilly).
3. Ole is arrested for Kitty's crime (told by Lubinsky).
4. Ole and Charleston in prison, 1938–40 (told by Charleston).
5. Ole is reunited with Kitty at Colfax's meeting to plan the heist (told by Charleston).
6. Ole and Colfax quarrel on the night before the heist (told by Blinky).
7. Kitty comes to Ole later that night and lies to him about the gang's decision to betray him (told by Kitty).
8. The heist takes place (visual flashback which accompanies the reading of a newspaper story by Riordan).
9. Ole robs the robbers at the rendezvous point (told by Blinky).
10. Kitty takes the money and ditches Ole in Atlantic City (told by Mary Dourghty, the maid listed as Ole's beneficiary).
11. Colfax discovers Ole at the Brentwood service station a few days before he is killed (told by Nick Adams).

The sequence of these flashbacks in the film is as follows—11, 10, 1, 2, 3, 4, 5, 8, 6, 9, 7. All but the heist flashback correspond to an interview Riordan is conducting, and their combined effect gives *The Killers* its all-important interplay between past and present.

By revealing Ole Andreson's past in such a way, the film transforms Hemingway's story into the detective novel he never wrote but should have. In so doing, it makes explicit themes which are only mysteriously hinted at in the story. Kitty Collins is one of the most important noir *femmes fatales* because she epitomizes the danger and evil of desire that is a major theme of the cycle. Ole's own desire results in an obession with her that is so strong that he must learn the truth the hard way. In betraying Ole, Kitty reveals the full extent of her heartless greed, while at the same time punishing him for being so trusting. After his betrayal, Ole's obssession with Kitty becomes an obsession with the past, and it is this second obsession which actually destroys him. Had he been able to put the past behind him, Ole could probably have avoided Colfax and his killers. Since he had no intention of doing this, Ole emerges as another passive victim actually very much responsible for his own fate.

Undercurrent (1946)

Director: Vincente Minnelli. *Screenplay*: Edward Chodorov, from the novel *You Were There* by Thelma Strabel. *Photography*: Karl Freund. *Music*: Herbert Stothart (excerpts from Brahms' Fourth Symphony). *Art Directors*: Cedric Gibbons, Randall Duell. *Film Editor*: Ferris Webster. *Producer*: Pandro S. Berman. *Production/release*: MGM, November, 1946. 116 minutes. **Cast**: Katharine Hepburn (playing Ann Hamilton Garroway), Robert Taylor (Alan Garroway). Robert Mitchum (Michael Garroway), Edmund Gwenn (Professor Hamilton), Jayne Meadows (Sylvia Burton), Marjorie Main (Lucy), Clinton Sundberg (Wornsley), Kathryn Card (Mrs. Foster), Dan Tobin (Professor Bangs), Leigh Whipper, Charles Trowbridge, James Westerfield, Billy McLain.

Ann Hamilton is the daughter of a respected college professor living in a small Midwestern town. When rich, handsome industrialist Alan Garroway visits her father on business, Ann is swept off her feet. Within a few weeks, they are married and returning to Alan's home in Washington, D.C. On their first night back, Alan throws a party for Ann, who is intimidated by the superficial sophistication of his high class friends. That same evening, Alan tells Ann about his "evil" brother Michael, and how he embezzled thousands of dollars from their business before the war. According to Alan, Mike had made his entire childhood miserable by taking advantage of their parents' favoritism. Mike disappeared after the embezzlement, and Alan hopes that he never has to see his brother again. Ann is sympathetic to Alan's tale, but in the weeks to come she begins to learn things which indicate that he wasn't being entirely truthful. When Alan leaves on a business trip, Ann persuades his aide to give her the keys to Mike's deserted ranch. A man who introduces himself as the caretaker shows her around, and they discuss Mike. That night, Alan shows up at the ranch and violently denounces Ann for sneaking behind his back to find out more about Mike. Alan apologizes later, but Ann is now even more curious about Mike. After Alan has returned to his business, Ann visits Mike's former girlfriend, Sylvia Burton, who tells of her suspicions that Alan murdered the missing brother years earlier. Ann is terrified that Sylvia might be right. Despite her fears, she travels to join Alan at the family estate in Middleburg. Ann arrives ahead of Alan, but someone else is lurking mysteriously on the grounds. When she stumbles across the remains of a distinctive cigar smoked by the caretaker of the ranch, Ann realizes that it is Mike. Thinking her nightmare is over, she anxiously waits for Alan to arrive. When he does, Mike meets him in the driveway and confronts him with the truth. Alan had framed Mike for embezzlement to cut him out of the family business. Then he murdered a German inventor who had just

Katharine Hepburn (playing Ann Hamilton) pays a visit to the office of her new husband, Robert Taylor (as Alan Garroway), in *Undercurrent* (MGM, 1946).

developed an invaluable long-distance plane control. The device helped win the war and gave Alan his much-needed success. Mike is not interested in revenge of any kind. All he asks is that Alan tell Ann the truth. Alan agrees, but before he can, she confesses all her fears and guilt regarding Mike. Thinking that Ann really loves Mike rather than him, Alan becomes violent and threatening. Ann fears for her life and tries to escape, but Alan catches her. In the midst of their struggle, a neighbor arrives with an invitation to go horseback riding. After getting rid of the witness by feigning an accident, Alan tries to kill Ann. As he is about to crush her with a rock, Alan's horse tramples him to death. The film then ends with the disturbing romantic meeting of Mike and Ann.

Ann's dream marriage is only a few weeks old when a shadow gradually emerges to threaten it. This shadow is associated completely with Michael. Little bits of evidence begin popping up which contradict Alan's characterization of him as a cruel heel. Ann's curiosity compels her to investigate on her own. After comparing Alan's drab, impersonal office with Mike's beautiful ranch, she begins to wonder if maybe Alan is the evil brother. This suspicion soon grows into the fear that Alan has murdered Mike. After one dreadful night of pondering that possibility, Ann learns that Mike is alive. In the very next scene, Mike confronts Alan and reveals the truth about him. It seems that Ann's relief was premature: Alan is a murderer after all. Not only has he deduced the facts of this murder, but Mike understands the tragic motivation which controls his brother. He knows that Alan's desperate need for success and power is a twisted attempt to feed the emotional insecurity produced by his childhood. Mike probably also knows that this insecurity arose because he got most of the parental love which should have gone to Alan. Because he knows these things, Mike refuses to turn Alan in to the police. Being the good brother, Mike displays both awareness and mercy.

Despite his evil past, Alan sincerely wants to make a new life for himself with Ann. The trouble is that Ann isn't as forgiving as Mike. The thought that her husband might be a murderer terrifies her. When he learns this, Alan realizes that he can't tell Ann the truth without losing her. Then she unloads the final blow which sends Alan over the edge. In a moment of extreme guilt, she admits that Mike was her obsession rather than his (as she had always maintained earlier). This confession activates Alan's insecurity in the worst way. He had already feared that Mike had again "stolen" his love from him, and this confession seems to prove it. Since this probably represents the ultimate emotional despair for Alan, it is not surprising that he begins to think of murder.

There follows an adequate build-up of suspense and Alan's unsuccessful attempt to do Ann in. After he has been killed by his own horse (a bit of Freudian symbolism typical of the period), the film concludes with a provocative coda which further underscores the tragic aspects of the story: Apparently recovered from the shock of her ordeal, Ann has sent for Mike. After opening the conversation by discussing the disposal of Alan's estate, Mike confesses his love for Ann. From the way she is acting, it appears that the feeling is quite mutual.

This romantic conclusion is so disturbing because it indicates that Alan was correct in his jealous suspicions. Ann couldn't make it with him because she was, in fact, saving her love for someone like Mike. Someone, that is, who could offer her a life which was free of the destructive phantoms of a dark and unhappy past.

The thematic content of *Undercurrent* can thus be described as Freudian determinism of the highest order. The parable of two brothers clearly illustrates this viewpoint by tracing the roots of their contrasting destinies to childhood treatment. The good brother grows up adjusted, happy and loved, primarily because he was loved as a child. The bad brother, on the other hand, grows up hopelessly insecure, emotionally misguided and ultimately doomed because he wasn't.

The Man I Love (1946)

Director: Raoul Walsh. *Screenplay*: Catherine Turney and Jo Pagano, from the novel *Night Shift* by Maritta Wolff. *Photography*: Sid Hickox. *Music Adaption*: Max Steiner. *Songs*: "The Man I Love" by George and Ira Gershwin, "If I Could Be with You" by Henry Creamer and Jimmy Johnson. *Art Directors*: Stanley Fleischer, Eddie Edwards. *Film Editor*: Owen Marks. *Producer*: Arnold Albert. *Production/release*: Warner Brothers, December 27, 1946. 96 minutes. **Cast:** Ida Lupino (playing Petey Brown), Robert Alda (Nicky Toresca), Andrea King (Sally Otis), Bruce Bennett (Sam Thomas), Martha Vickers (Virginia Brown), Dolores Moran (Gloria O'Connor), John Ridgely (Roy Otis), Don McGuire (Johnny O'Connor), Warren Douglas (Joe Brown), Alan Hale (Riley), Craig Stevens (Johnson), James Dobbs, William Edmunds, Patrick Griffin.

Manhattan torch singer Petey Brown decides to visit her family on the East Coast. Petey's older sister Sally lives in a modest apartment in Long Beach with her younger brother Joey, sister Virginia, and a seven-year-old son. When Petey arrives, Sally tells about her husband Roy, who's in a veteran's hospital suffering from mental exhaustion. Sally is very worried because Roy no longer seems to trust or love her. While they're talking, Joey arrives home from work at the nightclub of Nicky Toresca. Nicky is a slick womanizer who's latest interest is Sally. He has sent Joey home with a beautiful evening dress as a present to his sister. Sally tells Joey to take the dress back, but Petey stops her. After meeting Gloria and Johnny O'Connor, a young couple from across the hall, Petey heads for Nicky's club wearing the flashy dress. When Nicky sees Petey, he quickly forgets all about her sister. Within minutes, Petey has landed a singing job and become Nicky's new female interest. A few days later, Joey gets into a fight over a card game, and Petey goes to the jail to bail him out. They meet on the steps of the police station, and Joey proudly tells Petey how he conned the police into jailing the other guy instead of him. Since she knows that Joey started the fight, Petey feels that it's her duty to bail his victim out. The man's name is Sam Thomas. Petey seems interested in him, but he doesn't seem to want company, and they part after a brief meeting. Later that evening, Nicky takes Petey to hear the jazz band at a rival nightclub. While Nicky is talking business, Petey again meets Sam Thomas. To Petey's amazement, he is the same Sam Thomas who used to be a talented and successful jazz pianist in New York. Petey quickly ditches Nicky and invites Sam back to her place for a nightcap. With Petey's encouragement, Sam tells how he came to give up his music career. At the height of his success, Sam had fallen in love with a rich and beautiful society woman named Amanda Chandler. After a short period of marriage, Amanda had become dissatisfied with Sam.

Ida Lupino (as Petey Brown) and Bruce Bennett (as Sam Thomas) in *The Man I Love* **(Warner Bros., 1946).**

When her attempts to fit him into her elite social circle failed, Amanda divorced him. Sam took this rejection so hard that he gave up serious piano playing and signed up with the merchant marines. The night he was jailed, Sam missed his boat, and he's now waiting for another. By the time Sam is finished telling Petey his story, it is fairly clear that a new love has blossomed between them. Several days later, Nicky informs Petey that Amanda Chandler is in town. Since Sam didn't show up at the club as he had promised, both assume the obvious. When Petey returns home, she finds Sam waiting for her. At first she's relieved, but later, when Sam admits that he wanted to see Amanda, Petey has an outburst of possessive jealousy. Sam reacts with justifiable outrage and eventually walks out on Petey, supposedly for good. The next day at Sally's, Petey tells how she saw Gloria at Nicky's club with a man, instead of the girlfriend she was supposed to be out with. Johnny overhears this conversation and returns home to confront Gloria with her apparent infidelity. Johnny's accusations result in a vicious quarrel, which ends with Gloria walking out on him. Fed up with the responsibilities of marriage, Gloria heads straight for Nicky Toresca. A few days later, we see Nicky mulling over the problem of getting rid of the drunken Gloria. Since he doesn't want to be seen with Gloria in public, Nicky sends for Joey and orders him to drive her home. Figuring that she won't go if she knows where he's taking her, Joey offers to take Gloria out for some food. When she realizes where they're really going, Gloria jumps out of the car in the middle of a busy intersection. Not wanting to bother with her anymore, Joey starts to drive off. Gloria tries to run after him and is struck by a car, which kills her instantly. In the meantime, Sam has come to say goodbye to Petey at Nicky's club. As they are about to part, Petey embraces him and admits she was wrong to be jealous and possessive. Joey then returns to Nicky and fearfully tells him of Gloria's death. Afraid that he might be blamed, Nicky decides to tell the police that Joey murdered Gloria. Just as he's about to make the phone call, Petey barges into the room and stops him. Nicky offers to let Joey off the hook if Petey will be his girl. While they're still arguing about it, Johnny O'Connor appears with the intention of killing Nicky as revenge for Gloria's death. Petey quickly grabs Johnny's gun and slaps him back to his senses. Having saved Nicky's life, Petey confidently warns him not to go to the police about Joey. The next day, Sally's husband returns home from the veteran's hospital. After a brief reunion, Petey informs her family that she will be returning to New York that evening. In the last scene, Petey bids farewell to Sam at the dock. They agree to meet again, though they don't really know where or when.

The Man I Love features a large array of characters with a variety of problems adjusting to post-World War II American life. The literal readjustment problems of air force veteran Roy Otis are tacitly expanded to include a microcosmic group of people that are all maladjusted to some significant degree. Otis' mental illness is depicted entirely in the short flashback story told to Petey by Sally. It is quite clear from this sequence that Roy's mind has become a paranoid "battlefield" in which the whole world is his enemy. Unable to understand this condition, Sally becomes fearfully alienated from Roy and unwittingly reinforces his distrust. Petey apparently can see that Sally is Roy's only hope of being cured. Roy returns home at the end of the film largely because Petey encouraged Sally not to give up on her husband. Put simply, Roy's loss of faith in life can only be diminished by his wife's faith in him.

Roy Otis is an important character solely because his cynical lack of faith is mirrored in one way or another by most of the other characters in the film. The closest one comes to a villain is Nicky Toresca, an apparently successful businessman whose adjustment to life involves using others to satisfy his own desires. Near the end of the film, the viewer is given a brief glimpse of the destructive cynicism which lurks beneath Nicky's exterior of self-satisfied confidence. All it takes is one sentence delivered during the character's desperate attempt to prevent Petey from leaving town. "Come and live with me in my gutter," he tells her, and the strong implication is that a choice of gutters is all anyone really has in life. It is clear from this line alone that Nicky's cynical lack of faith provides the simplest kind of philosophical justification for his amoral selfishness. As far as he's concerned, everyone is out for himself and that's all there is to it.

Perhaps the clearest indication of Nicky's evil effect on others is given by his relationship to the misguided characters of Joey and Gloria. Impressed by his boss's power and money, Joey is in grave danger of acquiring the same selfish approach to life. If he is saved from this fate at the end, it is only because he directly experiences the full extent of Nicky's callous disregard for others by becoming his victim. This occurs when Joey tells Nicky of Gloria's death. Nicky responds to the news with a decision to frame Joey to protect himself. Since Gloria's death was clearly accidental, the viewer is initially unable to understand why Nicky feels compelled to draw the blame away from himself. The film's thematic structure holds the most satisfying answer to this question. On a pertinent spiritual level, Gloria's death is the result of her attitude toward life. When she walks out on Johnny, Gloria heads straight for Nicky because he expresses, in its most pure form, the selfish cynicism which undermines her marriage. In *The Man I Love*, evil arises from having destructive attitudes toward life, and Nicky epitomizes that evil more than any other character. That is why he anticipates being blamed for Gloria's death, and that is why Johnny tries to kill him.

As the film's protagonist-heroine, Petey is the one character who can handle Nicky. The strength and wisdom which allows her to do this is displayed generally in her supportive treatment of most of the other characters. Sam is the one exception to this pattern, primarily because she falls for him. When her own deepest emotions are involved, even Petey is somewhat confused and maladjusted. She falls so fast for Sam that she nearly destroys their love by becoming possessive and disrespectful of his emotional plight. Though he obviously feels something for Petey, Sam is still in the throes of an emotional loss of faith caused by his former wife. When Petey becomes jealous and possessive, Sam is forced to assert his own independence by walking out on her. This forces Petey to realize that she was wrong, and to re-examine her own emotional priorities. The result is a climactic reconciliation which represents a significant spiritual growth for our herione.

This growth is most clearly manifested in the last moment of the film, after Petey bids farewell to Sam. As she walks off into the darkness, a transcendental smile bursts onto her face. At that one moment, Petey truly feels the full power and meaning of a faith which has been gained from an ongoing confrontation with life's trials and tribulations. At that one moment, Petey understands the value of her independence and accepts the inevitable fact that security can only come from within oneself. At that one moment, Petey becomes totally purged of her possessiveness and realizes that the love within her is what really counts.

Brute Force (1947)

Director: Jules Dassin. *Screenplay*: Richard Brooks, from a story by Robert Patterson. *Photography*: William Daniels. *Special Photography*: David S. Horsely. *Music*: Miklos Rozsa. *Art Directors*: Bernard Herzbrun, John F. DeCuir. *Film Editor*: Edward Curtiss. *Producer*: Mark Hellinger. *Production*: Mark Hellinger Productions. *Release*: Universal-International, August, 1947. 98 minutes. **Cast**: Burt Lancaster (playing Joe Collins), Hume Cronyn (Capt. Munsey), Charles Bickford (Gallagher), Sam Levene (Louie), Howard Duff (Soldier), Art Smith (Dr. Walters) Roman Bohnen (Warden Barnes), John Hoyt (Spencer), Whit Bissell (Tom Lister), Jeff Corey (Freshman), Vince Barnett (Muggsy), Richard Gaines (McCallum), Yvonne DeCarlo (Gina), Ann Blyth (Ruth), Ella Raines (Cora), Anita Colby (Flossie), Frank Puglia (Ferrara), James Bell, Jack Overman, Sir Lancelot, Ray Teal, Jay C. Flippen, James O'Rear, Howland Chamberlain, Kenneth Patterson, Crane Whitley, Charles McGraw.

The rain pours down upon the ominous structure of Westgate Prison. From cell R17, five convicts watch Joe Collins return from solitary with head guard Captain Munsey. As the two men walk across the prison yard, Munsey pleads with Collins to reconsider his refusal to "cooperate." Collins' only answer is a hard stare filled with unspoken hatred. Back at his cell, Collins is reunited with his five cellmates — Soldier, Spencer, Muggsy, Freshman and Tom Lister. Collins tells the others that their only hope is a breakout. The next day, Collins visits the office of the alcoholic Dr. Walters, his only friend on the prison staff. Collins asks Walters for the time, and the scene abruptly shifts to the prison machine shop. As the convicts stage a diversionary brawl, Soldier, Spencer, and Muggsy force a fearful stool pigeon into a huge drill press with blow torches. When he gets the news of this fatal "accident," Dr. Walters realizes that Collins had been using him as an alibi, while his men disposed of the talkative informer. Collins knew that Walters would say nothing about this obvious set-up. At a meeting with Warden Barnes and Captain Munsey, we are given to understand Walters' position. The

Top: Burt Lancaster (left, playing Joe Collins) and Charles Bickford (as Gallagher, right); bottom: the prison riot at the conclusion. *Brute Force* (Universal-International, 1947).

convicts are justifiably restless and on edge due to poor and overcrowded facilities. Walters pleas for more understanding and tolerance under these conditions, but the Warden has doubts. His efforts at tolerance in the past have failed, and now he is receiving strong pressure from Munsey and government representative McCallum to take a more strict authoritarian approach. The meeting is adjourned with no conclusion, but things look bad for the future. In the next scene, Collins meets with convict leader Gallagher, who also is the editor of the prison newspaper. Collins wants Gallagher to go along on the breakout, but Gallagher refuses because he's up for parole soon. Collins leaves after implying that Gallagher's hope is just a pipe dream. Back at cell R17, the convicts discuss the importance of a calendar girl's picture on their wall. Newcomer Muggsy can't understand why an unknown girl's picture could mean so much to all of them. The silver-tongued orator of the group is Spencer, who explains that the picture makes each convict think of the women in his life. For the past several days, Spencer has been thinking about a beauty named Flossie. He met her one evening while having a run of good luck at roulette. A police raid busted up the fun, but Flossie saved Spencer from arrest by pocketing his gun and directing him to a secret exit. Spencer thought he had it made as they drove away together. That's when Flossie pulled his own gun on him. So surprised was Spencer that he didn't even protest as Flossie ordered him out of his car and drove away with his entire bankroll. And that, we are told, is a perfect example of how Spencer's life has gone. In the next scene, Collins visits a sick inmate who has a message for him from a recently deceased friend. Both men had been taken ill while working on Captain Munsey's mysterious pet project – the drainpipe just outside of the prison walls. The sick inmate tells Collins that his friend felt the drainpipe was the key to a successful escape. The friend's last words were, "Ask Soldier about Hill 633." Later that evening, while the rest of the convicts are at a movie, Tom Lister sits in his cell trying to write a letter to his wife. Unable to write, he gazes at the calendar picture and thinks back to his past. A flashback then begins with Tom returning from a typical day at his clerk job. His beautiful wife, Cora, sullenly prepares their dinner. Cora, it seems, is dissatisfied with their modest life. And Tom agrees that she deserves better. That is why he has brought home a present. It's the expensive fur coat Cora has always wanted. The catch is that Tom had to embezzle eight thousand dollars to buy it. An ominous knock comes at the door. Though it seems that Tom is in grave danger of apprehension, all Cora can think about is keeping her coat. Now that he's in prison for the crime, Tom is even more desperately in love with Cora. He stays in his cell night after night writing Cora letters because she's his only hope in life. Tom's remembrance is then interrupted by Captain Munsey, who demands that he cooperate by giving information about the drill press accident. When Tom refuses, Munsey informs him that Cora has gotten a divorce. With one carefully placed lie, Munsey has deftly destroyed another life. Since he no longer has any hope left, Tom hangs himself after Munsey leaves the cell. Munsey then uses Tom's death as an excuse for punishing the other convicts of cell R17. Despite their protest of innocence, Munsey orders them to report for work at the drainpipe in the morning. After Munsey leaves, Collins has Soldier explain the strategy of Hill 633, which turns out to be a two-sided attack upon a seemingly impregnable enemy position. Though nothing further is said, everyone knows they're not just discussing old war memories. The next morning, Gallagher receives word that all convict privileges have been revoked for an indefinite period. When he protests to Warden Barnes, Gallagher is told that all paroles have been canceled. For Gallagher, that is the last straw. He meets with Collins that evening to plan the breakout. Collins explains how working in the drainpipe will allow him and his men to attack the strategic guard tower from the rear, while Gallagher holds the guard's attention with a mass riot in the prison yard. Though Gallagher has doubts, Collins convinces him that their best chance is to plan the attack for a quarter past twelve the following day. Back at cell R17, Soldier dreams of his lost love. The setting is Italy near the end of the war. Soldier loves an Italian girl named Gina, who lives with her embittered father. Soldier has taken a chance by smuggling them food. Rather than being grateful, the girl's father feels that the Americans owe him this food because they have destroyed his country. As he is hurriedly gathering the supplies, the military police arrive. Instead of protecting Soldier, the father runs out to betray him. Filled with her own hatred, Gina instinctively grabs Soldier's gun and shoots her father down in the doorway. Soldier then grabs the gun back from her and takes the murder rap himself. After this flashback, the scene shifts to Warden Barnes' office. Doctor Walters makes a final plea for mercy, but it's no use. The Warden exits, leaving Munsey and Walters in his office. With his courage fortified by alcohol, Walters tells Munsey off in no uncertain terms. Walters knows that Munsey is a torturer and murderer. He sees through Munsey's rationalized higher purpose to the sick, psychopathic obsessions underneath. Munsey reacts to this analysis by striking Walters and proving everything he has said. Meanwhile, across the prison in cell R17, Collins lies in bed thinking of his past. A flashback begins in the middle of a robbery getaway. Collins asks three other men to wait in the car while he makes one short stop at the home of Ruth, a crippled girl he has fallen in love with. Collins has only recently turned to crime to get the money for an operation which may enable Ruth to walk, but he never tells her the truth about his "business." Instead, Collins simply reassures Ruth of his love and promises to return soon with the money for her operation. This ends the flashback which was, apparently, the last time Collins saw Ruth. Now, on the last night before the break, he hopes against hope to get back to her. The next scene shows Louie, Gallagher's "ace reporter," furtively delivering last minute messages about the break. When Louie tries to get a pass to go to the drainpipe, Munsey stops him. In the film's most horrifying scene, Munsey tortures Louie almost to death trying to get information about the break. Louie doesn't talk, but Munsey still knows all about the plan. This is the message that Walters delivers to Collins less than an hour before noon. Though he knows it's all a set-up, Collins decides to go ahead anyway. Minutes before zero hour, the prison population is told that Munsey has been named the new Warden. The timing is perfect for the start of the prison riot. As Gallagher and his men toss fire bombs at Munsey in the tower, Collins goes into action. Having discovered that Freshman turned stoolie, he ties him to the front of a railroad hand car and charges Munsey's secretly placed machine gun nest behind the tower. One by one, all of Collins' men and all of the tower guards are killed. Mortally wounded himself, Collins makes his way into the tower, knocks Munsey out and throws him into the prison yard. With his last dying breath, Collins realizes that the break is a complete failure. Even though he has captured the controls, the front gate still won't open because Gallagher has blocked it with a truck in his own futile attempt to free the inmates. In the film's last scene, Dr. Walters ponders over the tragic outcome of the day. Collins and his cellmates, Gallagher, Munsey and many others are all dead. Walters' conclusion: "Nobody ever really escapes."

All of the characters in *Brute Force* are doomed by fate and without hope. Though Collins succeeds in capturing the main guard tower, his plan still fails because fate (not bad luck) has sealed the only exit out of Westgate Prison. While Gallagher may have been the instrument of this fate, he cannot be blamed any more than anyone else in the prison. It was their fate to die and fail to free even one man.

But why must this be so? The convicts' answer is to blame all their trouble on the evil and injustice outside of themselves. And, admittedly, there was plenty of that around. Captain Munsey, in particular, is as vicious and evil as any screen villain in history. One can certainly see how the convicts (along with most viewers) could easily blame everything on him. But to do so is the total error which everyone is making. Munsey is actually the instrument of the convicts' fate, just as they are the instrument of his. He seems in control because he has the power and apparent free choice, but the film implies that everyone is equally trapped and responsible for that trap.

Munsey's position is as much a trap, rationalized and resulting from his view of life, as the convicts. He believes he's just doing his job in a world where the fit must control the unfit. Walters tries to tell him that his authoritarian philosophy is just a mask for his deeper obsession with "brute force," but Munsey is far too adept at washing his hands of such horrifying responsibility.

Prison becomes, at this point, an existential metaphor for all of society. It is really the great deterministic prison. No one breaks out because no one believes they chose this life of vicious conflict and pain. But they all did! Not only is Munsey as trapped as the convicts, but the convicts are just as free as Munsey.

The film's four flashbacks carefully illustrate how each doomed convict chose (admittedly or not) a love that was hopeless. In terms of fate, thematic context and a harsh psychological reality, this all but means they chose a life of doom. This point is further underscored by Collins' decision to go ahead with the break even though it's a set-up, and by Gallagher's ironic suicidal drive into the prison gates.

In the end, both of these men attempted to be martyrs. Like all martyrs, they failed to free anyone because fate is fate and destroying its instruments won't stop it. Writing everything off to the villain no longer works in the existential world. In a sense, this may even be the root of man's worst troubles.

The traditional prison theme of hatred for stool pigeons takes on a special significance in this connection. In a way, it represents the deepest guilt of all the convicts — that they refuse to sympathize or understand the very understandable vulnerability that many men have to Munsey's demands. To avoid being a stool pigeon, a convict had to be willing to sacrifice his life rather than talk. Every convict was expected to endure the ultimate pain, whether it was physical (Louie), or emotional (Tom Lister) or both (Collins). The ones that failed were hated and destroyed unmercifully.

The film's easily ignored moral theme indicates that Munsey and Collins had virtually the same values (demanding absolute obedience and discipline) because they both saw themselves as leading respective armies in a full scale war. The stool pigeon was caught right in the middle of this war. By fearing for his own life most of all, he put himself in this position. (Thus, Collins discovers that Freshman is a stoolie because he asks to bring up the rear of the break.) Munsey tries to play on this fear, while the convicts grow to hate it. To them, fear for one's own well-being is treason punishable by death. There is no room for the understandable failure to be a hero or martyr. Like Munsey, the convicts are anti-human because power is everything to them. They hate human weakness equally (which *is* the stool pigeon), and their obsession with power is what traps them.

The themes of *Brute Force* are so universal that Westgate Prison may even be viewed as the heritage of western culture in America, where most Americans are trapped because they believe so much in the importance of external circumstance, which is external power. This goes equally for oppressed and oppressors. Everyone is busy projecting the evil and responsibility onto everyone else. Their fate is inevitably tragic simply because they won't stop and accept their life as their own doing. Everyone thinks that their own trouble is caused by something outside of them, when the real trouble is inside each and every one of us.

The film's last line clearly means you can't escape yourself. Virtually all of the characters are doomed because they never realize what this means. As for Dr. Walters, he seems almost as doomed because he does, which poses the question of art and philosophy's answers. Aren't they of little use when the sickness is so widespread? From this view, Walters represents director Dassin and writer Richard Brooks, whose artistic awareness of the problem does them little good in terms of the real world they are talking about. Like Dr. Walters, they don't really feel free of responsibility because of their external power of movie making. They may (ironically enough) be attempting to escape from that responsibility into a world of dreams, but at least the dream is totally honest this time: no false *deux ex machina* or slick resolution to deaden the impact.

The Unsuspected (1947)

Director: Michael Curtiz. *Screenplay*: Ranald MacDougall, adapted by Bess Meredyth, from the novel by Charlotte Armstrong. *Photography*: Woody Bredell. *Special Effects*: David C. Kertesz, Harry Barndollar, Robert Burks. *Music*: Franz Waxman. *Art Director*: Anton Grot. *Film Editor*: Frederick Richards. *Producer*: Charles Hoffman. *Production*: Michael Curtiz Productions. *Release*: Warner Brothers, October 3, 1947. 103 minutes. **Cast**: Claude Rains (playing Victor Grandison), Joan Caulfield (Matilda Frazier), Audrey Totter (Althea Keane), Constance Bennett (Jane Moynihan), Hurd Hatfield (Oliver Keane), Michael North (Steven Howard), Fred Clark (Richard Donovan), Jack Lambert (Press), Harry Lewis, Ray Walker, Nana Bryant, Walter Baldwin.

The shadow of a murderer creeps stealthily through the rooms of a huge mansion. In the study a secretary is typing. The phone rings. It is Althea Keane, asking if her husband is home yet. The secretary, whose name is Roslyn, says he isn't. The murderer enters the room. Roslyn drops the phone and screams. Althea calls for Roslyn and is answered by the click of the phone being hung up. Althea asks her date for the time. He tells her it's exactly 9:37. A week later, Jane Moynihan reads a newspaper story telling about the suicide of Roslyn, secretary to the famous Victor Grandison. Jane, who also works for Grandison, then looks up to watch the beginning of his nationwide radio show. After being introduced as the renouned writer, art collector, and teller of strange tales, Grandison begins the narration of his eerie mystery program. Grandison tells of a certain suicide that is really murder. As he describes the inevitable guilt which racks the unsuspected murderer, four apparent suspects are introduced — Steven Howard on a train, Press in a cheap hotel room, and two men at Grandison's mansion — Richard Donovan and Oliver Keane. These last two men are among the guests at a surprise birthday party for Grandison. Steven Howard arrives and introduces himself to Althea, who is Grandison's niece. Althea is immediately fascinated by Steven's brooding sophistication. After introducing Oliver Keane as her drunk husband, Althea wisks Steven away from the guests. Steven sits transfixed by the stunning portrait of the beautiful Matilda Frazier. Althea tells him that Matilda, who was Grandison's ward, was killed on a ship which burned at sea last month. Steven then reveals that he married Matilda only three days before she took the fateful ship. Steven knows that Matilda loved Oliver and that Althea stole him from her. Grandison then arrives and meets Steven. When he is told of Matilda's marriage, Grandison thinks that Steven is after her estate. But this can't be, since Steven is already rich. All Steven wants is the painting. Grandison agrees and invites him to stay the night. The next day, Donovan reports to Grandison that Steven's story checks out. Grandison receives a telegram telling that Matilda is alive and will arrive in New York the following day. Grandison confronts Althea and Steven in the guest house and breaks the good news. Steven asserts his right to meet Matilda at the airport alone. On the drive home from the airport, Matilda tells Steven that she has never seen him before. To prove that they were married, Steven takes her to see the justice of the peace who performed the ceremony. This confuses Matilda even more. She just wants to get back to her home and see Victor, who she loves like a father. Back at the mansion, Grandison toys with a desperate murderer named Press. With a secret recording as evidence, Grandison is blackmailing Press. For what, we don't know yet. Matilda arrives home and confronts Althea. Matilda has learned a lesson from Oliver's marriage. She's tired of being pushed around by Althea and orders her back to her own room. Matilda is then reunited with the coddling Grandison, who admits that the beautiful mansion actually belongs to *her*. Grandison knows that Steven is lying but tells Matilda to play along with him. ("When the time comes, I'll know what to do with him.") The next day, Steven meets Jane in New York. Jane knows that Grandison is after

Left to right: Joan Caulfield (as Matilda Frazier), Claude Rains ((Victor Grandison), Michael North (Steven Howard) in *The Unsuspected* **(Warner Bros., 1947).**

Matilda's money and that Roslyn never committed suicide. For this reason, she is helping Steven with his clever plan. Back at the mansion, Matilda finds out that Roslyn was killed. Donovan, who has now been revealed as a police inspector, arrives at the mansion with Steven. Donovan meets with Grandison and explains the crucial evidence which proves that Roslyn was murdered. When Roslyn hung from the chandelier, a lamp was knocked over which unplugged the clock, giving the exact time of the hanging as 9:35. A record of a long distance call to Roslyn is listed at 9:34. This means that Roslyn saw the murderer and couldn't have committed suicide because she couldn't have hung up the phone. In the next scene, Matilda meets with Oliver. He loves her and begs her to stop avoiding him. She doesn't love him anymore, if she ever did. He thinks she loves Steven, and she doesn't deny it. A day later, Donovan is back snooping around in the cellar of the mansion. As the lights flicker on and off, Grandison tells Matilda that Roslyn was murdered. Matilda is badly shaken by this news and breaks down in

Grandison's arms. Donovan asks Grandison for his alibi. Grandison explains that he was giving his weekly radio broadcast that evening and couldn't have gotten home by 9:30. In the guest house, Steven starts to pump Althea, who tells him about calling Roslyn. Oliver then meets with Grandison and tells him he's going away. Althea comes in and has it out with Oliver. Grandison sneaks into his study and secretly records their conversation. Althea will do anything to keep Matilda from getting married. Oliver threatens to kill her if she doesn't discard her plan. Grandison gets rid of Oliver and then confronts Althea. He has overheard her telling Steven that it was he who murdered Roslyn. For this reason, she must die too! Grandison secretly records this murder scene, just as he did the previous quarrel. He then plants the gun (which also killed Roslyn) in Oliver's coat. Steven confronts Matilda in another part of the mansion. Steven tells Matilda that she's in grave danger from Grandison. She wants to believe him but can't. In the meantime, Grandison has spliced the recording of Althea's murder onto the recording of her quarrel with Oliver, so that it sounds like Oliver kills her. He then starts the doctored recording on high volume and times it so that Steven and Matilda "hear" Oliver shoot Althea just before they can get to her body in the study. The police are alerted to chase Oliver, whose brakes have been sabotaged by Grandison. Oliver is killed in a wreck before the police can get to him. A ballistics matchup on the gun found in the wreck appears to prove that Oliver murdered both Roslyn and Althea. Steven knows that Grandison has engineered the whole thing, but the police won't listen to him. Steven meets Matilda in New York and admits that he arranged the hoax of their marriage to get into Grandison's mansion. His real goal had been to avenge Roslyn, whom he had loved since childhood. Though it started out as just an act, Steven says that now he has fallen in love with Matilda. He desperately tries to warn her to stay away from Grandison, but she won't listen. Instead, Matilda returns to the mansion and admits to Grandison that she loves Steven. Grandison feigns fatherly approval as he carefully sets up Matilda's murder. By pretending to need help with a radio script, Grandison tricks Matilda into writing a suicide note. Steven arrives and beats Grandison to the study. He finds the incriminating recordings and phones the police just before Grandison throws him out. Press, who has been summoned by Grandison, attacks Steven in the garage and locks him in an old trunk. Grandison then gives Matilda the drugged champagne and leaves for his radio broadcast. Thanks to Steven's call, the police arrive at the mansion in time to wake up Matilda. The police then catch Press at a nearby dump, just in time to save Steven from being burned alive. At the broadcast, Grandison sees Matilda and Steven come in with the police. Realizing that he's been caught, Victor Grandison confesses to his audience that *he* is the unsuspected.

More than any other film noir, *The Unsuspected* is about the evil of popular art. The themes are simple and yet complex: Great beauty is inseperable from great power which is inseperable from great evil. The message of the film is as subversive as they come: to love this film is to love the evil and power as well as the sensual beauty of sight and sound. The villain is in control from the very start, and yet he is doomed. We watch for the murderer and then learn that it was the writer, the narrator, the artist, who has contrived a fascinating tale of his own attempt to escape an inevitable fate. As for irony, this is just the beginning. Victor Grandison's story is the most ironic because he is responsible for all that you see.

Grandison has everything. He is rich, famous and successful because he's an artistic genius with vast knowledge, abilities and creative talent. It is no mere twist of the plot that Grandison turns out to be the villain. On the contrary, this revelation is the key to an entire allegorical level of meaning which lurks (like a murderer) below the film's superficial who-done-it structure. Once this level is discovered, *The Unsuspected* becomes a sophisticated dialogue about the relationship between power, beauty, evil and art. Grandison, the artist, seems to own beauty just as he seems to own the mansion and Matilda Frazier (These are the two main symbols of beauty in the film, which are carefully linked by Matilda's painting.) As the complex plot unfolds, Grandison's ownership is exposed as manipulative exploitation of beauty for his own selfish ends. Grandison has everything, which is a power so vast that no man could withstand its corrupting, destructive pattern of cause and effect. No matter how ingeniously powerful he becomes, he must fail in the end because the stakes are just too high.

Grandison understands all this as well as anyone could, but his great awareness can't save him any more than his power and fame. Man is motivated by emotional needs which can never be satisfied by these worldly goals, no matter how refined they become. The more Grandison attempts to channel his basic emotional needs into the power-crazed exploitation of beauty, the deeper he becomes "enmeshed in his own incredible folly." One imagines that Grandison wants to love Matilda as a man (not a coddling father figure) but he knows she would never accept him that way. Thus he tries to murder her right after she confesses love for another. This motivation doesn't undercut the greed for her money; it adds to it the deepest emotional roots of a desperate, twisted selfishness.

Grandison's understanding of himself would probably include any psychological analysis we could make of him. As the self-conscious artist-genius, he even understands that an understanding of his sickness is no cure at all. And so, instead of helping him, Grandison's vast knowledge of himself and others is constantly being utilized by the twisted emotional forces that will stop at nothing to protect themselves. This sickness reaches its supreme expression in his ingenious murder schemes. These schemes are of crucial importance because the plot is devoted largely to uncovering them, and the entire theme of evil is developed through them. The method of these schemes is actually very simple. Grandison utilizes the recorded illusion which is art to fool and manipulate the police into believing he is innocent and someone else (Oliver Keane) is guilty.

To the degree that it is self-conscious, art is the power to manipulate the artist's audience for the precise desired effects. In the modern mystery thriller, this is done by arranging the plot to appear just the way the writer wants. The viewer is carefully manipulated for the maximum effects of suspense, curiosity and narrative attention. Grandison simply transfers this power of plot manipulation (through recorded illusion) to the real world. In a sense, he attempts to make the whole world his work of art by turning people into either characters or viewers which he, the all-knowing artist, cleverly manipulates. The degree to which art is a part of his evil is staggering because this evil is in every way a work of art.

Because he knows he is evil, Grandison must fail. This is made clear in the opening narration, which stresses that the unsuspected can never run away from his own guilt. It is this guilt which makes Grandison slip at the end, allowing Steven Howard to succeed in his daring attempt to catch the murderer. This character is not without his own importance in the film. In addition to being the film's hero, he is also a man primarily motivated by love (first of Roslyn, then Matilda). His conventional identity of goodness is primarily manifested through this ability to love. In the end, Steven wins Matilda and the mansion because his motivation is relatively pure. Art may be owned by the artist, but beauty can never be. True beauty, artistic or human, can only be "owned" by those who truly love.

This does not mean that Steven can do without worldly power. On the contrary, a crucial element of his heroism is his ability to challenge Grandison in his own sphere. Thus his scheme for getting into the mansion parallels the murder schemes. By arranging the evidence of a false past (plot), Steven shows that he too can pull the great artistic manipulation. Steven's scheme is so clever because it succeeds even though Grandison never really believes his story. By arranging for it to appear that he married Matilda, Steven forces Grandison to invite him to stay simply to protect his kind and understanding front. This gives our hero a chance to pursue his goal, which, of course, changes from avenging Roslyn to protecting Matilda. The ensuing power struggle with Grandison ends in a draw as far as successful manipulation is concerned. Steven soon knows that Grandison is the murderer, but Grandison knows he knows it and counters with clever plans of his own. It actually takes a slip by Grandison, some very good luck, and the efforts of several different people to produce the film's climactic justice. Steven Howard plays an important part in this climax, but one can't really say he outfoxes Grandison. No one could do that but Grandison himself, which brings us back to the importance of his guilt.

In the artist, this guilt is also an awareness that goodness (Steven and Matilda?) must triumph over him in the end. Grandison's guilt and his belief in an inevitable fate are inseparable. The rest of the characters do their part, but it is Grandison's own sense of morality which really makes the conventional denouement possible. When the theme is the evil of art, no one is more aware of that evil than the artist-villain himself. This awareness manifests itself through a guilt which reaches the breaking point as Grandison tries to murder Matilda. From this view, Grandison's slip is actually the triumph of his guilty conscience, which just manages to throw off his calculation enough to give Steven and Matilda a chance.

Grandison's surprisingly developed moral conscience helps to give him a black and white character which is perfectly consistent with the film's overall concept of art as the exaggeration of life's strongest impulses. In particular, the ironic juxtaposition of evil and beauty is emphasized through both style and narrative. Grandison, the artist, does bear a certain responsibility for the beauty which surrounds him, but the attainment of this goal has cost him his soul. Great success demands great ambition, which demands great selfishness, which ultimately becomes great evil. To experience or create the total beauty of great art involves a total commitment to art, which involves a dangerous relegation of life to a secondary position. When Grandison is forced to choose between Matilda and the mansion, he chooses against human beauty. The significance of the film's art theme makes this choice much more than a question of either greed or jealousy. On the deepest allegorical level, Grandison must keep the mansion at all costs because it represents his commitment to the ultimate in abstract, manmade beauty which is art.

The film's most powerful irony is structural because its themes don't save the viewer any more than awareness could save Grandison. If the film is successful, the viewer realizes that his attraction of its power and beauty is of the same order as Grandison's attraction to the mansion. Moral themes are all well and good, especially if they include the irrelevance of morality, but the primary effect and power of art is no longer seen as moral. Through the intensification and refinement of style, the emotional and sensual effect of art is exaggerated and clarified. Themes or no themes, this effect is dangerous because art invariably sets itself above life through its very formal perfection.

Implicit in all of these ideas is an inherent link between Grandison and director Michael Curtiz. The lush opulence of the mansion so dominates

The Unsuspected visually that it becomes an artistic metaphor for the film itself. From this view, Grandison setting the mansion above all else is also Curtiz setting the artistic beauty of his film above all else. Like Grandison, Curtiz is a sophisticated artist who knows too much. He knows that he has produced a work of great power and beauty. He also knows the price he had to pay to do it, and this is what the film is all about.

Out of the Past (1947)

Director: Jacques Tourneur. *Screenplay*: Geoffrey Homes (Daniel Mainwaring), from his novel *Build My Gallows High*. *Photography*: Nicholas Musuraca. *Special Effects*: Russell A. Cully. *Music*: Roy Webb. *Art Directors*: Albert D'Agostino, Jack Okey. *Film Editor*: Samuel E. Beetley. *Producer*: Warren Duff. *Production/Relase*: RKO, November 13, 1947. 94 minutes. **Cast**: Robert Mitchum (playing Jeff Bailey), Jane Greer (Kathie Moffat), Kirk Douglas (Whit Sterling), Rhonda Fleming (Meda Carson), Richard Webb (Jim), Steve Brodie (Fisher), Virginia Huston (Ann), Paul Valentine (Joe Stefanos), Dickie Moore (The Kid), Ken Niles (Eels).

A dark stranger drives into the small resort town of Bridgeport, California, and stops at Jeff Bailey's gas station. The stranger tells the deafmute boy working there that he is looking for Jeff. Informed of the stranger's arrival by the boy, Jeff returns from the mountains with his girlfriend Ann. Jeff confronts the stranger whom he knows as Joe Stefanos, a hired thug working for crooked gambler Whit Sterling. Stefanos tells Jeff that his boss wants to see him at Lake Tahoe. Realizing that he has no choice, Jeff drives to Tahoe accompanied by Ann. On the way he tells her of his past dealings with Sterling. This flashback story begins three years earlier with Jeff as a private eye in New York. Sterling hires him and his partner, Fisher, to find Kathie Moffat, Sterling's beautiful mistress, who ran off with $40,000 after trying to kill him. Assuring Fisher that he will get his cut of the large fee, Jeff sets out to track Kathie down. After a bit of clever detective work, Jeff finds Kathie in Acapulco. They meet and have a torrid love affair. She guesses his true identity and begs him not to take her back, saying that she never stole the $40,000. Blinded by love, Jeff agrees to run away with her. On the day they are to leave, Sterling and Stefanos arrive in Acapulco. Jeff makes up some clever lies to get rid of them and flees with Kathie. They travel to San Francisco, where they live a secretive existence haunting dark cinemas and small nightclubs. Their sanctuary is shattered when Jeff is seen by Fisher at the

Top: left, to right, Paul Valentine (playing Joe Stefanos), Kirk Douglas (as Whit Sterling) and Robert Mitchum (as Jeff Bailey); bottom: Jane Greer (as Kathie Moffat) and Mitchum. *Out of the Past* (RKO, 1947).

race track. Jeff and Kathie try to lose Fisher but can't. Fisher confronts them at a remote cabin in the mountains and admits that he's working for Sterling. For what's left of the $40,000, Fisher agrees to keep quiet. With Kathie looking on, a violent fist fight breaks out between the two men. As Fisher staggers from Jeff's blows, Kathie panics and shoots him. When she sees Jeff's shocked reaction, Kathie runs out, leaving him with a corpse and evidence that she did, in fact, have the $40,000. After burying Fisher, Jeff decides that he'd better continue to hide out. With a new name and profession, he settles in Bridgeport. As he finishes this story, Jeff arrives at Sterling's Tahoe estate. While Sterling is welcoming Jeff back to the fold, Kathie casually appears. The three of them sit down to break-fast, and Sterling explains Jeff's new assignment. A lawyer named Leonard Eels is blackmailing Sterling with documents proving his income tax evasion. With the help of Meda Carson, Eels beautiful secretary, Jeff is to steal back the documents. Against his better judgment, Jeff agrees to do the job. Kathie meets with Jeff furtively and tries to explain why she had to return to Sterling, but Jeff's not listening. Jeff then travels to San Francisco and meets with Meda Carson. When she directs him to visit Eels for cocktails, Jeff begins to suspect a double-cross. After leaving Eels, he follows Meda to the lawyer's office and sees her come out with a valise which probably contains the crucial tax records. Jeff then returns to Eels' apartment and finds the lawyer dead. Now knowing for sure that he is the fall guy, Jeff hides the corpse and drives to Meda's apartment. There Jeff watches Kathie carry out the final steps in Sterling's plan to frame him for Eels' murder. To insure prompt discovery of the body, Kathie phones the manager of Eels' apartment building and asks him to check up on Eels. To her surprise, the manager says the apartment is empty. As Kathie ponders what to do next, Jeff confronts her. Convinced that the plan has failed, Kathie tells Jeff about an affadivit which she signed that accuses him of murdering Fisher. By replacing the tax records with this affadivit, they made it look like Eels was blackmailing Jeff instead of Sterling. Kathie then tells Jeff that Meda took the tax records to the office of a North Beach gambling house owned by Sterling. Wasting no time, Jeff walks into the gambling house and steals back the records. When Sterling's men catch up with him, Jeff offers the records in exchange for the affa-davit. Meda then tries to retrieve the affadivit, but the police (who have just discovered Eels' body) beat her to it. Now wanted for two murders, Jeff flees to his mountain hideaway near Bridgeport. He sends the deaf-mute boy to Sterling's Tahoe estate, but Whit is not there. Kathie is, however, and she directs Stefanos to follow the boy back to Jeff and kill him. The boy saves Jeff's life by pulling Stefanos off a cliff with his fishing rod, just as the gunman is about to pull the trigger. That night, Jeff travels to Tahoe himself and confronts Sterling. In exchange for the tax records,

Jeff demands that Sterling turn Kathie in for Fisher's murder and provide him with transportation out of the country. Finally backed up into a corner, Sterling agrees to these demands and viciously forces Kathie to accept her fate. Jeff then drives to Bridgeport and says goodbye to Ann before returning to Tahoe and finding Sterling dead. Kathie arrogantly admits the killing and demands that Jeff run away with her. With all hope of clearing himself gone, Jeff pretends to go along with her. When she goes upstairs to get her bags, he calls the police. As their car meets the police roadblock, Kathie realizes that she's been double-crossed. She shoots Jeff and dies herself in the barrage of machine gun fire that riddles the car as it crashes into the roadblock. In the final scene, the boy tries to help Ann forget Jeff by telling her that he was indeed planning to run away with Kathie.

An unexpected reflexive theme emerges from the flashback and transforms *Out of the Past* into something more than just a standard 40s tale of betrayal and revenge. As a basic indication of this theme, Jeff's romantic entanglement with Kathie is directly linked with movies at several different points in the story. In the Acapulco scenes, it is Jeff who is associated with a bizarre movie theater which sits across from the cafe where the couple first meet. This shot, which shows Jeff in front of the cafe, is taken from an angle that makes the theater the only background. By repeating this shot several times, director Jacques Tourneur emphasizes its symbolic significance. During the final occurence of the shot, Jeff's narration attempts to describe the essential characteristics of his romance with Kathie. He doesn't know where she lives or if she'll try to skip out on him. All he is told is a time and a place to meet her. Despite the dangerous circumstances of their meeting, the couple is oblivious to past or future. In looking back, Jeff doesn't really know what they thought would happen. He can only allude to their trancelike state by saying, "Maybe we thought the world would end, or maybe we thought it was all a dream and we'd wake up with a hangover in Niagara Falls."

After some time passes and Jeff admits his true identity, the couple is no longer able to ignore the past. Nor is Jeff able to continue pretending that he will still do his job. And so they agree to run away together. Perhaps they were trying to escape the past all along, but now they must make an active effort to hide from it. And where do they hide but in a movie house. The sole sequence which characterizes the couple's secretive San Francisco existence shows them coming out of a movie theater. Through the narration, Jeff reinforces the symbolic implication that they practically lived there. When they are drawn away from this hiding place and into more public places like the race track, their past catches up with them in the person of Jeff's partner. After their futile attempt to elude him, Fisher confronts the couple. The moment he walks in the room we see a completely different Kathie. She tells Jeff to "break his head," but when he does beat Fisher up that's not enough for her. Kathie shoots Fisher, and Jeff's romantic dream is ended.

By associating Jeff's love for Kathie with escape from the past and movies, *Out of the Past* accomodates a reflexive interpretation in which Jeff represents the viewer and Kathie symbolizes the film itself. Close scrutiny of their early encounter reveals that Kathie did, in fact, cause Jeff to experience just what the film offers the viewer — suspense, mystery, danger and beauty. Jeff's romantic impulse is, like the viewer's motivation, an attempt to escape the grim (moral?) realities of the past into a dreamlike trance. Like the viewer, Jeff is completely ignorant of Kathie's life away from him (or off camera). All he knows is the time and place of their next "scene" together. There is even a symbolic reference to plot movement built into the romance, as Kathie leads the passive (except in the clinches) Jeff from place to place.

The reflexive symbolism of the flashback helps to indicate the importance of the deep link between the viewer and Jeff in *Out of the Past*. The desire of an ambiguous protagonist had always been implicitly associated with audience expectations in the film noir, but in this film the idea becomes somewhat more overt. Through Jeff, the viewer confronts the full implication of his urge to escape the past into the film's dream world. Escape from the past means escape from morality because of the importance of obligations and commitments. Thus the significance of Jeff's skipping out on his deal with Fisher and Sterling. In a sense, Kathie is right when she tells Jeff at the end that they deserve each other. An undeniable aspect of their mutual romantic yearnings is the urge to escape moral responsibility. The only difference between them is that Kathie is more fanatical and desperate in her twisted need for freedom.

This does not mean that the moral significance of murder is swept under the rug, only that the film seems just as concerned with deeper psychological impulses shared by all the characters. Since he was not exactly unaware of her reputation, Jeff's original fascination for Kathie is ultimately seen as a flirtation with evil. Jeff acts shocked when Kathie kills Fisher, but he shouldn't be. The fact that she might be a murderess was an important part of her alluring mystery all along.

Appropriately, all of Jeff's trouble and all of the film's themes come from "out of the past." As the film opens, that past is reaching out for Jeff like a spider for its prey. The job Whit has for him is actually a complex and diabolical trap designed to pay Jeff back for his past betrayal. Jeff spends the rest of the film trying to escape from this trap, and he almost succeeds. His one mistake, however, is in again underestimating Kathie, and this spells his doom.

This resolution, though harsh, does have its logic. Jeff plays with fire and then tries everything possible to avoid getting burned. By the time he realizes he cannot elude certain grim consequences of his involvement with Kathie, it's too late to make any compromises (with her or jail). And so he just sits back and watches his burns become fatal.

Criss Cross (1949)

Director: Robert Siodmak. *Screenplay*: Daniel Fuchs, from the novel by Don Tracy. *Photography*: Franz Planer. *Special Effects*: David S. Horsley. *Art Directors*: Bernard Herzbrun, Boris Leven. *Music*: Miklos Rozsa. *Film Editor*: Ted J. Kent. *Producer*: Michel Kraike. *Production/release*: Universal-International, January 12, 1949. 87 minutes. **Cast**: Burt Lancaster (playing Steve Thompson), Yvonne DeCarlo (Anna), Dan Duryea (Slim Dundee), Stephen McNally (Pete Ramirez), Richard Long (Slade Thompson), Tom Pedi (Vincent), Percy Helton (Frank), Alan Napier (Finchley), Griff Barnett (Pop), Meg Randall (Helen), Joan Miller (Lush), Edna M. Holland (Mrs. Thompson), John Doucette (Walt), Esy Morales, Marc Krath, James O'Rear, John Skins Miller, Robert Osterloh, Vincent Renno, Charles Wagenheim, Tony Curtis.

The camera pans over L.A. and comes down on Steve and Anna huddled in a parking lot. Steve tells Anna to wait for him at the beach house. She's very worried that Slim will find out or something else will go wrong. Inside the nightclub, Slim is waiting impatiently for Anna. She comes in and Slim cross-examines her. Anna tells Slim to leave her alone. Steve walks into the club and is met by police Lt. Pete Ramirez, who tries to stop him from going in. Steve pushes Ramirez away and confronts Slim and Anna in a private dining room. Slim welcomes Steve. Cut back to Ramirez who is told that Slim has a knife on him. Ramirez walks into the dining room and picks the knife off the floor. It looks like Steve and Slim have been fighting, but everyone denies that anything happened. We then follow everyone but Ramirez into the alley. A thug explains the plot. The fight was supposed to be staged, but it got a little carried away. The thug persuades Steve and Slim to shake hands because of the heist ("Boy, would Ramirez be surprised to know they're on a caper together"). The next day at the armored car company, Steve arrives for work. One of his compatriots is eliminated through a phone call telling him his wife is sick. That leaves only Steve and Pop to drive the armored car. Pop is worried, but Steve lies effectively, telling him everything will be all right. As they speed down the road, Steve reflects upon how he got himself into this situation.

Top: Yvonne De Carlo (as Anna) and Burt Lancaster (playing Steve Thompson) meet in a parking lot in the opening scene; bottom: left to right, De Carlo, Dan Duryea (as Slim Dundee), one of Slim's gangsters, and Lancaster. *Criss Cross* (Universal-International, 1949).

The flashback opens with Steve returning to L.A. after being away for a year. Through the narration, Steve assures us that he did not return because of Anna. He just wants to help out his folks and maybe get his old job back. Since no one is at his house, he goes downtown to phone his old friend Pete Ramirez. Pete isn't in either, so Steve casually wanders into "the club." Old memories crowd Steve's mind as he talks to the "new" bartender. Ramirez soon shows up and tells Steve to stay away from Anna. Back at home, Steve's family is introduced. After dinner, Steve's kid brother displays his manhood by necking with his fiancée in the parlor. Steve decides to go out and heads straight for the club. He is reunited with Anna and meets Slim Dundee, a shady looking character who appears to be her new boyfriend. Several days later, Anna meets Steve at a corner drugstore. They talk of the past and all the good times they used to have. (We learn they were married for seven months before Steve left town.) After assuring Steve that Slim means nothing to her, Anna proposes they they start seeing each other again. Steve tries to put her off for good, but changes his mind at the last second. They go out several times, and Steve soon falls in love with Anna again. Steve's mother tries to warn him to stay away from Anna. Steve won't listen. He goes to the club that evening and is told by the bartender that Anna has married Slim. Steve tries to forget Anna but fails miserably in this task. Then one day, he runs into her outside of the Union Station, and they go to his place. Steve is surprised to learn that Anna had good reasons for leaving him in the lurch. A few nights before the elopement, Pete Ramirez took Anna down to the police station and threatened to frame her for a crime if she didn't stop seeing Steve. Anna, who was already fed up with the pressure from Steve's family, decided she could take no more. When he hears this story, Steve realizes that Anna was a victim as much as he. Anna wants to come back to him now, but Slim poses a formidable problem. They need money to get away from the vicious gangster. Steve mulls over the situation and comes up with the idea of robbing the armored car company. Several days later, Anna comes to Steve at his home with a warning that Slim is after him. Almost immediately, the couple is confronted by Slim and his thugs. To prove that things are not as they seem, Steve proposes the armored car heist. Since Steve will be the inside man, Slim goes for the idea. They call in a big criminal mastermind named Finchley and carefully plan the robbery. A mass of details and intricate arrangements stretches into the night. Among other things, it is agreed that Anna will hold the money until the heat is off. At daybreak Steve meets furtively with Anna in an adjoining room. He tells her to go to the beach house after getting the money and wait several weeks for him. Anna is really worried. She now wishes they had never met. Having brought us right back to the start of the film, the flashback ends.

And now it is only a few minutes until the robbery. Steve continues to reassure Pop as they notice an ominous black car following them. After pretending to lose the car, Steve pulls into the armored car company lot. Smoke bombs saturate the area, and Slim's men close in just as Steve and Pop get out of the armored car. When he sees Slim murder Pop, Steve instinctively reacts by fighting off the criminals. As they drive off with Pop's half of the money, Steve passes out from a bullet wound in the arm. He wakes up in a hospital room surrounded by his family. When they leave, Steve passes out again. Hours later, he wakes up to see Ramirez standing in the corner of the blurry room. Having guessed the truth about Steve's complicity in the robbery, Ramirez proceeds to describe the baffling situation he is now in. Everything depends on Anna. If Steve's hope is answered and she doesn't double-cross him, Slim will send a killer to the hospital for revenge. Steve is safe only if Anna betrays him by returning to Dundee. Ramirez thinks the situation is pretty hopeless either way and leaves after wishing he had been even more foreceful in his attempts to keep Steve and Anna apart. Since he believes Anna will not betray him, Steve now knows he is in grave danger. In desperation he asks a man in the hall to stay in the room through the night. Several hours later, the man wakes Steve up and admits he is working for Slim. As the man prepares to sneak him out of the hospital, Steve passes out again. When he wakes up, Steve is in a car speeding down the highway. By offering the driver $10,000, Steve persuades him to drive to the beach house instead of Slim's. Anna is at the beach house, but not for long. She desperately fears Slim and has decided to take off by herself. Steve would be a dangerous burden with his wounded arm and notoriety. She is sorry but Steve is just going to have to grow up and face the world as it really is. Anna starts to leave but is back almost immediately with a look of terror on her face. It's Slim, of course, and he kills them both as the authorities close in.

The primary themes of *Criss Cross* center around one question: Why is its protagonist unable to escape from the clutches of a *femme fatale* that he knows will eventually spell his doom? Steve Thompson's answer to this question is conveyed primarily through his narration during the film's lengthy flashback sequence. By analyzing the chain of events which led up to his chance meetings with Anna, Steve attempts to prove that a power greater than man was responsible for his eventual tragedy. For a time this explanation looks very attractive, but eventually *Criss Cross* gives the viewer just enough information to see this viewpoint for what it really is — a doomed character's convenient excuse for his own destructive desires and dangerous lack of will power.

Steve's narrative attempts to prove the existence of fate reach their climax in the scene at Union Station, when he sees Anna for the first time since her marriage to Slim. The attractiveness of Steve's philosophical assertion is nowhere more evident than in his careful description of the fantastically precise timing that "made him" see Anna in the middle of the crowded station. Steve's narration is interwoven into this scene so perfectly that his fate argument is driven home at the exact moment when Anna catches his eye. The argument is deceptively simple and convincing: fate must be operating because the coincidence is so perfectly timed. Along with Steve, we have seen the evidence, and now we are encouraged to believe the apparent explanation.

What is really operating here is not fate at all (at least not the kind Steve is talking about), but the power of the film itself. While watching the film, the viewer is drawn into the protagonist's mind and accepts his explanations. Only after the film has ended does the viewer have time to see through Steve's subconscious rationalization. The occurrence of certain coincidences (no matter how fantastic) proves very little when Steve's will power is constantly crumbling in Anna's presence. The Union Station sequence illustrates this as much as any scene. So what if Steve happened to see Anna? Did this mean he must meet with her? Fate, whether it exists or not (and the film leaves this open), did not make Steve lose his will power. The underlying existential truth of *Criss Cross* is that only Steve can be held responsible for that.

Discounting the fate argument, we are left with a tragic-romantic portrait of Steve's helplessness before Anna. The real truth of their relationship is most clear in the drugstore scene, when Steve makes his greatest effort to establish his independence. Right after telling Anna goodbye forever, he changes his mind and asks her on a date. Nothing we are shown of the character is more revealing than this capitulation. Despite all his judgment to the contrary, Steve is simply unable to break free of Anna's hypnotic spell of love.

Criss Cross is tragic-romantic because this is its definition of love — an intoxicating and dangerous loss of control before the mysterious object of one's desire. Hollywood movies, generally, and this classic suspenser, in particular, are perfectly equipped to defend this viewpoint. Since the viewer of narrative films must always be passive, the love of these films must largely be based upon a certain loss of assertive self-control. *Criss Cross* exploits this aesthetic truth in ways which aren't readily apparent. The power and significance of loss of control are carefully utilized to make the viewer identify with Steve on levels which are much deeper than he realizes. The power of the film is like the power of Anna, devoid of moral considerations. Time after time, Siodmak demonstrates this through his precise manipulation of the narrative. Such heavy manipulation invariably makes one crucial point — the viewer's attention can be directed anywhere; anything or anyone can become fascinating in a good suspense film. Thus identification, which is the very heart of the cinema's power, need not have much to do with one's beliefs or attitudes. In this case, which is anything but an isolated example, it's much more a kind of delirious desire for the unpredictable beauty of Anna and *Criss Cross*.

Caught (1949)

Director: Max Ophuls. *Screenplay*: Arthur Laurents, from the novel *Wild Calendar* by Libbie Block. *Photography*: Lee Garmes. *Montage*: Michael Luciano. *Music*: Frederick Hollander. *Art Director*: P. Frank Sylos. *Film Editor*: Robert Parrish. *Producer*: Wolfgang Reinhardt. *Production*: Enterprise Productions. *Release*: MGM, February 17, 1949. 88 minutes. **Cast**: Robert Ryan (playing Smith Ohlrig), James Mason (Dr. Larry Quinada), Barbara Bel Geddes (Leonora Eames), Ruth Brady (Maxine), Curt Bois (Franzi), Frank Ferguson (Dr. Hoffman), Natalie Schaefer (Dorothy Daly), Art Smith (Psychiatrist), Sonia Darrin (Miss Chambers), Bernadene Hayes, Ann Morrison, Wilton Graff, Jim Hawkins, Vicki Stiener.

Carhop Leonora Eames is persuaded by a girlfriend to take a six-week charm school course so that she can meet a "decent" man with money. When the course is completed, Leonora gets a job modeling in an expensive department store. While at work, Leonora receives an invitation to a yachting party being given by millionaire Smith Ohlrig. Leanora meets Ohlrig, and he takes her out several times, but she won't sleep with him. Though he has no intention of getting married, Ohlrig changes his mind just to prove his psychiatrist wrong. Leonora accepts Ohlrig's proposal, and their marriage is front page news. Leonora is almost immediately dissatisfied with the wifely role that Ohlrig demands of her. On a typical day, she waits until after midnight for him to return from work. When he does show up, Ohlrig is accompanied by clients whom Leonora is expected to entertain. After this goes on for several months, Leonora has it out with Ohlrig. Since it is obvious that he has no intention of changing his lifestyle to accommodate her, Leonora decides to move out on Ohlrig. Determined to prove her independence, she takes a small Manhattan apartment and gets a job as a doctor's assistant. Leonora tries to do a good job, but it's very difficult to please the critical and dedicated Dr. Quinada. Then one evening, she receives a visit from Ohlrig and is persuaded to go out to dinner with him. Though Ohlrig is

Top: the first meeting of Barbara Bel Geddes (playing Leonora Eames) and Robert Ryan (as Smith Ohlrig); bottom: millionaire Ryan, in *Caught* (MGM, 1949).

able to sweet-talk her into bed, Leonora realizes the next morning that he has no real intention of changing. As a result, she returns to her job more determined than ever to please Dr. Quinada. Working day and night together, Leonora and Quinada soon fall in love. Not long after this, Leonora discovers that she is pregnant. Quinada wants to marry Leonora, but she is unable to tell him the truth about her other life. Instead, she returns to Ohlrig for the good of the baby. Quinada follows Leonora to Ohlrig's mansion and learns about their marriage. As Quinada is leaving, Leonora stops him and reveals her pregnancy. She admits her love for Quinada but is still torn between the two men because of the pregnancy. After Quinada finally leaves, Ohlrig threatens to have Leonora's baby taken away if she tries to divorce him. Certain that he would and could carry out this threat, Leonora begrudgingly stays with Ohlrig. For months she stays locked in her room at the mansion, seldom agreeing to see anyone. Then late one night, Ohlrig returns from work and demands that Leonora see him. When she refuses, Ohlrig has one of his hysterical heart attacks. As crowds of people gather around the prostrate millionaire, Quinada comes to rescue Leonora. He soon discovers that the shock of Ohlrig's attack has sent her into premature labor. Taking no chances, Quinada wisks Leonora off to the hospital in an ambulance. Several hours later, he learns that Leonora survived the operation but the baby didn't. Finally free to start a new life together, Quinada and Leonora are reunited in her hospital room.

Innocent, naive carhop Leonora Eames is seduced by a popular value system which stresses the importance of money and success. Leonora's overbearing roommate Maxine tells her over and over that marrying rich is her only hope of a secure and happy life. Maxine's plan of taking charm school and landing a modeling job works only too well for Leonora, who turns out to be the one girl in a million fated to hook a millionaire. Once she's married to Smith Ohlrig, Leonora learns just how wrong Maxine was about life. Instead of a man who has everything, Ohlrig turns out to be a man hopelessly trapped by everything he has.

The psychology of Smith Ohlrig assumes a primary thematic importance because it represents an explanatory demonstration of why and how a materialistic value system can be so destructive. The very root of Ohlrig's sickness lies in his belief that money and power are the only important goals in life. This belief has led him to the top of a world where everyone is just as selfish and manipulative as he is. In fact, the primary assumption of this "world of success" is that everyone operates from selfish motives. By reinforcing only the selfish greed of others, Ohlrig dooms himself to seeing people respond only in selfish ways, which, in turn, reinforces his cynical view of human nature. In an important sense,

Ohlrig's materialism forces him to deny the existence of the emotional needs which really motivate people. His cynical power approach to life is inevitably frustrating and self-destructive because it results in the pathological denial of that thing which he needs most—love. To put it even more ironically, Ohlrig is driven by a desperate need for something that he doesn't believe is possible. Elevating money and power as the primary goals in life forced him into this trap from which there seems to be no escape.

Maxine's belief that money brings security attains its own special irony in the light of Ohlrig's unbalanced character. If Ohlrig proves anything, it is that money breeds a self-perpetuating insecurity that prevents one from any real fulfillment or salvation. Since he has nothing but monetary advantages to offer people, Ohlrig correctly believes that this is the only reason why anyone ever shows an interest in him. This distrust of people's motives is exceptionally damaging to his relationship with Leonora. Though she attempts to deny it, Ohlrig and the viewer can see that Leonora did, in fact, marry him for his money. This is what aggravates his insecurity so badly, and this is what makes him treat Leonora like a hired servant. When she responds by rejecting him in ways that he cannot cope with, the situation becomes completely hopeless.

Leonora and Ohlrig are both "caught" by a sickness which pervades an entire society. The unparalleled role of media propaganda in perpetuating the continued prevalance of these false values is emphasized throughout the film. Magazines, newspapers, and even movies are presented as the insidious tools of a capitalistic establishment bent on reinforcing the public's obsession with money. With Smith Ohlrig as the thematic focal point, *Caught* carefully exposes the psychological, philosophical, and even metaphysical roots of this materialistic sickness. This latter dimension, which arises naturally from director Max Ophuls' radical visual style, is quite extraordinary for an American film of the period. By constantly asserting the significance of the physical space surrounding the characters, Ophuls extends the theme of materialism to the deepest levels of man's relationship with his environment. When put within a complete aesthetic context, *Caught*'s concept of materialism encompasses social man's unconscious assumptions about the nature of reality. To wit: the materialistic impulse has gone so far in Smith Ohlrig that he has come to treat people like physical objects (an idea which is stressed through the character's compulsive fixation for pool and pinball).

Ophuls' magnification of space helps to preserve the significance of a close parallel between social and physical environments. The two ways of life which end up fighting for Leonora are represented by characters on one level and overall composition on another. The huge, elegant rooms of Ohlrig's mansion are ironically contrasted with the cramped settings of

Leonora's "other life" with Quinada. Ironic because all that baroque deep-focus space in the mansion scenes actually oppresses the characters much more than the seemingly claustrophobic settings at Quinada's offices. The meaning of this visual contrast is implicitly obvious: in terms of the physical world, everyone is oppressed. True freedom must, therefore, involve a relative transcendence of that dimension's apparent supremacy.

As the only characters in the film who have approached this freedom, Doctors Quinada and Hoffman are two rare examples of unselfish, productive living. Significantly, their commitment to health overrides their technical roles as medical doctors who treat only physical ailments. In fact, one might even say that Quinada and Hoffman are good doctors because they understand the frequent interrelationship of the physical and the psychological. This point is clearly illustrated when Quinada becomes upset with Leonora for preaching charm school values to his patients. Though Leonora doesn't understand it at the time, Quinada gets so mad at her because he knows how unhealthy such ideas can be.

Ophuls' visual depiction of Quinada and Hoffman is even more thematic than his treatment of the other characters. While continuing to emphasize physical surroundings, Ophuls creatively modifies his camera placements to indicate their radically different (from Ohlrig and Leonora) relationship with those surroundings. Following Quinada through his offices by tracking through walls is the most literal example of this technique, but not the most outstanding. That occurs in a scene midway through the film, in which Quinada and Hoffman stand in their respective office doorways discussing Leonora's absence from work. In the most bizarre shot of the entire film, the camera is set up below and directly in front of Leonora's empty desk, which sits in the reception room between the two doctors. As Ophuls pans back and forth between them, the empty desk looms ominously in the center of the screen. While noting that the desk is the most obtrusive physical object in the film, the viewer also realizes that its meaning is completely different from all those protruding objects at Ohlrig's mansion. As a desk or even a part of the physical surroundings, the desk means nothing to Quinada and Hoffman. In stark contrast to the physical symbolism of Ohlrig's objects, the empty desk is so obtrusive only because it represents the glaring absence of a person who is sorely missed.

By ironically reversing the meaning of physical objects in this way, Ophuls cleverly indicates their proper place in a healthy environment. The life which Leonora and Quinada begin together at the end of the film may very well be cramped physically, but they will still be free as long as their attitudes are anti-materialistic. This is how some characters can be liberated in a film in which they all appear oppressed.

The Reckless Moment (1949)

Director: Max Ophuls. *Screenplay*: Henry Garson and Robert W. Soderberg, adapted by Mel Dinelli and Robert E. Kent, from the novel *The Blank Wall* by Elisabeth Sanxay Holding. *Photography*: Burnett Guffey. *Music*: Hans J. Salter. *Art Director*: Cary Odell. *Film Editor*: Gene Havlick. *Producer*: Walter Wanger. *Production*: Walter Wanger Productions. *Release*: Columbia, November, 1949. 82 minutes. **Cast**: James Mason (playing Martin Donnelly), Joan Bennett (Lucia Harper), Geraldine Brooks (Beatrice Harper), Henry O'Neill (Mr. Harper), Sheppard Strudwick (Ted Darby), Roy Roberts (Nagle), David Blair (David Harper), Frances Williams (Sybil).

Lucia Harper and her family live in an affluent suburban home on the California coast. With her husband away on business, Lucia has her hands full trying to ride herd on Bee, her seventeen-year-old daughter. As the film opens, Luica drives the 50 miles to L.A. and meets with Ted Darby, a middle-aged gigolo who's been seeing Bee. Lucia demands that Darby break off the relationship. Darby asks for payment and Lucia walks out. Back at home, Lucia tells Bee of Darby's demands, but she won't believe it. Lucia forbids Bee from seeing Darby, and they have a bitter quarrel. That evening, Bee sneaks out and meets Darby in the boat-house. When Darby admits asking for money, Bee becomes hysterical and hits him on the head with a flashlight. The next morning, Lucia finds Darby's body on the beach. Stunned by the flashlight blow, he had fallen onto an anchor and been killed. In a desperate attempt to protect her family from scandal, Lucia transports the body to another beach. News of the "murder" appears in the local papers the following day. That evening, a small-time blackmailer named Martin Donnelly visits the Harper home. He and his partner, Nagle, have in their possession a pile of love letters which Bee had written to Darby. Donnelly promptly demands $5,000 to keep them from showing the letters to the police. Lucia tries to put Donnelly off but fails. He returns the next day, and they drive to town together. After warning that Nagle won't wait long, Donnelly agrees to give Lucia a few more days. Lucia's anxiety increases as the murder investigation brings the police to her home. She tries to raise the money but is only able to get $800 by pawning some jewelry. When she offers this money to Donnelly, he informs her that another man has been picked up for Darby's murder. Lucia is concerned because she knows the man is innocent. She tells Donnelly that *she* killed Darby. Though he's skeptical about this confession, Donnelly says that the man deserves whatever he gets, even if he is innocent. Since the arrest lets Lucia off the hook, Donnelly advises her to do nothing. Still pondering her next move, Lucia returns home to find Nagle waiting for her in the boathouse. The man

Top: Joan Bennett (playing Lucia Harper) and James Mason (as Martin Donnelly); bottom: Mason with the corpse, Roy Roberts, of his partner (a man named Nagle). *The Reckless Moment* (Columbia, 1949).

who had been picked up earlier has now been released, and the blackmail is back on. While Nagle is threatening Lucia, Donnelly arrives. In an ironic attempt to save Lucia, Donnelly attacks and strangles his ruthless partner. When Lucia runs into the house to get bandages for his wounds, Donnelly drives off with Nagle's body. Lucia and her maid follow in their car. A few miles down the road, they find Donnelly pinned underneath the car which he had deliberately crashed. As Lucia clutches at him in tears, Donnelly tells her to leave to avoid the police. Despite her grief, she does as he says. Later that evening, Lucia learns that Donnelly confessed to Darby's murder just before dying.

The Reckless Moment portrays a devoted American mother as hopelessly trapped by the responsibilities and prejudices of her social role. Lucia Harper's primary motivation seems to be the protection of her family's respectable autonomy. In the course of the film, three "unsavory" lower-class characters emerge to threaten this autonomy. When Ted Darby is accidentally killed, Lucia acts to prevent scandal by disposing of the body. Almost immediately, Martin Donnelly appears to replace Darby as a threat to the Harper family. The character of Donnelly is so important because he explodes every stereotype that Lucia and the viewer might have regarding the desperate lower classes which he represents. In fact, Donnelly seems to be on the verge of a profound social perspective closely related to the film's ultimate theme. He clearly indicates this theme when he says to Lucia, "We're all involved with each other, one way or another. You have your family. I have my Nagle." Donnelly knows that both he and Lucia are trapped by their lives, but implies that this mutual entrapment represents an important link between them. Though both are forced to play out the social roles which make them enemies, Donnelly can see beyond the roles to the mutual humanity which is being stifled by them. Lucia, on the other hand, is lost in her role, primarily because she has a life worth protecting.

Lucia's protective values mask the assumption that the lower classes deserve, by their own inferiority, to be "down." This is because her goal of respectability is based upon freedom from (and over) them. One is respectable if one does not associate with the unrespectable, and if one remains unsoiled by the sins and scandals which threaten one's social image. Lucia cannot see that to base one's attitudes towards people on their social image represents a profound denial of their humanity. Since her primary concern for her own family involves that image, she denies their humanity as well. Her misguided motive of protection isolates her from her family because it represses intimate communication. Protecting one's outward image means denying one's inward reality, and this is what Lucia is constantly doing to herself and everyone around her.

The Reckless Moment carefully hints that things like sensitivity, awareness and honesty are much more healthy values than respectability. The film's subversive irony arises from the fact that Donnelly is the only character who possesses these traits to any significant degree. Ironic because he should be the villain. But that's just the point. Lucia and the viewer must be proved wrong to assume that Donnelly is as unsavory or evil as outward appearances indicate. Thus we are given a sympathetic view of a character who has been trapped by the morally debilitating effect of his social circumstances. In a way, this evil effect is represented by Donnelly's ruthless alter ego, Nagle. Thanks to him, Donnelly has been approaching the end of his rope for some time. The blackmailing of Lucia Harper represents the last straw. When his sympathy for her reaches a peak, Donnelly strikes out at Nagle with all his desperate anguish. Then, after destroying the influence that had made him hate his life so much, Donnelly destroys himself. Nagle or no Nagle, he is unable to salvage any hope or faith in his own life. Instead he decides to sacrifice it all for someone who has something worth living for.

The film's final, disturbing question remains whether or not that sacrifice is worth much. Though Donnelly ends the threat of scandal and breaks through to Lucia on some emotional level, he cannot end her repressive entrapment. This is the meaning of the final scene, in which Lucia continues to lie to her husband while framed behind the foreboding bars of a staircase in her home. All Donnelly has really accomplished is to put Lucia right back where she started before Ted Darby was killed. In terms of the film's themes, the inherent pessimism of this ending is undeniable. The power of social circumstances is ultimately too great for both of the main characters. Donnelly is freed only by death, while Lucia remains safe and secure behind the bars of her home.

The File on Thelma Jordon (1949)

Director: Robert Siodmak. *Screenplay*: Ketti Frings, from a story by Marty Holland. *Photography*: George Barnes. *Special Effects*: Gordon Jennings. *Music*: Victor Young. *Art Directors*: Hans Dreier, Earl Hedrick. *Film Editor*: Warren Low. *Producer*: Hal B. Wallis. *Production*: Hal B. Wallis Productions. *Release*: Paramount, December 31, 1949. 100 minutes. **Cast**: Barbara Stanwyck (playing Thelma Jordon), Wendell Corey (Cleve Marshall), Paul Kelly (Miles Scott), Joan Tetzel (Pamela Marshall), Stanley Ridges (Kingsley Willis), Richard Rober (Tony Laredo), Minor Watson (Judge Calvin Blackwell), Gertrude W. Hoffman (Aunt Vera Edwards), Harry Antrim (Sidney), Kate Lawson, Theresa Harris, Byron Barr, Geraldine Wall, Jonathan Corey, Robin Corey.

I. *The Affair.* Frustrated about his wife's social conformity, Assistant District Attorney Cleve Marshall spends his wedding anniversary at the office drinking. When Thelma Jordon arrives to report some recent burglary attempts at her rich aunt's home, Marshall asks her out for a drink. Though she fends off his advances that evening, Thelma continues to see Marshall and they soon begin an illicit affair. Thelma eventually confesses that she is married to a gambler named Tony Laredo, who left her some time ago. Marshall seems torn between Thelma and his wife, who soon guesses that he's having an affair.

II. *The Murder.* Thelma's aunt gets out of bed to investigate noises in the house. She disappears into the den and a single shot rings out. Marshall calls the house and Thelma answers. Thelma tells Marshall that something is wrong. When he meets her outside, she is in a confused daze. She tells him that her aunt has been murdered, supposedly by an unknown burglar. Marshall becomes upset when Thelma admits wiping off her fingerprints. He follows her back to the house and has her replace the evidence of her presence. A neighbor is aroused, and this causes the butler to discover the body. Before it has a chance to get off the ground, the couple's plan is a disastrous failure, dependent as it was upon Thelma's finding and reporting the body. Marshall tells her to pretend to be in bed and escapes out the window in the nick of time.

III. *The Investigation.* Chief Investigator Miles Scott feels certain that Thelma is guilty. The butler overheard her conversation with Marshall, but he doesn't know Marshall's identity. Thelma refuses to divulge it, and he becomes known as Mr. X. Both this conversation and Thelma's fingerprints represent strong evidence against her, since she claimed to be in bed. In addition, Thelma is left all of the aunt's money, which gives her the perfect motive. When the jewels from the safe are recovered and it is learned that Tony was in Chicago on the night of the murder, the police are confident that they have an airtight case.

IV. *The Trial.* Marshall gives Thelma the money to hire Kingsley Willis, "the best defense lawyer in the country." On the advice of Mr. X, Willis pulls a clever trick which gets the District Attorney disqualified from the case and replaced by Marshall. When it looks like he, Marshall, might win, Marshall (as Mr. X) again contacts Willis and tells him not to put Thelma on the stand. Willis' big closing argument is based on the possibility that Mr. X was the murderer and Thelma is protecting him because of love. By referring to trial transcripts, Willis proves that Mr. X could have killed the aunt and still had time to call Thelma when he did. (Marshall had implied that the call cleared Mr. X.) The jury buys this argument and Thelma is acquitted.

V. *Denouement.* Back at the house, Thelma is with Tony. He alludes to their plan and tells her to get rid of Marshall for good. Just

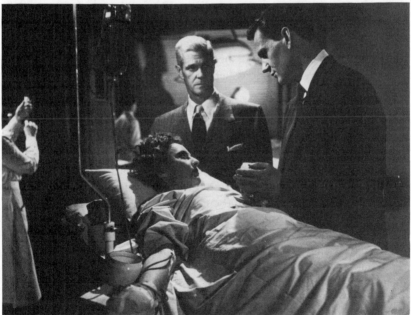

Top: Wendell Corey (as Cleve Marshall) and Barbara Stanwyck (playing Thelma Jordon) in an early scene; bottom: Stanwyck, Paul Kelly (as Miles Scott), and Corey. *The File on Thelma Jordon* (Paramount, 1949).

then, Marshall shows up. As Tony listens, Thelma confesses the truth to Marshall. She tells him that he was a part of the plan but the aunt's murder wasn't. The plan was to rob the aunt's jewels and have the police believe it was an anonymous burglary. When the aunt caught her at the safe, Thelma was forced to shoot. After this confession, Tony knocks Marshall out and leaves with Thelma. Thelma attacks Tony with a cigarette lighter in the car, and a violent crash results. Tony is killed and Thelma is mortally wounded. At the hospital, Thelma confesses her guilt to Scott but refuses to reveal the identity of Mr. X. Minutes later she is dead. Scott then informs Marshall that he knows Marshall is Mr. X. Scott intends to turn Marshall in for disbarment, but Marshall has already turned himself in. After admitting that he will probably go back to his wife, Marshall walks off to try and pick up the pieces of his life.

In *The File on Thelma Jordon*, Siodmak magnifies the film noir's frequent tendency toward characters with unclear motives and uses that concept as the basis of the film's suspense. With Marshall's frustrated motivation apparently established in the first scene, the viewer's initial curiosity and distrust is focused upon Thelma. Siodmak keeps this curiosity at a peak through a rhythmic alteration of contradictory clues, which increase the mystery of her character without revealing much of anything. When the murder takes place, all the viewer really knows about Thelma is that she hasn't been completely truthful with Marshall. From that point on, curiosity about her builds in a more conventional way, since nothing she says or does before the climax sheds any light on the truth.

The mystery of Thelma's character is based primarily upon facts (about her relationship with Tony) that aren't revealed to Marshall or the viewer until the end. Once she does make her confession to Marshall, Thelma's earlier behavior makes pretty good sense. Under the evil influence of Tony, she set out to use Marshall as a part of a plan to rob the rich aunt. When she was forced to shoot the aunt, Thelma ended up using Marshall to gain acquittal from the murder charge. In the meantime, she began to love Marshall and hate Tony. This emotional reversal apparently reached its climax with her confession to Marshall. Since Tony had no intention of letting her go, Thelma struck out at him in a spontaneous act which had definite suicidal undertones. Always tragically "soiled" in life, Thelma attains moral purity in death by taking the full blame for the aunt's murder and refusing to reveal the identity of her beloved Mr. X.

In contrast to Thelma, confusion about the motivation of Marshall is fairly subtle and never really cleared up. Much of one's doubts about his motives centers upon the crucial and fascinating scene in which he directs Thelma to replace her fingerprints on the body of the murdered aunt. The scene moves so quickly that the viewer is never really able to get his bearings. Without realizing it at the time, the viewer is really in the same boat as Thelma. Both are swept up by Marshall's quick, decisive directions, and both assume that he is simply trying to protect her. When his plan turns into an ironic blunder which has the effect of implicating Thelma even more than she would have been without his help, I for one begin to question what Marshall was really up to. Perhaps he wasn't trying to protect Thelma when he directed her to replace her fingerprints. Once the neighbor was aroused, it must have been obvious to him that Thelma wouldn't be able to "discover" the body before someone else found it. Given that probability, he must have known that the fingerprints would implicate rather than protect her. And yet, he still had her go ahead with the plan.

Confusion about Marshall's real intentions continues into the trial. When he gets himself appointed prosecutor, the big question becomes whether or not he is really trying to throw the case. Marshall's treatment of a key juror is apparently crucial, but one never really learns much from this because of confusion about just what effect he is trying to have on the woman. Marshall does indicate to Thelma that he is afraid of his prosecutor's instincts taking over. Because of that fear, he advises the defense attorney not to put her on the stand. Thanks to this and some clever arguments by the defense regarding the possible guilt of Mr. X, Thelma is acquitted. Just what Marshall's real reaction is, no one can tell.

Cleve Marshall's psychological dilemma is ultimately more complex than Thelma's because it involves several different but interrelated emotional and moral conflicts. First, there is the strictly emotional conflict between his love for Thelma and his love for his wife. There is, of course, a basic moral issue involved here, but Marshall seems to ignore it. Next, there is the question of Thelma's guilt. There are strong indications that Marshall's assumption of her innocence was mainly a deception (of her, or himself, or both). When Thelma finally does confess, Marshall replies, "I guess I knew it all the time." If one accepts this statement on face value, then Marshall must have been trying to protect her despite her guilt. Somehow this explanation seems very attractive, though I would never be willing to go all the way with it. Perhaps his need to protect her prevented him from fully admitting that he believed she was guilty.

Deep speculation along these lines is largely futile since the film goes out of its way to withhold any final answers. One can only assume that Marshall was vacillating because of the confusion which all of these problems caused within him. If he never really believed Thelma was innocent, his protective action must be considered a victory for love over the moral and legal standards which had previously guided his life. By the time his ordeal is over, Marshall has confronted psychological ironies which he never knew existed and learned that simplistic moral standards are helpless in the face of such profound conflicts. In other words, moral ambiguity and psychological ambiguity go hand in hand. That is why there are no strictly positive characters in *The File on Thelma Jordon*, and that is why Thelma is seen much more as a tragic victim than as an evil *femme fatale*.

D.O.A. (1950)

Director: Rudolph Maté. *Screenplay*: Russell Rouse and Clarence Greene. *Photography*: Ernest Laszlo. *Music*: Dimitri Tiomkin. *Art Director*: Duncan Cramer. *Film Editor*: Arthur H. Nadel. *Producer*: Leo C. Popkin. *Production*: Harry M. Popkin Productions. *Release*: United Artists, April 21, 1950. 83 minutes. **Cast**: Edmond O'Brien (playing Frank Bigelow), Pamela Britton (Paula Gibson), Luther Adler (Majak), Beverly Campbell (Miss Foster), Lynn Baggett (Mrs. Phillips), William Ching (Halliday), Neville Brand (Chester), Henry Hart (Stanley Phillips), Laurette Luez (Marla Rakubian), Jess Kirkpatrick, Cay Forrester, Virgina Lee, Michael Ross.

Frank Bigelow walks into the Los Angeles homicide bureau to report his own murder. Bigelow then proceeds to tell his story, which is depicted in flashback. Bigelow comes from a small town in the desert named Banning. He runs a small business as an accountant and notary public. He is engaged to his secretary, Paula Gibson. Paula is hurt because Bigelow doesn't want her to come on his impulsive trip to San Francisco, but she eventually agrees that he should be free to get away for awhile. Bigelow arrives at a San Francisco hotel filled with wild conventioneers. Paula calls to tell Bigelow that a Mr. Phillips is trying to reach him. Bigelow is invited to a party next door by a Mr. Haskell. Mrs. Haskell takes a big interest in Bigelow, and the party moves to a bar on the waterfront called "The Fisherman." Caught between a promiscuous wife and her jealous husband, Bigelow escapes by talking to another woman. During this conversation a mysterious stranger (whose face you never see) switches Bigelow's drink. The next day, Bigelow wakes up with a bad stomachache. He goes to a doctor who discovers the presence of a deadly but slow-acting poison in his system. Bigelow is told that he has from one day to a week to live. Bigelow is understandably outraged and shocked at this diagnosis. He goes to another doctor who says the same thing. When this doctor calls the police, Bigelow runs out. He goes to the Fisherman bar, but it's closed. He then returns to his hotel, where he receives another call from Paula. She tells him that a Mr. Phillips, who had been looking for him, has mysteriously died. Bigelow decides that this is the lead he must follow. He flies to L.A. and goes to the office of the Phillips' Import-Export Company. There he meets "the controller," Mr. Halliday, and his secretary, Miss Foster. Halliday tells Bigelow that Phillips committed suicide and that he doesn't know why his boss wanted to see him. Bigelow then visits Phillips' beautiful widow. She tells Bigelow that Phillips killed himself because he was being charged for selling stolen merchandise. Bigelow returns to his hotel and receives another call from Paula. She has discovered in their records that Phillips had a certain bill of sale notarized several months earlier. This bill of sale proves that Phillips bought the stolen merchandise from a Mr. Reynolds. Bigelow guesses that Reynolds first killed Phillips, and then tried to kill *him* to cover up all evidence of the theft. Bigelow visits a beautiful model, Marla Rakubian, who Phillips saw just before his death. She is in the middle of packing and acts very guilty. Bigelow finds a picture of Reynolds in her suitcase. He goes to the photographer who took the picture, hoping to find out Reynolds' address. The photographer has no address but reveals Reynolds' real name, which is Raymond Rakubian. Upon leaving the photographers', Bigelow is fired upon. He chases the sniper, but loses him after finding clues indicating that this same person was probably his poisoner. Bigelow then returns to Halliday and asks him if he recognizes the picture of Rakubian. Halliday denies ever seeing Rakubian and expresses resentment about Bigelow's suspicions. Back at his hotel room, Bigelow is met by three vindictive thugs. They take him to see their boss, Mr. Majak, who is accompanied by Marla Rakubian. Asked why he is poking his nose into "all this," Bigelow tells Majak that he wants to find Raymond Rakubian, whom he believes to be his killer. Majak replies that Rakubian died five months ago. It's a dead end for Bigelow in more ways than one. Majak can't afford to risk the ten years in jail that Bigelow's knowledge could get him. Majak orders Chester, his chief henchman, to dispose of Bigelow as quickly as possible. After some tense moments, Bigelow escapes the vicious psychopath, who is then killed by police when he starts to use his gun in a drugstore. Bigelow then returns to his hotel, where he is met by Paula. She knows that Bigelow is in some kind of trouble, but he is unable to tell her the truth. After declaring his unwavering love to Paula, Bigelow leaves to continue his search. On a hunch, he goes to the home of Halliday's secretary. There he encounters Stanley, who is suffering from a certain familiar stomachache. Stanley tells of discovering that Mr. Phillips was having an affair with Halliday, and of confronting the guilty couple with evidence to that effect. Bigelow then realizes that Halliday and Mrs. Phillips are also behind his own murder. They had to kill to protect the explanation of Phillips' death as

Above: Edmond O'Brien (as the doomed Frank Bigelow) tells the L.A. police how he hunted his own murderer; opposite: Neville Brand (playing psychopath Chester) hovers over O'Brien. *D.O.A.* (United Artists, 1950).

suicide. (Since Bigelow's bill of sale would have saved Phillips from prosecution, its existence proved that Phillips had no reason to kill himself). Having figured out all the motives, Bigelow confronts the widow with her guilt. She tells him how Halliday pushed her husband out of the window when he produced the letter indicating their illicit affair. Certain that Halliday is also his own murderer, Bigelow goes after him. On the way, he is pursued by Majak and his men. Eventually eluding them, Bigelow arrives at the Phillips Import offices just in time to confront Halliday. A gun battle ensues, and Bigelow kills his murderer. Having completed his story, Bigelow falls to the homicide bureau floor dead.

As his marriage to Paula Gibson draws near, Frank Bigelow begins to feel trapped. His trip to San Francisco is a response to this feeling. Paula's initial reaction to the trip is extreme disappointment that she can't go along. This reaction understandably reinforces Bigelow's feelings of enclosure. Once they discuss the situation at a local bar, Paula realizes that the whole point of the trip is to get away from her. Understanding

Bigelow's need to be free to pursue other desires and possibly even reconsider his marriage plans, Paula changes her tune and encourages him to
follow his impulse. She knows that he must feel that he is freely entering
into the marriage commitment, and that the trip to San Francisco represents the testing of that freedom.

The San Francisco that Bigelow initially encounters reveals a lot about the internal conflict which motivates him. He is not the only one that comes to the city in an attempt to break free of his responsibilities and commitments. Upon his arrival, he seems to identify completely with the wild conventioneers who just want to enjoy the hedonistic pleasures of wine, women and song. Haskell invites him to join his group, and Bigelow becomes a part of the gay throng. The fun doesn't last long, however. Mrs. Haskell's lust for Bigelow soon activates her husband's possessive jealousy. Bigelow quickly escapes this situation, but not before an important thematic point has been made. Mrs. Haskell represents the irresponsible desire which underlies the hedonistic urge for freedom that Bigelow shares with the conventioneers. His need to reconsider marriage to Paula is actually a need to pursue the irresponsible desire which stands opposed to the love commitment. This specific theme of moral danger is further underscored when the truth behind Bigelow's murder is uncovered. The desirous villainy of Halliday and Mrs. Phillips clearly takes the form of their disregard for the marriage commitment. Bigelow's murder simply arises from a need to cover up their illicit affair and the murder of Mr. Phillips which it resulted in.

D.O.A. can be seen as a modern parable in which this conflict between the love commitment and the selfish urge for freedom is clarified and resolved. Consistent with most other noirs of the period, the city is associated almost completely with the negative side of the film's thematic oppostition. The many people who Bigelow encounters represent the evil desire, alienation and greed which underlies the glamour and excitement of urban life. The conflict is ironically resolved by Bigelow's death. Only by confronting the reality of death can he truly appreciate the importance of making the love commitment. The point seems to be that there is never time to waste with selfish desire because death may strike at any time. When death looms over him, Bigelow experiences a feeling of love for Paula that he never knew was possible. He wishes that he had never come to the city because somehow (even though it doesn't make strict causal sense) his death represented the harshest lesson regarding his urge to break free of Paula.

The film makes a big point of Bigelow's being already dead as soon as he finds out about the poison. When he sees the second doctor and knows for sure about his terminal condition, Bigelow realizes that death is one thing he cannot escape. At that moment, he decides that he must accomplish one task before he dies—he must find the person who murdered him and get revenge. Though he soon realizes that he was wrong to leave Paula and question their love commitment, Bigelow's impending death leaves little time for love. He resolves his conflict between emotional commitment and selfish freedom only after it is too late and he has taken the wrong road. Bigelow cannot avoid this road, and the first-person detective structure of the film insures that the viewer walks it along with him. Both protagonist and viewer can now recognize the moral which indicates he should never have come to the city, but they don't have any time to leave it or the pathological motivations which plague it.

Bigelow puts every bit of life he has left into a quest which ultimately proves quite futile. His successful revenge seems so meaningless because Halliday's act of murder was so totally impersonal. Halliday killed Bigelow only because he notarized a paper, something he routinely did for a living. Bigelow's death seems to have been caused more by fate than by Halliday. Only fate could have arranged the timing of Halliday's poisoning to coincide so perfectly with Bigelow's first attempt to hustle a strange girl in the city. Halliday was simply the desperate instrument of the fate, which was teaching Bigelow the harshest lesson regarding his urge to escape Paula. Channeling all of his energy into discovering Halliday seems so futile because that discovery has so little to do with the meaning of his impending demise. Tracking down the logical causes of that demise represents an attempt to deny its deeper meaning, which has to do with a more universal, ever-present threat of death and its connection to the love commitment which Bigelow hesitated to make. That such a hesitation may prove fatal is the sobering moral graphically illustrated by *D.O.A.*

In a Lonely Place (1950)

Director: Nicholas Ray. *Screenplay*: Andrew Solt, adapted by Edmund H. North, from the novel by Dorothy B. Hughes. *Photography*: Burnett Guffey. *Music*: George Antheil. *Art Director*: Robert Peterson. *Film Editor*: Viola Lawrence. *Producer*: Robert Lord. *Production*: Santana Productions. *Release*: Columbia, May 17, 1950. 94 minutes. **Cast**: Humphrey Bogart (playing Dixon Steele), Gloria Grahame (Laurel Gray), Frank Lovejoy (Brub Nicolai), Carl Benton Reid (Capt. Lochner), Art Smith (Mel Lippman), Jeff Donnell (Sylvia Nicolai), Martha Stewart (Mildred Atkinson), Robert Warwick (Charlie Waterman), Morris Ankrum (Lloyd Barnes), William Ching (Ted Barton), Steven Geray (Paul), Hadda Brooks, Alice Talton, Jack Reynolds, Ruth Warren, Ruth Gillette, Guy Beach, Lewis Howard.

Arrogant, alienated screenwriter Dixon Steele drives to Paul's Restaurant in Hollywood, where he meets his agent, Mel Lippman, and several other acquaintances who work in pictures. Steele has been offered a job adapting a popular novel and must read the book that evening to decide if he will take the assignment. Figuring that the book is no good, Steele invites an innocent hat check girl named Mildred Atkinson home to tell him the plot. Quickly realizing that the novel's turgid story is all he's going to get out of the girl, Steele sends Mildred home with twenty dollars for cab fare. Early the next morning, police detective Nicolai arrives at Steele's and informs him that Captain Lochner wants to see him for questioning. At police headquarters, Steele learns that Mildred Atkinson was murdered hours after leaving his place, and that he is a major suspect. Laurel Gray, a new neighbor of Steele's, than arrives and corroborates the screenwriter's claim that he sent Mildred home early. Lochner lets Steele go, but is very suspicious of his smug reaction to the whole affair. Back at their apartment complex, Steele flirts with Laurel Gray and then asks her out. Though she puts him off, Laurel is obviously attracted to Steele. Later that evening, Steele demonstrates his expert knowledge of crime by dramatizing the Atkinson murder, with Nicolai and his wife as the actors. At the end of the evening, the Nicolais exchange impressions of Steele. Mrs. Nicolai thinks Steele is sick, but Brub dismisses her reaction, saying that the screenwriter is just "an exciting guy." Steele returns to Laurel Gray, and they begin a romantic interlude. Several days later, Mel Lippman arrives to find Steele working feverishly on his new script (thanks to Laurel's love and support). In the meantime, the murder investigation continues. Steele has a long record of brawls and near arrests which adds to Captain Lochner's feelings that he may be the murderer. Laurel is again called in for questioning, and Lochner warns her that it may be very dangerous to trust Steele. Laurel is beginning to think that he may be right. On a picnic with the Nicolais, Steele flies into a paranoid rage upon learning that Laurel has seen Captain Lochner without telling him. He jumps into his car and drives like a maniac until he sideswipes a young college student. When the boy makes a threat, Steele gets out of his car and starts a very one-sided fight. Only Laurel's terrified scream prevents Steele from bashing the student's head in with a rock. The next day, Steele finishes the script and proposes to Laurel. She accepts out of fear, but plans to run out on him at the last minute. Laurel then goes to Mel and tells him of her plans to leave Steele. Mel begs her to wait, at least until Steele has had some success to offset such a blow. Laurel reluctantly agrees and then gives Mel the finished script, which she hopes will represent that success. That evening, Steele throws an informal engagement party at Paul's Restaurant. When he learns that Mel has taken the script without his permission, Steele flies into another rage and knocks his most devoted friend to the floor. The party breaks up and Steele follows Laurel back to her apartment. Realizing that

Art Smith (center, playing Mel Lippman) tries to restrain Humphrey Bogart (as Dixon Steele), while Gloria Grahame (right, as Laurel Gray) and friends (Robert Warwick, Alice Talton) look on — *In a Lonely Place* (Columbia, 1950).

she plans to run out on him, Steele attacks Laurel. Just as he is about to strangle her, Steele stops himself and the phone rings. It is the police with news that he is no longer suspected of killing Mildred Atkinson. Steele is unable to appreciate the call, since he has lost Laurel forever.

In a Lonely Place focuses on an artist-protagonist whose extreme alienation dominates all of his social relations. Among strangers, Dixon Steele looks for fights and often finds them. Outside of his devoted agent and a washed-up actor who's now a drunkard, he has no real friends. The mysterious murder of Mildred Atkinson causes him to meet Laurel Gray and be reunited with police detective Brub Nicolai, a former comrade in World War II. Steele needs friends and love desperately because of his isolation, but his alienation causes him to distrust everyone. If he feels the slightest bit betrayed by a friend, his violent and destructive cynicism is immediately activated.

When she first meets Steele, Laurel Gray seems confident that he is not a murderer. His violent temper activates her insecurity, which takes the form of a fear of painful involvement. (Steele is not the only one with emotional scars.) Laurel then begins to suspect, along with Lochner, that maybe Steele *is* capable of murder. Steele finds out about her suspicions, and this sends him over the edge, resulting in the car incident. Luckily, Laurel is able to stop him from really hurting someone.

Steele realizes at this point that his relationship with Laurel is in deep trouble: she has seen his scary potential for evil, and it is too much for her. As they drive home, Steele mentions some poetic lines from the screenplay he is writing — "I was born when you kissed me. I died when you left me. I lived a few weeks while you loved me."

Steele knows that his "few weeks" are probably up, but he still makes a desperate effort to prevent the inevitable by proposing. Laurel is too afraid of him to tell him the truth, so she lyingly accepts. When he catches her trying to run out, Steele nearly strangles her to death. Then comes the phone call from Lochner which, as it turns out, is minutes too late to help matters. If it had come before Steele's attack, things might have been different. As it is, the call ironically adds to the apparent hopelessness of his fate.

Dixon Steele's artistic awareness and temperament make him a hotbed of contradictions and emotional conflicts. To put it bluntly, there is nothing that is not extreme about the character. On the one hand, he's attractive, exciting, sensitive and creative, but on the other, he's resentful, vicious, cruel and violent. Mel certainly knows what he's talking about when he tells Laurel that "you've got to take the good along with the bad" to maintain a relationship with Steele. But Laurel, like most people, is only attracted to his good side; when the bad side is exposed, she just wants to run away.

Steele definitely loves and needs Laurel, but his artistic temperament demands an honesty which makes the suppression of his bad side impossible. Since this bad is closely related to the character's feelings about (or anticipation of) the inability of others to accept it, Laurel's fear just makes it worse, which makes her worse, etc.

In a Lonely Place presents a tragic view of the modern artist as caught between his need for people and his uncontrollable tendency to reject their normal perceptions of life. His insecurities are great because he has so much trouble with relationships. The love which he needs for creative inspiration and fulfillment is always short-lived ("I lived a few weeks while you loved me") because it is only a matter of time before a normal person's insecurities force them to reject him. This, in turn, makes the artist even more alienated and insecure, which starts the whole vicious circle all over again.

Kiss Tomorrow Goodbye (1950)

Director: Gordon Douglas. *Screenplay*: Harry Brown, from the novel by Horace McCoy. *Photography*: J. Peverell Marley. *Special Effects*: Paul Eagler. *Music*: Carmen Dragon. *Production Design*: Wiard Ihnen. *Film Editors*: Truman K. Wood, Walter Hannemann. *Producer*: William Cagney. *Production*: A William Cagney Production. *Release*: Warner Brothers, August 19, 1950. 102 minutes. **Cast**: James Cagney (playing Ralph Cotter), Barbara Payton (Holiday Carleton), Helena Carter (Margaret Dobson), Luther Adler (Cherokee Mandon), Ward Bond (Inspector Weber), Steve Brodie (Jinx Raynor), Barton MacLane (Reece), Rhys Williams (Vic Mason), Herbert Heyes (Ezra Dobson), John Litel (Chief of Police Tolgate), William Frawley (Byers), Robert Karnes (Gray), Kenneth Tobey (Fowler), Dan Riss, Frank Reicher, John Halloran, Neville Brand.

The film opens at the beginning of a trial in which seven people are charged with various crimes, including murder, robbery and extortion. After condemning the evil of these defendants, the prosecutor calls his first witness. As a prison guard starts his testimony, the film's main plot begins in flashback.

Notorious criminal Ralph Cotter accompanies a fellow inmate on an escape from a prison farm. When his accomplice tries to turn back, Cotter shoots him. A woman named Holiday and a driver named Jinx pick Cotter up. Holiday had arranged the escape for her "innocent" brother, and Cotter tells her that he was killed by a prison guard. The three fugitives arrive at the garage of Vic Mason. When he learns that Holiday owes Mason for engineering escape, Cotter promises to get the money. After quickly seducing Holiday, Cotter gets Jinx to help him rob a local grocery store. Cotter then goes back to Mason, who is furious about the robbery because the store was so near his garage. Mason takes the money owed to him and tells Cotter to get out. Mason then calls two crooked policemen, who go to Holiday's apartment and give Cotter the big shakedown. After pocketing the money from the heist, Inspector Weber orders Cotter and Holiday to get out of town on separate buses. Cotter isn't about to give up that easily. He takes Jinx's share of the loot and returns to Vic Mason. He offers the crooked garage owner $2,000 for a car to drive out of town. Mason refuses and calls Weber, telling him that Cotter has held out on him. Having overheard the call, Cotter beats Mason up and returns to Holiday's apartment. When Weber arrives for a second shakedown, Cotter has their conversation secretly recorded. Cotter intends to use the tape in an elaborate blackmail scheme, but first he must find a go-between. Jinx knows of a former doctor, who now runs a respectable business teaching mystical philosophy. After obtaining the

JAMES CAGNEY

Hotter than in 'White Heat' in

Kiss Tomorrow Goodbye

PRESENTED BY **WARNER BROS.**

BARBARA PAYTON · HELENA CARTER · WARD BOND   LUTHER ADLER · BARTON MacLANE   Screen Play by Harry Brown   WILLIAM CAGNEY   GORDON DOUGLAS
A CAGNEY Production   Directed by WARNER BROS.

name of a powerful and corrupt lawyer, Cotter hustles the doctor's beautiful young assistant. While courting the rich and classy Margaret Dobson by night, Cotter continues his devious criminal ventures by day. He meets crooked lawyer Cherokee Mandon, who acts as a go-between in the extortion of Inspector Weber. Armed with the threat of the recording, Cotter demands that Weber destroy his criminal record and issue him a legal gun permit. After those demands are met, Cotter forces Weber to go along with his plan to rob the collectors of the city's gambling racket. Weber isn't too happy about this because he gets a cut in exchange for legal protection of the gambling. The day before the heist, Cotter secretly marries Margaret Dobson. That night Margaret's father catches them in bed together. When he is shown their marriage certificate, Ezra Dobson promptly demands an annulment. The next morning, Cotter signs a paper agreeing to the annulment and relinquishing all claims to Margaret's money. Both Dobsons are really surprised when Cotter declines the $25,000 which is offered for his trouble. Later that day, Cotter pulls the gambling heist without a hitch. After splitting the money with Jinx and Weber, Cotter learns that Ezra Dobson wants to see him. The powerful financier was so impressed by Cotter's display of integrity that he now wants him for a son-in-law. Confessing that Margaret is worth more money than he is, Dobson offers Cotter control of her estate as a part of the marriage bargain. Cotter decides to accept, and Margaret joyfully proposes that they go away on a luxurious honeymoon. Cotter agrees to the trip and returns to Holiday's to pick up his money. As Cotter is about to leave her forever, Holiday pulls out a gun. After telling him that she has learned the truth about her brother's death, Holiday viciously kills Cotter with two shots from her revolver. The police (who had obtained Holiday's name from Mason) arrive just in time to see Cotter die.

Cut to the courtroom and a shot of the seven defendants, all of whom the viewer now recognizes. They are all staring at a tape recorder that is playing the recording with which Cotter blackmailed Weber. When the recording is finished and Cotter's voice is verified, the prosecutor rests his case.

Ralph Cotter, the protagonist of *Kiss Tomorrow Goodbye*, is a classic gangster villain who will stop at nothing to get what he wants. What makes this film so cynical is that every character seems motivated by the same greed and desire that results in Cotter's relentless evil. With the introduction of characters like Inspector Weber and Cherokee Mandon, one soon realizes that the American society being depicted is extremely corrupt. Cotter is a temporary success in this environment because he understands its evil motivation so well. One almost admires the way he blackmails the blackmailers and robs the Mafia. In a world devoid of good, Cotter at least has a certain morbid class.

While questing for money and power in a male realm by day, Cotter satisfies more basic urges by night. Of the two women he becomes involved with in the course of the film, the first is somewhat less deceived. Holiday knows that he is evil, but she can't seem to help herself. Her motivation is slickly characterized through their initial embrace—desperate emotional need with a strong element of sexual desire. Once she falls for Cotter, Holiday is unable to resist his evil. She vacillates from hating him and herself to wallowing in the immoral pleasure which he offers. Eventually resigning herself to the relationship, Holiday tells Cotter, "I guess I'm just what you make me." Despite this resignation, Holiday still attempts to fight Cotter's evil. For awhile it looks like she has lost the fight, but she avenges herself and her brother in the end (though even this act has undertones of simple jealousy).

Cotter takes a big step upward when he meets and seduces Margaret Dobson. Cherokee Mandon warns Cotter to stay away from her because it would only be a matter of time before he would tangle with her father. Cotter ignores Mandon's warning, confident that he can handle even Ezra Dobson. This confidence proves to be correct, mainly because "the most powerful man in the state" approaches life in terms of greed just like the less respectable men in the film.

When Dobson learns that Cotter has married his daughter, he assumes that this stranger is only after her money. Once Cotter has displayed some surprising integrity, Dobson wants him for a son-in-law. He tells Cotter, "I almost gave up trying to find a man that could stand up to Margaret." This does not mean, however, that Dobson believes Cotter is morally pure. On the contrary, Dobson ironically sees Cotter for what he is: a big time operator who can't easily be bought off.

Dobson isn't looking for a son-in-law who's not after Margaret's money. He's looking for a son-in-law who can handle that money and the power position that goes along with it. In a sense, he's looking for a man who can think and act like he does about such matters. Cotter proves that he is that man, and in so doing he drives home the film's most radical thematic point: a cold-blooded villain and "the most powerful man in the state" are virtually two of a kind.

The film's highly cynical content is presented in a unique flashback form. What appears to be the standard single flashback plot is given a new twist in *Kiss Tomorrow Goodbye*. The flashback begins when the prosecutor's first witness opens his testimony. Cotter's story continues uninterrupted almost to the end, but not completely. Right after the gambling heist, we are returned to the trial in the film's present. The prosecutor asks the witness, who turns out to be Jinx, how he felt at "that point." Jinx says that he was scared, and the flashback resumes with a few lines of his voice-over narration. This sole interruption, in what is otherwise a single, unified flashback narrative, demonstrates that Cotter's story is told collectively by all the prosecutor's witnesses.

By dispensing with the usual return to the present as each speaker changes, *Kiss Tomorrow Goodbye* gives a standard noir flashback structure, one more stylistic turn of the screw. Perhaps more important than this, however, is the structure's subtle implication that the story is biased against Cotter and the other defendants. As with many other noir flashback structures, one main purpose of this narrative form is to undercut the story's apparent objectivity. One notes that the ending comes before the defense can utter a word. Having seen the vindictive zeal with which the prosecutor denounced all of the defendants in the opening scene, one can probably assume that the unknown witnesses who tell Cotter's story have been carefully picked to give the most incriminating view of the dead villain and his fellow criminals. Though several crooked officials are involved, you can bet that the prosecutor made no mention of the corrupt society which forms the basis of the film's strongest themes. Society can never be expected to admit any of the blame for the criminals it produces. Such a task is left mainly to the artist.

Dark City (1950)

Director: William Dieterle. *Screenplay*: John Meredyth Lucas and Larry Marcus, adapted by Larry Marcus. *Photography*: Victor Milner. *Music Score*: Franz Waxman. *Songs*: "If I Didn't Have You" by Jack Elliot and Harold Spina, "That Old Black Magic" by Johnny Mercer and Harold Arlen, "I Wish I Didn't Love You So" by Frank Loesser, "I'm in the Mood for Love" by Jimmy McHugh and Dorothy Fields, "Letter from a Lady in Love" by Judy Bennett and Maurice Ellenhorn. *Art Directors*: Hans Dreier, Franz Bachelin. *Film Editor*: Warren Low. *Producer*: Hal Wallis. *Production*: Hal Wallis Productions. *Release*: Paramount, October 18, 1950. 88 minutes. **Cast**: Charlton Heston (playing Danny Haley), Lizabeth Scott (Fran), Viveca Lindfors (Victoria Winant), Dean Jagger (Capt. Garvey), Don Defore (Arthur Winant), Jack Webb (Augie), Ed Begley (Barney), Henry Morgan (Soldier), Walter Sande (Swede), Mike Mazurki (Sidney Winant), Mark Keuning, Stanley Prager, Walter Burke.

Danny Haley runs a small bookie operation along with two-bit gamblers Augie and Barney. After the third police raid in as many months, Danny decides that he must close down the illegal business. Unsure of his plans, Danny puts off a girlfriend named Fran, who is afraid he is going to leave town. While watching Fran sing at a local club, Danny meets Arthur Winant, a naive businessman from Los Angeles. After seeing a check for $5,000 in Arthur's wallet, Danny agrees to let him sit in on a poker game along with Augie and Barney. Arthur is easily hustled by the three gamblers, who let him win the game so they can up the stakes the following evening. The plan works like a charm, and Arthur is eventually forced to sign over the check, which isn't even his own money. The next day, Danny learns that Arthur has committed suicide. Danny tries to deny responsibility for Arthur's death, but dangerous complications arise. After complaining about being followed, Barney is found murdered in his apartment. As a result, Danny and Augie are called in for questioning by Police Captain Garvey. They are told that Arthur Winant's brother Sidney is a psychopath who flew into a rage when told of the suicide. Garvey believes that Sidney intends to kill the three gamblers, who he considers responsible for Arthur's death. Barney appears to have been Sidney's first victim, but Garvey can't get Danny and

Top: Lizabeth Scott (playing Fran) and Charlton Heston (as Danny); bottom: left to right, Ed Begley (as Barney), Heston, Don Defore (as Arthur Winant) and Jack Webb (Augie). *Dark City* (Paramount, 1950).

Augie to admit their involvement in the incident. Now aware that they are in grave danger, Danny and Augie fly to L.A. to try to find out what they can about Sidney. Masquerading as an insurance investigator, Danny approaches Victoria Winant, Arthur's widow. He tells her that Arthur had a $10,000 life insurance policy payable to Sidney. He asks her for help in locating the phantom brother, specifically a photograph of him. Victoria stalls Danny for several days, and they become somewhat involved. Victoria eventually confesses that she destroyed all photographs of Sidney because she's afraid of seeing him. The couple's passion explodes in one desperate embrace, and Danny reveals his true identity. Unable to forgive him for her husband's death, Victoria asks Danny to leave. When he returns to his hotel, Danny finds Augie dead. Minutes later, the police arrive and arrest Danny. Captain Garvey shows up at the jail the next day and assures the local authorities that Danny didn't kill Augie. After warning him to come clean, Garvey orders Danny to leave town. Danny heads for Las Vegas, where he meets up with Soldier, a feeble-minded veteran who had worked for him earlier. Soldier gets Danny a job dealing blackjack at the Swede's Casino. Fran arrives in town, and she too is hired by the Swede. On her opening night, Fran receives a phone call from Victoria, warning her that Sidney is on his way to Las Vegas. When Fran finds Danny, he is in the midst of a tremendous winning streak at the craps table. Danny seems almost relieved to learn of Sidney's impending arrival. He directs Fran to send his winnings to Victoria and then drives to his apartment to wait for the killer. Sidney jumps out of a closet, and they become locked in a life and death struggle. Just as Sidney is about to strangle Danny, Captain Garvey arrives to save him. After thanking Garvey, Danny races to find Fran. He arrives at the airport just in time to stop her from boarding a plane, and tells her that he doesn't want to be alone anymore.

It is established quite early that Fran loves Danny desperately. It is fairly obvious that Danny has strong feelings for her, but he repeatedly refuses to admit these feelings or make any type of emotional commitment. Fran is certain that Danny's unwillingness to get involved stems from a past experience with another woman. Danny admits that there was another woman, but refuses to give Fran any details. Captain Garvey uncovers the truth through a routine investigation of his own. During the war, Danny discovered that his best friend was having an affair with his wife. A fight broke out between the two men, and the friend died of injuries he received. As a result, Danny was court-martialed and never saw his wife again. This tragic incident shattered Danny's faith in human nature and transformed his entire attitude toward life. Danny came to feel that his previous emotional vulnerability was naive and innocent. His personality hardened into a cynical alienation which involved a bitter refusal to ever love or need anyone again.

Danny's criminal involvement and friends are the direct result of this attitude, and their plan to hustle Arthur Winant is a typical example of their overall approach to life. When Fran tries to stop Danny from carrying out the plan, he defends his action by saying that Arthur deserves whatever he gets ("He was plenty willing to take *our* money"). As far as Danny is concerned, he's almost doing the poor schmuck a favor by teaching him a lesson in the harsh ways of the jungle. Unfortunately, Arthur's loss of innocence is just too much for him. Rather than becoming stronger, he simply becomes dead. Danny tries to shirk responsibility for Arthur's death by stressing that Augie did the cheating and that he simply set out to beat the guy at poker.

Danny can rationalize all he wants, but there's one person who isn't listening. Sidney Winant cares only about killing the three men who he believes drove Arthur to suicide. The character of Sidney represents a kind of personified poetic justice which Danny and his accomplices deserve. Having taken advantage of the weaker Arthur, it is only fitting that they should have to defend themselves against the vengeance of his stronger brother. Psychopathic or not, Sidney has his own rules, just like Danny and Augie. His feeling that the gamblers were responsible for Arthur's death is generally shared by the film. Personal revenge is the logical result (especially since Sidney knows the law will do nothing to punish the gamblers). Danny hustled Arthur according to the law of the jungle, and Sidney seeks revenge according to the same law.

By taking steps to protect himself against Sidney, Danny places himself in a position which allows him to face his own guilt and realize the evil of his cynical alienation. This personal transcendence is made possible largely by Victoria Winant. Getting to know her renews Danny's faith in the potential goodness of mankind and beauty of life. She respected the crucial need man has for love so much that she remained devoted to Arthur even though she "hardly knew him after the war."

From the moment he first meets Victoria, Danny begins to waver in his strictly self-protective motives (Why else leave open the possibility of giving her the fictitious insurance payment?) When they become emotionally involved, Danny scraps his original plan altogether and ends his masquerade. This revelation ironically causes Victoria to terminate the relationship, since she still harbors deep resentment regarding Arthur's death. As he walks out the door, Danny again indicates that he has changed, by promising to return the $5,000 to its rightful owners.

In Las Vegas, Danny continues to wrestle with his guilt. The Swede tells him of his own great sin, the man he killed in the ring years earlier. On the day of the victim's funeral, the Swede tried to give all the money he had to the man's mother. She didn't want the money, and the Swede had to live with the guilt for the rest of his life. To this day, a picture of the Swede's victim still hangs in his office, the implication being that this incident and the guilt it produced had a lasting impact on his life. For Danny, the lesson of the Swede's conveniently parallel experience is clear. Even though he never set out to kill Arthur Winant, he must still accept a significant degree of responsibility for the man's death.

In the very next scene, Victoria calls to warn Danny that Sidney is on his way to Vegas. The thematic link between Danny's acceptance of guilt and his inevitable confrontation with the vengeful psychopath is thus maintained right up to the end. The confrontation itself reinforces the main theme, which so strongly indicates that Danny can no longer make it alone. He needs Captain Garvey's help to survive Sidney's attack, just as he needs Fran to go on living afterwards. The cynical independence which prevented him from making that commitment has been revealed as evil, and the character attains an almost spiritual redemption by overcoming this attitude at the end of the film.

Ace in the Hole (1951)

(also, *The Big Carnival*)

Director and Producer: Billy Wilder. *Screenplay*: Billy Wilder, Lesser Samuels, and Walter Newman. *Photography*: Charles B. Lang. *Music*: Hugo Friedhofer. *Song*: "We're Coming, Leo" by Ray Evans and Jay Livingston. *Art Directors*: Hal Pereira, Earl Hedrick. *Film Editors*: Doane Harrison, Arthur Schmidt. *Production/release*: Paramount, May 8, 1951. (released in July, 1951, as *The Big Carnival*). 112 minutes. **Cast**: Kirk Douglas (playing Chuck Tatum), Jan Sterling (Lorraine), Robert Arthur (Herbie Cook), Porter Hall (Jacob Q. Boot), Frank Cady (Mr. Federber), Richard Benedict (Leo Minosa), Ray Teal (Sheriff), Lewis Martin (McCardle), John Berkes (Papa Minosa), Frances Dominguez (Mama Minosa), Gene Evans (Deputy Sheriff), Frank Jacquet (Smollet), Harry Harvey (Dr. Hilton), Bob Bumps (Radio Announcer), Geraldine Hall, Richard Gaines, Paul D. Merrill, Steward Kirk Clawson.

Having been thrown out of several big city newspapers, ambitious and cynical newsman Chuck Tatum finds himself broke in Albuquerque, New Mexico. Tatum lands a job on the local paper, knowing that his only chance for a return to his previous success in the big time is an exclusive nationwide story. After a year in the sticks, Tatum's opportunity presents itself.

The scene of newspaperman Chuck Tatum's big story, in *Ace in the Hole/The Big Carnival* **(Paramount, 1951).**

Leo Minosa, the proprietor of an obscure tourist shop in the mountains, has become trapped in a cave while hunting for Indian treasure. Tatum happens upon the scene and immediately begins to organize the entire rescue operation into his own personal ticket for success. Tatum begins milking the story for every cheap angle he can think of, and tourists flock to the site of the man's ordeal by the thousands. When she realizes all the money there is to be made off of the incident, Lorraine, Leo's selfish wife, drops her plans to leave him in his hour of need. Tatum gains complete control of the rescue operation by making an underhanded deal with the corrupt local sheriff. With this cheap official's help, Tatum forces the engineer in charge of the diggings to take a long route in order to insure the story's length of one week. Tatum knows that this will give him enough time to make the story as big as possible. Lorraine makes repeated advances to Tatum, who responds with disgust at her total unconcern for Leo. After four days, Tatum quits the Albuquerque paper and offers to his former paper in New York exclusive rights to the story in exchange for his old job back. The editor agrees and it seems that Tatum is going to be successful in his plan to contrive that big break. Everything falls apart, however, when the doctor tells Tatum that Leo has only twelve hours to live. Tatum decides to switch the drilling operation back to the fast

Kirk Douglas (as Tatum) and Jan Sterling (playing Lorraine) in *Ace in the Hole*.

approach, but the engineer informs him that it is now too late for that since the drill has made the caves unsafe to enter. The desperate Tatum tries to take it out on Lorraine by attacking her failure as a wife. Lorraine becomes hysterical and stabs Tatum. Refusing to tend to his wound, Tatum gives up on the story and tries in vain to keep Leo alive until the drilling is completed. When Leo dies, Tatum tells all of the thrillseekers to go home and returns to his Albuquerque paper, where he collapses dead on the newsroom floor.

Ace in the Hole depicts an American society that is corrupt and decadent on every level. Yellow journalism is not so much the film's specific target as it is a central manifestation of modern society's decay. The protagonist of this film is a supercynical opportunist who manipulates others by revealing their selfish ambition and greed. Tatum gains control over the corrupt sheriff and Lorraine by cutting them in on large shares of the profits from Leo's "circus." He sees the public as parasites that feed upon others' misery, and Wilder almost agrees with him.

Ace in the Hole is subtly ironic in unexpected ways because Tatum's cynicism is the root of his evil. He gains success by giving the public what they want, and every good newspaperman knows what that is. The only news is bad news, and the most popular news is a personal tragedy. Tatum sardonically explains to a novice reporter why one person's death means a lot more to the public than hundreds or thousands. Tatum understands how the public becomes fascinated with misfortune when the victim has an identity carefully sketched by a skillful media. Successful news has little to do with the truth because the public doesn't want the truth. They want the kind of contrived, sensationalistic story that Tatum makes Leo's ordeal into. Tatum is ambitious, so he goes out and grabs this success any way he can, but he hates the world and himself for being so rotten.

Tatum's relationship with Lorraine is so important because she becomes the primary external object of his disgust with humanity. In developing this relationship, Wilder clearly explores the crucial link between guilt and destructive cynicism. Leo's innocent trust finally gets to Tatum when he realizes how much this simple man actually loves Lorraine. The protagonist's resultant feeling of guilt is so destructive because he is unable to keep it separate from his disgust with Lorraine. The more guilty he feels about Leo's plight, the more he torments Lorraine with *her* guilt. This strong element of guilt projection makes Tatum's death suicidal even though Lorraine did the stabbing. (This meaning is underscored by Tatum's refusal to tend to his wound.) Tatum's insidious cynicism represents the simultaneous manifestation of his own evil and that of others. He pursues his own "success" by offering the same to others, and when most of them accept his offer, his cynicism is reinforced.

Though Wilder consistently condemns Tatum, he is largely unable to challenge his protagonist's cynical view of contemporary society. The Federber family, tourists that are the first to arrive on the scene in response to the news story, seem to represent strong evidence in favor of Tatum's parasite view of the public. They are ignorant sheep easily captured by the attraction and motivated by their own selfish interests. (When interviewed on the radio, Mr. Federber tries to get in a plug for his insurance company.) Wilder tries to escape Tatum's attitude in the final shot of Mr. Federber consoling his tearful wife after Leo's death. The implication seems to be that these typical people *are* capable of genuine sympathy for the victim, but such a small gesture could never offset the overall thematic attack upon the public's motives unleashed by the film. At best, this gesture modifies the film's view of the public from parasites to pawns (a term that is also more consistent with Leo's function as the exploited victim). This would appear to increase the media's responsibility for social decay and undercut Tatum's "giving the public what they want" argument. By this view, the only news is bad news largely because this is what the public has been saturated with to the point of indoctrination.

There may be deeper psychological reasons for the public's vulture syndrome, but they are not dealt with in this film. Wilder is more interested in focusing on the corrupt immorality of those in power positions and simply taking it for granted that such corruption would not be possible without a mass public that is easily manipulated. In this light, the question of relative responsibility for society's decadence appears superfluous. Those in power bear a grave responsibility for society's follies, while the masses have their own disturbing kind of guilt.

Detective Story (1951)

Director and Producer: William Wyler. *Screenplay*: Philip Yordan and Robert Wilder, from the play by Sidney Kingsley. *Photography*: Lee Garmes. *Art Directors*: Hal Pereira, Earl Hedrick. *Film Editor*: Robert Swink. *Production/ release*: Paramount, November 6, 1951, 103 minutes. **Cast:** Kirk Douglas (playing Detective James McLeod), Eleanor Parker (Mary McLeod), William Bendix (Detective Lou Brody), Horace McMahon (Lt. Monahan), Cathy O'Donnell (Susan Carmichael), George Macready (Karl Schneider) Craig Hill (Arthur Kindred), Joseph Wiseman (Charles Genini), Michael Strong (Lewis Abbott), Bert Freed (Dakis), Lee Grant (Shoplifter), Gladys George (Miss Hatch), Gerald Mohr (Tami Giacoppetti), Frank Faylen (Gallagher), Luis Van Rooten (Joe Feinson), Warner Anderson (Sims), Grandon Rhodes, William "Bill" Phillips, Russell Evans.

Detective Story chronicles one fateful day at the 21st Precinct Police Station, New York City. In the middle of three main subplots (involving three pending criminal arrests) is Detective James McLeod. The protagonist's most recent case involves the morning's arrest of Arthur Kindred for stealing funds from the business where he is a clerk. Susan Carmichael, a "close friend," tries to get the charges dropped by paying back the money. Despite her efforts and the attempted intervention by Detective Brody on Kindred's behalf, McLeod refuses to allow the indecisive boss to drop the charges. McLeod's administration of the Kindred case is periodically interrupted by two other cases. The first involves the apprehension of two chronic burglars named Charley and Lewis. McLeod helps to question them and gets Lewis to betray Charley for holding out on him. The other case becomes the main focal point of the film. For over a year, McLeod has been trying to get Dr. Karl Schneider convicted for abortion. This time McLeod feels sure that he can make the charge stick, since he has an eyewitness in addition to the patient. When the witness changes her testimony and the patient dies, McLeod loses control and beats up Schneider. McLeod is then charged by Schneider's attorney with having personal motives for the mistreatment of his client. The attorney has evidence that McLeod's wife Mary was given an abortion by Schneider years earlier. The attorney thinks McLeod wants revenge because of this, but McLeod doesn't even know about it. When Lt. Monahan tells him, McLeod goes off the deep end. He makes one attempt to sustain his love for Mary, but is ultimately unable to forgive her or restrain himself from expressing revulsion and disgust regarding her past. Mary walks out on McLeod for good, after admitting that he had always been a cruel and vengeful man, incapable of forgiveness. McLeod is critically shaken by the loss of his wife. When Charley steals a gun from another officer in a desperate attempt to escape life in prison, McLeod taunts him into shooting and is fatally wounded. With his last dying breaths, McLeod attempts to redeem himself by asking for Mary's forgiveness and letting Arthur Kindred go free.

The essential thematic target of *Detective Story* is the moral absolutism of its protagonist. To James McLeod, there are only two kinds of people, good and bad. If you're a criminal, you're bad and you deserve no sympathy or compassion. The Arthur Kindred case serves to reveal the full extent of McLeod's heartless moral judgments. Like the innocent shoplifter, Kindred is obviously anything but a hardened criminal. He is just a young, sensitive man whose hopeless love for a beautiful model resulted in a mistake he now regrets. Kindred is the perfect example of someone deserving of mercy, forgiveness and a second chance, but McLeod refuses to give him any of these things. His mind is much more occupied by the Karl Schneider case. When he finds out that his wife was "treated" by the abortionist, the carefully arranged order of his life is shattered. As he confronts his wife with her "guilt" McLeod says, "I thought you were everything good and pure." McLeod's moral absolutism renders him unable to deal with Mary's past. For him to love her as he did, he had to believe that she was completely innocent of the evil with which he dealt every day on the job. McLeod's life was carefully arranged to accomodate his black-and-white moral code. When his love became directly associated with the evil he hated so much, McLeod was forced to make a choice between that love and his split view of the world. Almost as he is doing it, McLeod realizes that he has chosen against love. His suicidal death merely completes the full and tragic meaning of that choice.

A seemingly trivial sequence midway through the film serves to indicate its highly integrated structure. When Detective Brody returns with the stolen goods discovered at Charley's apartment, he and two other

Left to right: Russell Evans (as Barnes), Kirk Douglas (playing the hard-hearted detective Jim McLeod), and William Bendix (as Lou Brody), in *Detective Story* **(Paramount, 1951).**

detectives get on three separate phones to inform the theft victims that their possessions have been recovered. The three conversations overlap, both orally and visually, as the three detectives sit, one in front of the other, all perfectly framed in a provocative deep-focus shot. The detective nearest the camera completes his call, and the camera pulls past him to frame the other two, whose simultaneous conversations continue. Once again, the detective nearest the camera completes his call, and the camera pulls past him to focus on the last remaining caller. His conversation is taking so long because he happens to know the theft victim and he is asking her for a date.

This sequence directly links Wyler's long-take technique to the thematic concerns of the play. The concept of overlapping subplots which dominates the play's structure is temporally reduced to the concept of overlapping action within certain key scenes. This concurrent dramatic structure is closely related to the play's theme in a way which is signified by the phone sequence. The last caller's business call turned into a private call, and in so doing it became a reference to McLeod's split life. Unlike the tragic protagonist, the last caller integrates his private and professional lives with comic ease.

McLeod's absolutism and his inability to integrate the disparate subplots of his life are inseparable. The exaggerated tendency to organize one's world into preconceived conclusions about people becomes the black-and-white psychological stereotyping that supports moral absolutism. Intuitive integration of one's life supposedly makes such stereotyping impossible. McLeod's tragedy was that he could never break out of the narrow puritanical view of life that dictated his harsh moral righteousness. Sidney Kingsley's play implies, through its structure, that there are as many moral viewpoints as there are characters or people in the world. In addition, it clearly suggests that without large doses of compassion and understanding of others, morality can never be anything but a weapon.

As has been indicated, Wyler's direction plays an important role in preserving the play's confusing juxtaposition of different subplots, behavior and viewpoints. Wyler's goal here is a refusal to reduce the play to one easily comprehensible narrative with characters who all have clear-cut moral positions. Visual complexity inevitably denotes moral complexity (and vice versa), since the screen is ceaselessly dominated by a myriad of different characters and situations. This, in turn, can only be described as a perfect melding of dramatic form with thematic content. Wyler's objective technique denies the existence of any single moral grid along which his characters might be placed, while the play's content carefully attacks the psychological and moral assumptions that such grids are based on. In this way, the only true alternative to the film's evil of moral absolutism is directly communicated to the viewer.

The Big Combo (1955)

Director: Joseph H. Lewis. *Screenplay*: Philip Yordan. *Photography*: John Alton *Special Effects*: Jack Rabin, Louis DeWitt. *Music*: David Raksin. *Production Design*: Rudi Feld. *Film Editor*: Robert Eisen. *Producer*: Sidney Harmon. *Production*: Security-Theodora. *Release*: Allied Artists, February 13, 1955. 89 minutes. **Cast**: Cornel Wilde (playing Lt. Leonard Diamond), Richard Conte (Brown), Jean Wallace (Susan Lowell), Brian Donlevy (McClure), Robert Middleton (Peterson), Lee Van Cleef (Fante), Earl Holliman (Mingo), John Hoyt (Dreyer), Helen Walker (Alicia), Jay Adler (Sam Hill), Ted de Corsia (Bettini), Helene Stanton (Rita), Roy Gordon, Whit Bissell, Steve Mitchell, Baynes Barron, James McCallion, Tony Michaels, Brian O'Hara.

Police Lieutenant Leonard Diamond has been obsessively investigating powerful racketeer Brown and his crime syndicate for several years. Diamond's boss, Captain Peterson, absorbs the heat from upstairs and tries to back up his best officer. Peterson thinks that Diamond's obsession with arresting Brown comes from his frustrated love for Susan Lowell, Brown's beautiful mistress. Though she once loved Brown, Susan is now held captive by a humiliating sexual bond from which there seems to be no escape. Susan attempts suicide through an overdose of sleeping pills, but is found in time and raced to the hospital. Diamond questions Susan while she is still delirious, and she keeps mumbling something about Alicia. Though he has never heard of Alicia, Diamond becomes convinced that this woman represents an important clue. Diamond arrests every known member of Brown's organization and asks them about Alicia. No one talks, so Diamond hauls Brown in for questioning. A polygraphic test confirms the importance of Alicia and yields the name of Bettini. Brown's men retaliate by capturing Diamond and conducting their own interrogation. Despite some bizarre torture, Diamond refuses to tell Brown anything about the investigation. The next day, Diamond learns that Bettini was a major figure in the organization before Brown took over. Diamond finds Bettini in hiding and questions him about Alicia. Bettini tells Diamond that Alicia was Brown's first wife. She disappeared several years earlier while traveling to Sicily with Brown and Frazi, the former head of the organization. Bettini thinks that Brown had Alicia killed and sunk to the bottom of the ocean by the ship's anchor. Diamond searches out Dreyer, the captain of that ship who is now an aristocratic antique dealer. Diamond questions Dreyer but finds out nothing. Fearing that Dreyer may have talked, Brown has him killed. In Dreyer's safe deposit box, Diamond finds a picture of Alicia, Grazi and Brown. Diamond also learns of a ship's log which holds incriminating information, but Brown has it burned before he can get to it. Stuck without a lead, Diamond goes to Susan in desperation. Diamond tells Susan about Alicia and begs her for help, but she says nothing. Fearing that Susan has talked, Brown panics and orders that Diamond be killed. Brown's gunsels shoot up Diamond's apartment, but only manage to kill a burlesque dancer named Rita that he occasionally slept with. Diamond is enraged by Rita's death and again hauls in Susan. When he tells her about Rita's senseless murder, Susan agrees to cooperate. She boldly walks out on Brown and brings Diamond a recent picture of Alicia from the racketeer's safe. Diamond then deduces that it was Grazi, and not Alicia, that Brown murdered on the ship. Using a blowup of Alicia's picture, Diamond locates her in a mental home upstate. McClure, Brown's second in command, follows Diamond and finds out about Alicia. For years Brown has led McClure to believe that Grazi was running the organization from exile in Sicily. Now realizing that Brown secretly killed Grazi on the trip to Sicily, McClure decides to betray the betrayer. He

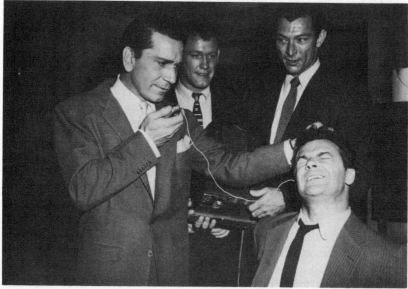

Top: Cornel Wilde (playing Lt. Leonard Diamond) talks backstage with Helene Stanton (as Rita); bottom: Wilde is tortured with a hearing aid by Richard Conte (playing Brown) as Earl Holliman (second from left, as Mingo) and Lee Van Cleef (as Fante) watch. *The Big Combo* **(Allied Artists, 1955).**

arranges to have Brown's gunsels kill their master, but the plan backfires and the gunsels shoot him instead. Brown then eliminates the gunsels and kidnaps Susan. Diamond appeals to Alicia for help in finding Brown and Susan. Alicia tells Diamond about a secret airport that Brown used for quick getaways. Diamond arrives at the airport while Brown and Susan are still waiting for the getaway plan. With Susan's help, Diamond finally captures Brown. Then he and Susan walk off into the night together.

The Big Combo deals quite creatively with the anti-desire theme that pervades many films noirs. Brown, the film's ruthless villain, perfectly represents all of the worst psychological and philosophical implications of a life based completely on desire. Brown's single-minded quest for power has its roots in a primitive expression of masculine sexuality. This sexuality is tested in the timeless jungle where men battle each other for the power that satisfies all their desires. Since the winner is seen as the superior man, it is viewed as just that he should get the most money and "best" women as his prizes.

Brown's all-pervasive tyranny comes from the influence of his attitudes on the other characters. Rita tells Diamond that women don't care what their men do for a living, only how they make love. The general truth of this statement represents strong evidence in favor of Brown's view of life. His "superior" masculinity attracted and won the superior femininity of Susan. Their relationship is based completely on the desire that Brown worships. In exchange for possessing the beautiful Susan, Brown gives her all the physical pleasure and monetary luxury she can handle. Susan cannot escape from Brown because she believes he is right about life. She tells Diamond that her life is a twisted maze in which all paths lead back to Brown. Even though Susan hates Brown, she can't get away from him because of her own desire.

As further proof of Brown's influence, even Diamond seems partially controlled by primitive desires. He sleeps with Rita purely out of sexual need, and his interest in Susan obviously has a strong physical base. Brown thinks that Diamond's righteousness is mostly self-deceptive and masks envy. He thinks that Diamond hates him so much because he wants to be in his place. In so far as Susan is concerned, this is true. Who is to say that Diamond's love is more pure than Brown's? Eventually, the plot implies it by emphasizing Diamond's genuine morality. The protagonist's hatred may not be any purer, but his love is, simply because he believes in moral commitment, which is the only path of escape from the corrupting vortex of selfish desire. This is what Diamond tells Susan and what makes betraying Brown her only salvation. Brown's totally desirous approach to life is the film's definition of evil, and thus he is evil personified. Susan can free herself from Brown only by recognizing his absolute villainy and rejecting it by betraying him to Diamond. In doing this, she has rejected desire as controlling life and supposedly chosen real (moral) love with Diamond.

Through a deeper reflexive level of meaning, *The Big Combo* subtly extends the scope of its anti-desire theme. This seemingly obscure pattern of associations begins with classical music as a symbol for art. Susan's love for music apparently preceded her love for Brown, and the film indicates a psychological connection between the two interests. The significance of this connection becomes clear only after the pattern is followed to the other symbolic use of music. This occurs in the bizarre torture scene. By turning up McClure's hearing aid, Brown turns the artistic experience of music into an ironic way of torturing Diamond. The scene strongly underscores the hearing aid's function as a device for manipulating sensual sensation. The key word here is sensual. Brown ingeniously utilizes the hearing aid to turn the sensual pleasure of music-art into sensual pain. The idea of sensuality also clarifies the meaning of the earlier connection between Susan's interest in art and her interest in Brown. Both attractions afford a kind of sensual pleasure and may come from the same desirous motivation.

A further development of these ideas occurs in the last hearing-aid scene. McClure lures Brown out to the secret airport, thinking that the two gunsels are now working for *him* and will kill Brown. McClure turns out to be wrong, and the gunsels turn their machine guns on him instead of Brown. As he backs up against the wall, McClure begs Brown for mercy. Brown takes away his hearing aid and says, "I'll do you a favor. You won't have to hear it." McClure's death is then depicted from his subjective viewpoint, with the guns blasting away silently. For one crucial moment, the hearing aid controls both the doomed character's sense of hearing and the viewer's.

The sensual aspect of art now being dealt with is the soundtrack of this movie. Withholding the sound of the gunshots indicates a specific definition of that aspect through its effect on the scene's climax. The content is not changed because we still know that McClure is being killed. Withholding the sound at this point only modifies the form of the murder's depiction. In this way, the hearing aid defines the sensual aspect of film art as form, as opposed to content.

The viewer's attention is directed to the form-content polarity because it holds a special significance for the film noir. The cynical content of these films often seemed to be overbalanced by an aesthetic formal beauty which encompassed intricate narrative structures, expressionistic visuals and audacious musical soundtracks. This formalism was implicitly decadent and ironic since it often had the effect of undermining a film's (apparent) thematic drift. By accentuating the formal aspects of the medium, the ugliness of society could be conveyed with a stunning beauty that transformed its grim reality into stylized art. This is exactly what occurs in the depiction of McClure's death. Through a clever dash of expressionistic manipulation, a brutal murder is portrayed entirely as the abstract beauty of the machine gun's flashing lights.

The Big Combo's sensuality theme is an attempt at explaining the full implications of this structural irony. Just as Susan's interest in classical music is consistent with her overall desirous motivation, so the viewer's interest in the formal beauty of *The Big Combo* could reinforce an amoral, escapist motivation which ignores its moral content. The idea of sensuality thus links the expressionistic formalism of the film noir to its own evil of desire. A general association of art with evil was, in fact, a frequent noir theme. By relating that theme to noir aesthetics, *The Big Combo* clarifies its significance in a unique and creative way.

The Killing (1956)

Director: Stanley Kubrick. *Screenplay*: Stanley Kubrick, from the novel *Clean Break* by Lionel White. *Photography*: Lucien Ballard. *Art Director*: Ruth Sobotka Kubrick. *Film Editor*: Betty Steinberg. *Producer*: James B. Harris. *Production*: Harris-Kubrick. *Release*: United Artists, July, 1956. 83 minutes. **Cast**: Sterling Hayden (playing Johnny Clay), Coleen Gray (Fay), Vince Edwards (Val Cannon), Jay C. Flippen (Marvin Unger), Marie Windsor (Sherry Peatty), Ted de Corsia (Randy Kennan), Elisha Cook, Jr. (George Peatty), Timothy Carey (Nikki Arane), Joe Sawyer (Mike O'Reilly), Jay Adler, Kola Kwarian, Joseph Turkel, James Edwards.

Ex-con Johnny Clay has devised a complex plan for robbing a big city racetrack. As the film opens, the first stage of Clay's plan is being put into effect. Clay's partner, Marvin Unger, contacts Mike O'Reilly, a track bartender, and George Peatty, a cashier, about a meeting regarding the heist. These four men are joined by Randy Kennan, a crooked cop who has a large gambling debt to pay off. Both O'Reilly and Peatty hope to give their stagnating marriages a new start with big money. George Peatty's wife is a classic *femme fatale* who totally dominates him. When Sherry Peatty learns of the heist, she plans with her lover to rob the robbers. She follows George to a second meeting of the conspirators and is caught listening at the keyhole. Clay has Sherry pegged immediately but stupidly believes she will settle for her husband's share of the loot. Clay informs the group that he will hire two other professional accomplices to create two separate diversions and occupy the track police at the time of the actual robbery. Clay contacts a former wrestler who agrees to start a fight in the track lobby and a psychopathic gun freak who will shoot the lead horse in the race which will be taking place at the time of the robbery. After Clay arranges for the money's drop point at a deserted motel, the day of the heist arrives. O'Reilly plants a gun in the track locker room, and Peatty lets Clay into the employees quarters, while the wrestler diverts the attention of the police. Clay grabs the gun, puts on a mask, and smoothly robs the main office of two million dollars. After hustling the frightened workers into the locker room, Clay throws the money and gun out of a window and makes his getaway. Randy Kennan, who has been waiting in his squad car outside the appointed window, picks up the money and transports it to the drop point. In the next scene, the four accomplices impatiently await Clay's arrival with the money. Fifteen minutes after Clay is to arrive, Sherry Peatty's boyfriend bursts through the door demanding to see the money. Realizing that his wife has betrayed him in more ways than one, George Peatty starts blasting away, and everyone is killed but him. Mortally wounded, Peatty staggers out of the hotel just as Clay arrives with the money. Peatty heads home to kill his wife, while Clay drives to the airport. When he arrives, Clay meets his girl Fay and checks in at the ticket office. Clay demands the right to carry the suitcase of money on the plane, but an airline official says it's too big and must be checked with the rest of his luggage. When the officials offer to refund his ticket money, Clay is forced to accede to their demand. As he stands waiting to board the plane, Clay watches the baggage truck being driven toward the plane, with his suitcase perched precariously atop the pile. Suddenly a passenger's small dog runs out of the crowd and chases after the truck. When the driver swerves to avoid the dog, Clay's suitcase is knocked off the pile. The suitcase flies open even before it hits the ground, and two million dollars in small bills are blown to the wind by the plane's gyrating propellors. Clay can't believe his eyes. Fay desperately tries to hustle him away from the airport, but everything works against her. After several futile attempts to hail a taxi, the couple looks up to see two plainclothes detectives coming at them with drawn revolvers. Realizing he's a beaten man, Clay says, "What's the difference?" and gives himself up.

The most conspicuous characteristic of *The Killing* is its formal structure. In his depiction of the big heist, Kubrick opts against the conventional attempt to preserve temporal continuity through parallel editing. Instead he follows each character through his day separately. The result is a stunning temporal fragmentation that dominates the tone of the film. Kubrick himself admits that this was the primary concept behind

Top: Sterling Hayden (as Johnny Clay, mastermind of the racetrack heist) asserts one form of power; bottom: psychopathic gun freak Timothy Carey (as Nikki Arane) doing his job. *The Killing* (United Artists, 1956).

The Killing: "Jim Harris and I were the only ones at the time who weren't worried about fragmenting time, overlapping and repeating action that had already been seen, showing things again from another character's point of view. In fact, this was just the structure in Lionel White's thriller, *Clean Break*, that had appealed to us and made us want to do the film. It was the handling of time that may have made this more than just a good crime film" (from an interview in *The Observer* [London], Dec. 4, 1960).

For Kubrick, the big heist is an almost allegorical portrayal of his characters' doomed power quest. All of the conspirators believe that money is the answer to their personal problems and criminal power is their shortcut to money. The heist is an intricate attempt to manipulate a large business operation into a vulnerable position so that it can be successfully robbed. In other words, the robbers are attempting to gain power over the racetrack for a short but crucial period of time. Since the plan involves the synchronized actions of at least six different men, precise temporal control is an indispensable element of the power necessary to pull off the heist.

The mastermind behind the plan is Johnny Clay, an experienced criminal adept at every type of power. In the course of the film, Clay utilizes all of his skills, from the subtle psychological manipulation of Marvin Unger, to the brute force which becomes necessary when a policeman blocks his exit from the track. Clay's power is challenged not so much by the police as by Sherry Peatty. Through the treatment of her husband, this deadly *femme fatale* demonstrates a talent for psychological manipulation which exceeds Clay's. Though George is determined not to reveal the day of the heist, Sherry induces him to tell her by focusing his insecure jealousy onto Clay. She then tells her lover when and where the split is to take place, so that he can rob the robbers. Clay misses the resulting shootout only because a twist of fate causes him to arrive fifteen minutes late for the split. Ironically, his failure to stick to the all-important timetable is what saves him from almost certain death.

Throughout the film a monotoned narrator painstakingly notes the exact time of each scene. This obtuse narration is, in effect, the primary method which Kubrick employs to make the film's fragmented style so conspicuous. Among other things, this style clearly indicates an implicit link between Clay's role in arranging the heist and Kubrick's role (as writer-director) in arranging the film's narrative. While everything goes smoothly, this link is perfectly preserved and Kubrick's fragmented narrative is literally identified with the complex heist plan which Clay worked out in his head. For this reason, it may be said that Clay's project is an attempt to maintain, for a specified period of time (the length of the film?), a god-like power which is virtually synonymous with Kubrick's artistic control over the film.

Right when it appears to have succeeded, Clay's plan goes completely awry. Kubrick's "fateful" intervention (making Clay late for the split) is necessary to save the protagonist from the deadly result of Sherry Peatty's power, and this sets the stage for the second twist of fate that seals his doom at the airport.

That this incredible bad luck is actually Kubrick's second god-like intervention is exactly the point. In *The Killing*, fate represents Clay's eventual failure to retain the god-like power which he so skillfully wielded in the planning and execution of the heist. Through his fateful interventions, Kubrick demonstrates that his power was much greater all along. Clay's total control early in the film was actually an illusion. At any time, Kubrick could have gummed up the works with an occurrence that Clay couldn't have planned for.

This leads to the obvious question of why Clay *must* fail in his quest. For the answer, we must consider an isolated sequence which occurs midway through the film: When psychopathic gun freak Nikki Arane pulls into the parking lot from which he is to shoot the lead horse in the seventh race, he is confronted by a black parking attendant who informs him that the lot is closed. Realizing that he must change the attendant's mind, Nikki is carefully diplomatic and offers him a large tip. The attendant appreciates Nikki's apparent friendliness as well as his money and lets him pass. As the race approaches, the attendant comes up to Nikki and offers him a horseshoe for luck. Since he no longer needs the attendant, Nikki tells him to get lost. The black man is outraged and throws the horseshoe on the ground as he leaves. Nikki then shoots the lead horse and starts to pull his car out of the lot to make his getaway. A policeman yells at Nikki, whose car won't seem to budge. Nikki is then shot to death by the policeman, and Kubrick's camera pans down to reveal that the fateful horseshoe had caused him to have a flat tire.

This sequence is so important because it gives us the most complete information regarding the fate which we now know is Kubrick's self-conscious and premeditated manipulation of the events depicted. The horseshoe is an overt and fairly obvious symbol of the fateful control, and it is directly linked to Nikki's relationship with the black parking attendant. The implication seems to be that if he had been nice to the attendant and accepted the horseshoe, Nikki would have escaped successfully. This was, of course, impossible because of the kind of person Nikki was. He could only be nice to the attendant when he thought he needed him. Once that need no longer seemed to be present, Nikki expressed his true feelings toward the guy. Bizarre (or comical) as it may seem, this confrontation is Kubrick's testing of the Nikki Arane character. Though Nikki doesn't know it, the horseshoe offer really *is* an offer of the good luck which is necessary for his survival. Revealing his true feelings toward the attendant necessarily involves refusal of the gift of luck, and that's why Nikki dies.

Though he's not as blatant as Nikki Arane, Clay also treats people as a means to his own selfish, greedy ends. Each person that he conspires with is absolutely necessary to the success of the plan, and that is the only reason why Clay cuts them in. As with Nikki, the fate which dooms Clay is self-consciously based on Kubrick's negative moral judgment of the character. This judgment is somewhat ironic because Clay's immorality is inseparable from his quest for a god-like power so closely linked to Kubrick's control over the film. In setting fate against Clay (and the other characters), Kubrick is drawing the crucial line between the artist's and the criminal's power. Clay must fail, not because he is breaking the law, but because his inner-most motives are immoral and totally misguided. His power may have appeared god-like for awhile, but it was actually very worldly, and that is why fate was so against him. The artist's role, according to Kubrick, is to justify his own god-like position by teaching this basic moral lesson. In a sense, his power exists at the expense of worldly men, who must always grapple with fate and lose.

Annotated Filmography

Annotated Filmography

The following 490 films represent an attempt at a comprehensive listing and documentation, with major credits and short descriptions, of all films noirs. Previous attempts at such a listing (which have included up to 250 or so films from the noir period and which usually have included significant mistakes) have fallen short of such a goal. This list, rather than based on strict or even general critera, was compiled by extrapolation from selected index films—representative and widely recognized films noirs that could serve, collectively, as a definition of the cycle. In this way, certain borderline controversies and confusions have been remedied.

By way of example, the question of whether or not certain forties and early fifties gangster films should be included was solved by comparison with *White Heat* (Walsh, 1949), which is generally considered *the* noir gangster film of the period, *Kiss Tomorrow Goodbye* (Douglas, 1950), which is surveyed in this book, and a number of other recognized films noirs (such as *Key Largo*, *The Enforcer*, and *The Racket*) that have strong gangster elements. As another example, the problem of whether to include certain right-wing police films was solved through comparisions with *T Men* (Mann, 1948) and *He Walked by Night* (Werker, 1948), two widely recognized films noirs with stringent law-and-order viewpoints. In both of the above examples and in all other cases (from the period thriller to isolated films that in the past have been overlooked or char acterized as "simply genre pieces"), the noir classifications were sustained primarily by appealing to the vagaries of tone, mood, narrative structure and psychological orientation. Visual style was also considered; however, not all films noirs have that expressive interplay of light and shadow which is so distinctively associated with a large number of the most well-known entries in the cycle.

This index-film method is more effective than any kind of criteria or guidelines because the many different types, shadings and degrees of the films noirs make it impossible to derive such criteria without becoming overly judgmental. Some movies pose no problem whatever since they invariably contain an abundance of elements associated with the noir trend.

However, there are numerous films less in the noir style than these that still retain enough appropriate elements to belong on any list purporting to include all films noirs. The strongest evidence in favor of this assertion is the fact that some of these less noirish films have always appeared on noir lists of the past.

Another consideration that underscores the superiority of this method is the developmental nature of movies in general and films noirs in particular. No matter what stylistic or psychological elements are isolated from obvious or widely recognized noirs, it will never be possible to derive a basic noir essence that can be used to identify all films in the cycle simply because the medium cannot and never will be static enough to allow such an exercise. The film noir went through several marked changes (and many subtle ones) in its twenty years and previous writers who have attempted to reduce the significance of these changes, in an effort to derive noir criteria or define a noir essence, have unnecessarily limited the scope of this category. Of course there is a point at which lines of definition must be drawn, no matter how difficult. The present work attempts to draw these lines at a less reductive or judgmental, and thus at a more inclusive, level.

Analysis of the index films yields a primary time period of 1940–1959. Noir oriented films made before this period are more properly termed precursors and those made after are better labeled postnoir. Further conditions are that all of the films be in black and white and that all be crime dramas or psychological melodramas of one sort or another. (For lists of films noirs from other genres as well as some precursors and postnoirs, see the Appendices, beginning on page 201.) Finally, it was decided that all entries be English language films, with British films included only if their director had already established himself in Hollywood. If there is such a thing as a British noir cycle or a French noir cycle (and there very well may be), it is left to others to define and list such films.

1. *Abandoned* (1949) Universal. *Dir* Joseph M. Newman. *Sc* Irwin Gielgud, from articles in the *Los Angeles Mirror*. *Ph* David S. Horsley. *Mus* Walter Scharf. *Cast* Dennis O'Keefe, Gale Storm, Jeff Chandler, Raymond Burr, Marjorie Rambeau, Mike Mazurki. 78 min.

Newspaper reporter helps girl search for her dead sister's baby; together they uncover an insidious adoption racket. Standard exposé melodrama with effective noir look.

2. *The Accused* (1949) Paramount. *Dir* William Dieterle. *Sc* Ketti Frings, from the novel *Be Still, My Love* by June Truesdell. *Ph* Milton Krasner. *Mus* Victor Young. *Cast* Loretta Young, Robert Cummings, Wendell Corey, Sam Jaffe, Douglas Dick. 101 min.

When one of her students makes sexual advances, a matronly psychology professor panics and accidentally kills him. Nightmare thriller similar in concept to *The Woman in the Window.*

3. *Ace in the Hole* [also titled **The Big Carnival**] (1951) Paramount.

Billy Wilder's story of an unscrupulous newsman's big break is an outstanding example of extreme noir cynicism. See page 105.

4. *Act of Violence* (1949) MGM. *Dir* Fred Zinnemann. *Sc* Robert L. Richards, from a story by Collier Young. *Ph* Robert Surtees. *Mus* Bronislau Kaper. *Cast* Van Heflin, Robert Ryan, Janet Leigh, Mary Astor, Phyllis Thaxter, Barry Kroeger. 81 min.

Fearful veteran is hunted by man who blames him for wartime massacre. Significant chronicle of respected citizen's flight into dark, menacing night world strong on resonance and imagery.

5. *Affair in Havana* (1957) Allied Artists. *Dir* Laslo Benedek. *Sc* Burton Lane and Maurice Zimm, from a story by Janet Green. *Ph* Allen Stensvold. *Mus* Ernest Gold. *Cast* John Cassavetes, Raymond Burr, Sara Shane, Lilia Lazo, Sergio Pena. 77 min.

American piano player in Cuba is drawn into a deadly love triangle.

6. *Affair in Trinidad* (1952) Columbia. *Dir* Vincent Sherman. *Sc* Oscar Saul and James Gunn, from a story by Virginia Van Upp and Berne Giler. *Ph* Joseph Walker. *Mus* George Duning. *Cast* Rita Hayworth, Glenn Ford, Alexander Scourby, Valerie Bettis, Torin Thatcher. 98 min.

Man seeks the killer of his brother in Trinidad, falls for but still suspects the victim's widow. Interesting return to the terrain of *Gilda.*

7. *All My Sons* (1948) Universal. *Dir* Irving Reis. *Sc* Chester Erskine, from the play by Arthur Miller. *Ph* Russell Metty. *Mus* Leith Stevens. *Cast* Edward G. Robinson, Burt Lancaster, Mady Christians, Louisa Horton, Howard Duff, Frank Conroy. 94 min.

A young man discovers that his wealthy, prominent father knowingly manufactured defective airplane parts during World War II, causing the death of American flyers. The dark side of Middle America's two most sacred institutions (family and business).

8. *All the King's Men* (1949) Columbia. *Dir* Robert Rossen. *Sc* Rossen, from the novel by Robert Penn Waren. *Ph* Gert Anderson. *Mus* Louis Gruenberg. *Cast* Broderick Crawford, Joanne Dru, John Ireland, John Derek, Mercedes McCambridge, Shepperd Strudwick. 109 min.

Idealistic small-town lawyer becomes a vicious, corrupt political boss. Hard-hitting noir adaption of Warren's eloquent novel.

9. *Among the Living* (1941) Paramount. *Dir* Stuart Heisler. *Sc* Lester Cole, Garrett Fort, from a story by Cole and Brian Marlow. *Ph* Theodor Sparkuhl. *Cast* Albert Dekker, Susan Hayward, Harry Carey, Frances Farmer, Gordon Jones. 67 min.

Man tries to catch his insane twin brother before he kills again. Eerie thriller with evocative early-noir visuals.

10. Angel Face (1953) RKO. *Dir* Otto Preminger. *Sc* Frank Nugent and Oscar Millard, from a story by Chester Erskine. *Ph* Harry Stradling. *Mus* Dimitri Tiomkin. *Cast* Robert Mitchum, Jean Simmons, Mona Freeman, Herbert Marshall, Leon Ames, Barbara O'Neil. 91 min.

Ambulance driver falls for a beautiful heiress with murder in her heart. Preminger's masterpiece of fatalistic sexual psychology.

11. Angels Over Broadway (1940) Columbia. *Dir* Ben Hecht and Lee Garmes. *Sc* Hecht. *Ph* Lee Garmes. *Mus* George Antheil. *Cast* Douglas Fairbanks, Jr., Rita Hayworth, Thomas Mitchell, John Qualen, George Watts. 80 min.

Girl and inebriate playwright help inspire cynical hustler to aid desperate, suicidal businessman. Significant, prototypic early noir with flamboyant Hecht dialogue.

12. Another Man's Poison (1952) United Artists. *Dir* Irving Rapper. *Sc* Val Guest, from a play by Leslie Sands. *Ph* Robert Krasker. *Mus* Paul Sawtell. *Cast* Bette Davis, Gary Merrill, Emlyn Williams, Anthony Steel. 88 min.

Female mystery writer kills her husband, then is blackmailed by criminal on the run.

13. Appointment with a Shadow (1958) Universal. *Dir* Richard Carlson. *Sc* Alec Coppel and Norman Jolley, from a story by Hugh Pentecost. *Ph* William E. Snyder. *Mus* Joseph Gershenson. *Cast* George Nader, Joanna Moore, Brian Keith, Virginia Field, Frank DeKova. 73 min.

While trying to scoop a big story, an alcoholic reporter becomes the target of a killer.

14. Appointment with Danger (1951) Paramount. *Dir* Lewis Allen. *Sc* Richard Breen and Warren Duff. *Ph* John F. Seitz. *Mus* Victor Young. *Cast* Alan Ladd, Phyllis Calvert, Paul Stewart, Jan Sterling, Jack Webb, Henry Morgan. 89 min.

Post office investigator tangles with hoodlums planning a million-dollar mail robbery.

15. Armored Car Robbery (1950) RKO. *Dir* Richard Fleischer. *Sc* Earl Felton and Gerald Drayson Adams, from a story by Robert Angus and Robert Leeds. *Ph* Guy Roe. *Mus* Roy Webb. *Cast* Charles McGraw, Adele Jergens, William Talman, Douglas Fowley, Steve Brodie. 67 min.

Criminal mastermind double-crosses the men who implement his plan to rob an armored car. Tough, fast-moving early caper film.

16. The Arnelo Affair (1947) MGM. *Dir* Arch Oboler. *Sc* Oboler, from a story by Jane Burr. *Ph* Charles Salerno. *Mus* George Bassman. *Cast* John Hodiak, George Murphy, Frances Gifford, Dean Stockwell, Eve Arden. 86 min.

Neglected wife becomes involved with husband's shady business client. Stylish, sincere "woman's thriller" with good psychological impact.

17. The Asphalt Jungle (1950) MGM. *Dir* John Huston. *Sc* Ben Maddow and Huston, from the novel by W.R. Burnett. *Ph* Harold Rosson. *Mus*

Miklos Rozsa. *Cast* Sterling Hayden, Louis Calhern, Jean Hagen, James Whitmore, Sam Jaffe, John McIntire, Marc Lawrence, Marilyn Monroe. 112 min.

A group of criminals are brought together for an elaborate jewel robbery. The quintessential noir heist film, which evokes with great intensity a dark universe of fatalistic desperation.

18. *Backfire* (1950) Warner Brothers. *Dir* Vincent Sherman. *Sc* Larry Marcus, Ivan Goff and Ben Roberts, from a story by Marcus. *Ph* Carl Guthrie. *Mus* Daniele Amfitheatrof. *Cast* Virginia Mayo, Gordon MacRae, Edmond O'Brien, Dane Clark, Viveca Lindfors, Ed Begley. 91 min.

A war veteran searches for his missing friend, finds a twisting path of violence and murder.

19. *Backlash* (1947) 20th Century–Fox. *Dir* Eugene Forde. *Sc* Irving Elman. *Ph* Benjamin Kline. *Mus* Darrell Calker. *Cast* Jean Rogers, Richard Travis, Larry Blake, John Eldredge. 66 min.

Jealous lawyer tries to frame wife for his own murder.

Beautiful Stranger see *Twist of Fate*

Before I Wake see *Shadow of Fear*

20. *Behind Locked Doors* (1948) Eagle Lion. *Dir* Bud Boetticher. *Sc* Malvin Wald and Eugene Ling, from a story by Wald. *Ph* Guy Roe. *Mus* Albert Glasser. *Cast* Lucille Bremer, Richard Carlson, Douglas Fowley, Thomas Browne Henry. 62 min.

Attempting to track down story of judge's disappearance, ambitious reporter gets himself committed to a suspicious mental hospital.

Betrayed see *When Strangers Marry*

21. *Between Midnight and Dawn* (1950) Columbia. *Dir* Gordon Douglas. *Sc* Eugene Ling, from a story by Gerald Drayson Adams and Leo Katcher. *Ph* George E. Diskant. *Mus* George Duning. *Cast* Mark Stevens, Edmond O'Brien, Gale Storm, Donald Buka, Gale Robbins, Roland Winters. 89 min.

Two close-knit L.A. cops attempt to bring in savage hoodlum for murder, with violent and tragic results.

22. *Beware, My Lovely* (1952) RKO. *Dir* Harry Horner. *Sc* Mel Dinelli, from his play and story. *Ph* George E. Diskant. *Mus* Leith Stevens. *Cast* Ida Lupino, Robert Ryan, Taylor Holmes, Ruth Williams. 76 min.

War widow and her new handyman suspect and fear each other. This offbeat thriller's moderate psychological depth is given extra mileage by Lupino and Ryan.

23. *Bewitched* (1945) MGM. *Dir* Arch Oboler. *Sc* Oboler, from his story. *Ph* Charles Salerno, Jr. *Mus* Bronislau Kaper. *Cast* Phyllis Thaxter, Stephen McNally, Edmund Gwenn, Henry H. Daniels, Addison Richards, Kathleen Lockhart. 65 min.

On the eve of her engagement, a demure young woman becomes the victim of a split personality and murders her fiance. Little-known, disquieting psychological melodrama that is Hollywood's first depiction of schizoid psychosis and, in turn, an important early treatment of the noir Doppelgänger (ghostly double) theme.

24. *Beyond a Reasonable Doubt* (1956) RKO. *Dir* Fritz Lang. *Sc* Douglas Morrow. *Ph* William Snyder. *Mus* Herschel Burke Gilbert. *Cast* Dana Andrews, Joan Fontaine, Sidney Blackmer, Philip Bourneuf, Shepperd Strudwick, Arthur Franz. 80 min.

Novelist makes secret agreement with publisher to incriminate himself in an unsolved murder for a book discrediting capital punishment. Lang's last American film is a slick B thriller with several neat plot twists.

25. *Beyond the Forest* (1949) Warner Brothers. *Dir* King Vidor. *Sc* Lenore Coffee, from the novel by Stuart Engstrand. *Ph* Robert Burks. *Mus* Max Steiner. *Cast* Bette Davis, Joseph Cotten, David Brian, Ruth Roman, Dona Drake, Regis Toomey. 97 min.

Passionate depiction of a restless woman's misguided attempt to escape her modest small town life.

26. *The Big Bluff* (1955) United Artists. *Dir* W. Lee Wilder. *Sc* Fred Freiberger, from a story by Mindret Lord. *Ph* Gordin Avil. *Mus* Manuel Compinsky. *Cast* John Bromfield, Martha Vickers, Robert Hutton, Rosmarie Bowe, Eve Miller. 70 min.

A man plots murder when the doomed woman he married for money recovers from her illness. Rehashing of *The Glass Alibi* (1946).

The Big Carnival see *Ace in the Hole*

27. *The Big Clock* (1948) Paramount. *Dir* John Farrow. *Sc* Jonathan Latimer, adapted by Harold Goldman from the novel by Kenneth Fearing. *Ph* John F. Seitz. *Mus* Victor Young, *Cast* Ray Milland, Charles Laughton, Maureen O'Sullivan, George Macready, Rita Johnson, Elsa Lanchester. 93 min.

The brilliant editor of a national crime magazine engages in a life-and-death battle of wits with his tyrannical boss. The ultimate noir statement on the world of American business, whose sheer artistry makes everything circular.

28. *The Big Combo* (1955) Allied Artists.

Stylish, sensual tale of a cop's obsession with nabbing a big-time mobster. See page 112.

29. *The Big Heat* (1953) Columbia. *Dir* Fritz Lang. *Sc* Sydney Boehm, from the novel by William P. McGivern. *Ph* Charles B. Lang. *Mus* Daniele Amfitheatrof. *Cast* Glenn Ford, Gloria Grahame, Jocelyn Brando, Alexander Scourby, Lee Marvin, Jeanette Nolan. 90 min.

Despite pressure from all sides, a police lieutenant doggedly pursues a suicide investigation linked to the city's powerful crime czar. Lang's most popular noir subverts its own moral victory through violence, tragedy and death.

30. *The Big Knife* (1955) United Artists. *Dir* Robert Aldrich.

Sc James Poe, from the play by Clifford Odets. *Ph* Ernest Laszlo. *Mus* Frank DeVol. *Cast* Jack Palance, Ida Lupino, Wendell Corey, Jean Hagen, Rod Steiger, Shelley Winters, Evertt Sloane. 111 min.

The fame of a Hollywood star becomes an agonizing trap from which there is only one escape. Extremely harsh, uncompromising late-noir cynicism.

31. *The Big Night* (1951) United Artists. *Dir* Joseph Losey. *Sc* Stanley Ellin and Joseph Losey, from Ellin's novel *Dreadful Summit*. *Ph* Hal Mohr. *Mus* Lyn Murray. *Cast* John Barrymore, Jr., Preston Foster, Joan Lorring, Howard St. John, Dorothy Comingore, Philip Bourneuf. 75 min.

Confused teenager seeks man responsible for beating up his father. Unique, moving film of a protagonists quest for manhood in a harsh, uncaring world.

32. *The Big Sleep* (1946) Warner Brothers. *Dir* Howard Hawks. *Sc* William Faulkner, Leigh Brackett and Jules Furthman, from the novel by Raymond Chandler. *Ph* Sid Hickox. *Mus* Max Steiner. *Cast* Humphrey Bogart, Lauren Bacall, John Ridgeley, Martha Vickers, Dorothy Malone, Elisha Cook, Jr., Bob Steele. 118 min.

Philip Marlowe is retained by a wealthy family to deal with a case of blackmail. Many different creative talents combine here for a distinctive and vastly entertaining depiction of Raymond Chandler's L.A. netherworld.

33. *Black Angel* (1946) Universal. *Dir* Roy William Neill. *Sc* Roy Chanslor, from the novel by Cornell Woolrich. *Ph* Paul Ivano. *Mus* Frank Skinner. *Cast* Dan Duryea, June Vincent, Peter Lorre, Broderick Crawford, Constance Dowling. 83 min.

Woman believes her husband is innocent of murdering sultry *femme fatale*, gets alcoholic songwriter to help her find the real killer. Important, stylish B noir, featuring Dan Duryea as the ironic central character.

34. *The Black Hand* (1950) MGM. *Dir* Richard Thorpe. *Sc* Luther Davis, from a story by Leo Townsend. *Ph* Paul C. Vogel. *Mus* Alberto Colombo. *Cast* Gene Kelly, J. Carrol Naish, Teresa Celli, Marc Lawrence, Frank Puglia. 92 min.

At the turn of the century, a son seeks revenge for the Mafia murder of his father in New York City's "Little Italy."

35. *Black Tuesday* (1954) United Artists. *Dir* Hugo Fregonese. *Sc* Sydney Boehm, from his story. *Ph* Stanley Cortez. *Mus* Paul Dunlap. *Cast* Edward G. Robinson, Peter Graves, Jean Parker, Milburn Stone, Warren Stevens, Jack Kelly. 80 min.

On the day of his planned execution, a vicious gangster pulls off an elaborate escape.

36. *Blind Spot* (1947) Columbia. *Dir* Robert Gordon. *Sc* Martin Goldsmith, from a story by Barry Perowne. *Ph* George B. Meehan. *Mus* Paul Sawtell. *Cast* Chester Morris, Constance Dowling, Steven Geray, Sid Tomack, James Bell. 73 min.

Mystery writer gets enmeshed in sordid circumstances of his craft, ends up charged with publisher's murder.

37. *The Blue Dahlia* (1946) Paramount. *Dir* George Marshall. *Sc* Raymond Chandler. *Ph* Lionel Lindon. *Mus* Victor Young. *Cast* Alan Ladd, Veronica Lake, William Bendix, Howard da Silva, Doris Dowling, Hugh Beaumont. 98 min.

Man just released from the service is prime suspect in murder of his unfaithful wife. Raymond Chandler's only original screenplay emphasizes the major noir theme of a war veteran's difficult, disillusioning return to the states.

38. *The Blue Gardenia* (1953) Warner Brothers. *Dir* Fritz Lang. *Sc* Charles Hoffman, from a story by Vera Caspary. *Ph* Nicholas Musuraca. *Mus* Raoul Kraushaar. *Cast* Anne Baxter, Richard Conte, Ann Sothern, Raymond Burr, Jeff Donnell, Richard Erdman. 90 min.

Newspaper columnist aids a girl who thinks she killed her blind date.

39. *Bluebeard* (1944) PRC. *Dir* Edgar G. Ulmer. *Sc* Pierre Gendron, from a story by Arnold Phillips and Werner H. Furst. *Ph* Jockey A. Feindell. *Mus* Leo Erdody. *Cast* John Carradine, Jean Parker, Nils Asther, Ludwig Stossel. 73 min.

Sensitive puppeteer is driven to kill beautiful young women. Sincere, meaningful narrative of a sympathetic artist-murderer.

40. *A Blueprint for Murder* (1953) 20th Century-Fox. *Dir* Andrew L. Stone. *Sc* Stone. *Ph* Leo Tover. *Mus* Lionel Newman. *Cast* Joseph Cotten, Jean Peters, Gary Merrill, Catherine McLeod, Jack Kruschen. 76 min.

Man has trouble proving that his sister-in-law is a clever poison murderer.

41. *Blues in the Night* (1941) Warner Brothers. *Dir* Anatole Litvak. *Sc* Robert Rossen, from a play by Edwin Gilbert. *Ph* Ernest Haller. *Mus* Heinz Roemheld. *Cast* Priscilla Lane, Betty Field, Richard Whorf, Lloyd Nolan, Jack Carson, Wallace Ford, Elia Kazan, Howard da Silva. 88 min.

The various members of a small swing band struggle with life. Little-known early Warners noir that posits the cycle's recurrent link with popular music of the day.

42. *Body and Soul* (1947) United Artists. *Dir* Robert Rossen. *Sc* Abraham Polonsky. *Ph* James Wong Howe. *Mus* Hugo Friedhofer. *Cast* John Garfield, Lilli Palmer, Hazel Brooks, Anne Revere, William Conrad, Joseph Pevney, Canada Lee. 105 min.

A fighter claws his way to the top, only to find that success is a very costly business. The first noir boxing film, memorable for a coherence of style and Garfield's gritty performance.

43. *Bodyguard* (1948) RKO. *Dir* Richard Fleischer. *Sc* Fred Niblo, Sr. and Harry Essex, from a story by George W. George and Robert B. Altman. *Ph* Robert de Grasse. *Mus* Paul Sawtell. *Cast* Lawrence Tierney, Priscilla Lane, Philip Reed, Steve Brodie, Frank Fenton. 62 min.

An ex-detective framed for murder poses as a bodyguard to obtain evidence of his innocence.

44. *Boomerang* (1947) 20th Century-Fox. *Dir* Elia Kazan. *Sc* Richard Murphy, from an article by Anthony Abbot. *Ph* Norbert Brodine. *Mus*

David Buttolph. *Cast* Dana Andrews, Jane Wyatt, Lee J. Cobb, Cara Williams, Arthur Kennedy, Sam Levene, Robert Keith, Ed Begley. 88 min.

When a popular clergyman is murdered in a small eastern town, great political and social pressure almost results in the conviction of an innocent man. Inciteful, realistic depiction of the crucial point at which government responsiveness loses all integrity.

45. *Border Incident* (1949) MGM. *Dir* Anthony Mann. *Sc* John C. Higgins, from a story by Higgins and George Zuckerman. *Ph* John Alton. *Mus* André Previn. *Cast* Ricardo Montalban, George Murphy, Howard da Silva, Arnold Moss, Charles McGraw, Alfonso Bedoya. 92 min.

Immigration agents infiltrate a crooked rancher's alien labor racket. Impressive, violent police film, set in Southwest border region.

46. *Born to Be Bad* (1950) RKO. *Dir* Nicholas Ray. *Sc* Edith Sommer, from Charles Schnee's adaption of the novel *All Kneeling* by Ann Parish. *Ph* Nicholas Musuraca. *Mus* Frederick Hollander. *Cast* Joan Fontaine, Robert Ryan, Zachary Scott, Mel Ferrer, Joan Leslie. 94 min.

Scheming woman's marriage to wealthy businessman doesn't stop her from keeping a successful novelist on the line. Sophisticated story of an alluring, heartless *femme fatale*.

47. *Born to Kill* (1947) RKO. *Dir* Robert Wise. *Sc* Eve Greene and Richard Macaulay, from the novel *Deadlier than the Male* by James Gunn. *Ph* Robert de Grasse. *Mus* Paul Sawtell. *Cast* Claire Trevor, Lawrence Tierney, Walter Slezak, Philip Terry, Audrey Long, Elisha Cook, Jr. 92 min.

Self-serving woman falls for a man she knows is a killer. Stark film filled with ugly, dangerous characters that is just one of many significant noirs produced by RKO.

48. *The Brasher Doubloon* (1947) 20th Century–Fox. *Dir* John Brahm. *Sc* Dorothy Hannah, adapted by Dorothy Bennett and Leonard Praskins, from the novel *The High Window* by Raymond Chandler. *Ph* Lloyd Ahern. *Mus* David Buttolph. *Cast* George Montgomery, Nancy Guild, Conrad Janis, Roy Roberts, Fritz Kortner. 72 min.

Search for a valuable stolen coin casts Philip Marlowe into complex maze of violence, blackmail and murder. Last noir adaption of a Chandler novel.

49. *The Breaking Point* (1950) Warner Brothers. *Dir* Michael Curtiz. *Sc* Ranald MacDougall, from the novel *To Have and Have Not* by Ernest Hemingway. *Ph* Ted McCord. *Mus* Ray Heindorf. *Cast* John Garfield, Patricia Neal, Phyllis Thaxter, Juano Hernandez, Wallace Ford, Sherry Jackson. 97 min.

The owner of a small charter boat struggles to make ends meet and still retain his self-respect. A faithful, distinguished adaption of Hemingway's novel.

50. *The Bribe* (1949) MGM. *Dir* Robert Z. Leonard. *Sc* Marguerite Roberts, from a story by Frederick Nobel. *Ph* Joseph Ruttenberg. *Mus* Miklos Rozsa. *Cast* Robert Taylor, Ava Gardner, Charles Laughton, Vincent Price, John Hodiak. 98 min.

Federal agent attempts to break up South American smuggling ring, but his involvement with a sultry woman causes complications.

51. *Brute Force* (1947) Universal.

Flashbacks reveal the pasts of five inmates as they are driven to the point of desperation resulting in a violent prison break. Despite significant cuts in Dassin's original footage, *Brute Force* is still the ultimate noir prison film and one of the high points of the cycle. See page 52.

52. *The Burglar.* (1957) Columbia. *Dir* Paul Wendkos. *Sc* David Goodis, from his novel. *Ph* Don Malkames. *Mus* Sol Kaplan. *Cast* Dan Duryea, Jayne Mansfield, Martha Vickers, Peter Capell, Mickey Shaughnessy, Stewart Bradley. 90 min.

Burglar and his gang steal valuable diamond necklace, are tailed by crooked cop who wants the prize for himself. Late-noir character study with highly stylized visuals.

53. *Bury Me Dead* (1947) PRC. *Dir* Bernard Vorhaus. *Sc* Karen DeWolf and Dwight V. Babcock, from the radio play by Irene Winston. *Ph* John Alton. *Mus* Emil Cadkin. *Cast* Cathy O'Donnell, June Lockhart, Hugh Beaumont, Mark Daniels. 71 min.

Woman shows up for her own funeral, foiling the plans of a philandering husband.

54. *C-Man* (1949) Film Classics. *Dir* Joseph Lerner. *Sc* Berne Giler. *Ph* Gerald Hirschfeld. *Mus* Gail Kubik. *Cast* Dean Jagger, John Carradine, Lottie Elwen, Harry Landers. 75 min.

Customs agent tracks down murderous jewel thieves. Semidocumentary thriller with some good atmosphere and a surprising electronic music score.

55. *Caged* (1950) Warner Brothers. *Dir* John Cromwell. *Sc* Virginia Kellogg and Bernard C. Schoenfeld. *Ph* Carl Guthrie. *Mus* Max Steiner. *Cast* Eleanor Parker, Agnes Moorehead, Ellen Corby, Hope Emerson, Betty Garde, Jan Sterling, Lee Patrick, Jane Darwell. 97 min.

After being implicated in a crime committed by her husband, an innocent young woman is sent to prison and undergoes innumerable hardships and cruelties. The most polished and stylish of all women's prison films depicts with great power the destructive, hardening effect of life behind bars.

56. *Calcutta* (1947) Paramount. *Dir* John Farrow. *Sc* Seton I. Miller. *Ph* John F. Seitz. *Mus* Victor Young. *Cast* Alan Ladd, Gail Russell, William Bendix, June Duprez, Lowell Gilmore. 83 min.

Commercial pilot in India attempts to avenge friend's murder.

57. *Call Northside 777* (1948) 20th Century-Fox. *Dir* Henry Hathaway. *Sc* Jerome Cady and Jay Dratler, adapted by Leonard Hoffman and Quentin Reynolds, from articles by James P. McGuire. *Ph* Joe MacDonald. *Mus* Alfred Newman. *Cast* James Stewart, Richard Conte, Lee J. Cobb, Helen Walker, Betty Garde. 111 min.

A newspaper reporter uncovers evidence that a man was wrongly convicted of murder twelve years earlier. Notable example of the late forties semidocumentary noir style.

58. *Canon City* (1948) Eagle Lion. *Dir* Crane Wilbur. *Sc* Wilbur.

Ph John Alton. *Mus* Irving Friedman. *Cast* Scott Brady, Jeff Corey, Whit Bissell, Charles Russell, Stanley Clements, DeForest Kelley. 82 min.

Realistic drama of inmate's unwilling involvement in a prison break.

59. *Captive City* (1952) United Artists. *Dir* Robert Wise. *Sc* Karl Kamb and Alvin M. Josephy, Jr., from a story by Josephy. *Ph* Lee Garmes. *Mus* Jerome Moross. *Cast* John Forsythe, Joan Camden, Harold J. Kennedy, Ray Teal, Marjorie Crossland, Victor Sutherland, Martin Milner. 90 min.

Midwest newspaper editor learns that his town is controlled by the mob.

60. *The Capture* (1950) RKO. *Dir* John Sturges. *Sc* Niven Busch. *Ph* Edward Cronjager. *Mus* Daniele Amfitheatrof. *Cast* Lew Ayres, Teresa Wright, Victor Jory, Jacqueline White, Jimmy Hunt, Duncan Renaldo. 81 min.

A man sets out to catch a robber, ends up on the run himself. Interesting and atypical noir, set in Mexico.

61. *Caught* (1949) MGM.

Max Ophuls' striking tale of a woman's marriage to money was purportedly inspired by the real life character of Howard Hughes. See page 75.

62. *Cause for Alarm* (1951) MGM. *Dir* Tay Garnett. *Sc* Mel Dinelli and Tom Lewis, from a story by Larry Marcus. *Ph* Joseph Ruttenberg. *Mus* André Previn. *Cast* Loretta Young, Barry Sullivan, Bruce Cowling, Margalo Gillmore. 74 min.

Menacing nightmare thriller of woman's desperate attempt to prevent her insanely jealous husband from framing her for his own murder.

63. *Champion* (1949) United Artists. *Dir* Mark Robson. *Sc* Carl Foreman, from a story by Ring Lardner. *Ph* Franz Planer. *Mus* Dimitri Tiomkin. *Cast* Kirk Douglas, Marilyn Maxwell, Arthur Kennedy, Ruth Roman, Paul Stewart, Lola Albright. 90 min.

An egotistical fighter will stop at nothing to get to the top. Similar to *Body and Soul*, only with a more thoroughly black ending.

64. *The Chase* (1946) United Artists. *Dir* Arthur Ripley. *Sc* Philip Yordan, from the novel *The Black Path of Fear* by Cornell Woolrich. *Ph* Franz Planer. *Mus* Michel Michelet. *Cast* Michele Morgan, Robert Cummings, Steve Cochran, Lloyd Corrigan, Peter Lorre. 86 min.

Man tries to run away with racketeer's wife, putting them both in extreme danger. Woolrich's paranoid nightmare is reconceived as a dark, hypnotic coalescence of dream and reality.

65. *Chicago Deadline* (1949) Paramount. *Dir* Lewis Allen. *Sc* Warren Duff, from the novel *One Woman* by Tiffany Thayer. *Ph* John F. Seitz. *Mus* Victor Young. *Cast* Alan Ladd, Donna Reed, June Havoc, Irene Harvey, Arthur Kennedy, Shepperd Strudwick. 87 min.

Chicago reporter becomes obsessed with dead girl's past. Flashbacks reveal sordid details of one life in the dark urban jungle.

66. *Christmas Holiday* (1944) Universal. *Dir* Robert Siodmak. *Sc* Herman J. Mankiewicz, from the novel by Somerset Maugham. *Ph* John P.

Fulton. *Mus* Hans J. Salter. *Cast* Deanna Durbin, Gene Kelly, Richard Whorf, Gale Sondergaard, Dean Harens, Gladys George. 93 min.

Soldier meets distraught girl who tells him the sad story of her tragic marriage to a misguided New Orleans gentleman. With this significant early film, Siodmak masterfully establishes the noir aesthetic conception of subverting traditional narrative expectations.

67. *Circumstantial Evidence* (1945) 20th Century-Fox. *Dir* John Larkin. *Sc* Robert Metzler, adapted by Samuel Ornitz, from a story by Nat Ferber and Sam Duncan. *Ph* Harry Jackson. *Mus* David Buttolph. *Cast* Michael O'Shea, Lloyd Nolan, Trudy Marshall, Billy Cummings, Roy Roberts. 67 min.

Innocent reporter escapes from prison on the eve of his planned execution.

68. *City Across the River* (1949) Universal. *Dir* Maxwell Shane. *Sc* Shane and Dennis Cooper, from the novel *The Amboy Dukes* by Irving Shulman. *Ph* Maury Gertsman. *Mus* Walter Scharf. *Cast* Stephen McNally, Thelma Ritter, Luis Van Rooten, Jeff Corey, Tony Curtis, Richard Jaeckel. 90 min.

Two members of a tough Brooklyn street gang accidentally kill one of their teachers. Realistic, uncompromising noir study of urban juvenile delinquency.

69. *City of Fear* (1959) Columbia. *Dir* Irving Lerner. *Sc* Steven Ritch and Robert Dillon. *Ph* Lucien Ballard. *Mus* Jerry Goldsmith. *Cast* Vince Edwards, Lyle Talbot, John Archer, Steven Ritch, Patricia Blair. 81 min.

Escaped convict steals metal box he thinks is filled with heroin, but actually it contains dangerous radioactive material.

City on a Hunt see *No Escape*

70. *City That Never Sleeps* (1953) Republic. *Dir* John H. Auer. *Sc* Steve Fisher. *Ph* John L. Russell, Jr. *Mus* R. Dale Butts. *Cast* Gig Young, Mala Powers, William Talman, Edward Arnold, Marie Windsor, Wally Cassell, Chill Wills. 90 min.

Chicago patrolman faces temptation and danger as the spirit of the city looks on. Peculiar B noir with an interesting assortment of nighttime characters.

71. *Clash by Night* (1952) RKO. *Dir* Fritz Lang. *Sc* Alfred Hayes, from the play by Clifford Odets. *Ph* Nicholas Musuraca. *Mus* Roy Webb. *Cast* Barbara Stanwyck, Robert Ryan, Paul Douglas, J. Carroll Naish, Marilyn Monroe, Keith Andes. 104 min.

A world-weary woman tries to settle down in a New England fishing village, gets caught between two men, one handsome, brooding and cynical, and the other reliable but unexciting. Darkish, moody character study with depth and good acting, especially by Ryan.

72. *The Clay Pigeon* (1949) RKO. *Dir* Richard Fleischer. *Sc* Carl Foreman. *Ph* Robert de Grasse. *Mus* Paul Sawtell. *Cast* Bill Williams, Barbara Hale, Richard Quine, Richard Loo, Frank Fenton. 63 min.

Just back from overseas prison camp, amnesia victim wakes up in hospital and learns that he's accused of being a traitor. Obscure RKO thriller with a nicely interwoven mixture of strong noir elements.

73. *The Come-On* (1956) Allied Artists. *Dir* Russell Birdwell. *Sc* Warren Douglas and Whitman Chambers, from the novel by Chambers. *Ph* Ernest Haller. *Mus* Paul Dunlap. *Cast* Anne Baxter, Sterling Hayden, John Hoyt, Jesse White, Walter Cassell. 83 min.

Woman on the make wants love but won't pay the price; result: murder.

Confidential Report see *Mr. Arkadin*

74. *Conflict* (1945) Warner Brothers. *Dir* Curtis Bernhardt. *Sc* Arthur T. Horman and Dwight Taylor, from a story by Robert Siodmak and Alfred Neumann. *Ph* Merritt Gerstad. *Mus* Frederick Hollander. *Cast* Humphrey Bogart, Alexis Smith, Sydney Greenstreet, Charles Drake, Rose Hobart. 86 min.

A man murders his grasping wife and then tries to take up with her beautiful young sister. Absorbing, fatalistic Warners thriller, which displays a mature, Germanically influenced noir style and features a strong Bogart performance as the sinister, doomed protagonist.

75. *Convicted* (1950) Columbia. *Dir* Henry Levin. *Sc* William Bowers, Fred Niblo and Seton I. Miller, from a play by Martin Flavin. *Ph* Burnett Guffey. *Mus* George Duning. *Cast* Glenn Ford, Broderick Crawford, Millard Mitchell, Dorothy Malone, Carl Benton Reid, Frank Faylen, Will Geer. 91 min.

Serving time in prison for a murder he didn't commit, a man becomes hard and embittered. One of several noirs which were remade from appropriate thirties crime pictures.

76. *Cornered* (1945) RKO. *Dir* Edward Dmytryk. *Sc* John Paxton, from a story by John Wexley. *Ph* Harry J. Wild. *Mus* Roy Webb. *Cast* Dick Powell, Walter Slezak, Micheline Cheirel, Nina Vale, Morris Carnovsky, Steven Geray, Luther Adler. 102 min.

Canadian pilot, recently released from prisoner of war camp, seeks revenge for his French wife's war-related death. Wartime thriller that becomes noir due to the effective psychological portrayal of an emotionally scarred protagonist in an alien world.

77. *Crack-Up* (1946) RKO. *Dir* Irving Reis. *Sc* John Paxton, Ben Bengal and Ray Spencer, from a story by Fredric Brown. *Ph* Robert de Grasse. *Mus* Leigh Harline. *Cast* Pat O'Brien, Claire Trevor, Herbert Marshall, Ray Collins, Wallace Ford. 93 min.

Controversial member of art museum staff has vivid memories of a train wreck that never occured. Significant nightmarish thriller which utliizes subtle irony in its depiction of a corrupt, decadent art world.

78. *Crashout* (1955) Filmakers. *Dir* Lewis Foster. *Sc* Hal E. Chester and Foster. *Ph* Russell Metty. *Mus* Leith Stevens. *Cast* William Bendix, Arthur Kennedy, Luther Adler, William Talman, Gene Evans, Marshall Thompson, Beverly Michaels, Gloria Talbot. 90 min.

Brisk, hard-hitting film about six men on a prison break.

79. *Crime of Passion* (1957) United Artists. *Dir* Gerd Oswald. *Sc* Jo Eisinger. *Ph* Joseph LaShelle. *Mus* Paul Dunlap. *Cast* Barbara Stanwyck, Sterling Hayden, Raymond Burr, Fay Wray, Royal Dano, Virginia Grey. 85 min.

An ambitious, strong-willed woman will stop at nothing to obtain promotions for her police detective husband. Claustrophobic nightmare of fifties suburbia.

80. *Crime Wave* (1954) Warner Brothers. *Dir* André de Toth. *Sc* Crane Wilbur, adapted by Bernard Gordon and Richard Wormser, from a story by John and Ward Hawkins. *Ph* Bert Glennon. *Mus* David Buttolph. *Cast* Gene Nelson, Phyllis Kirk, Sterling Hayden, James Bell, Ted de Corsia, Charles Bronson. 73 min.

Ex-con trying to go straight is forced to cooperate with two former prison acquaintances that are planning a holdup. Well-crafted low budget melodrama which builds sympathy for a protagonist seeking to escape his criminal past.

81. *The Crimson Kimono* (1959) Columbia. *Dir* Sam Fuller. *Sc* Fuller. *Ph* Sam Leavitt. *Mus* Harry Sukman. *Cast* Victoria Shaw, Glenn Corbett, James Shigeta, Anna Lee, Paul Dubov. 82 min.

Two L.A. police detectives, who are also best friends, investigate the murder of a stripper. This potent film is actually the first of a series of distinctive, noir-oriented thrillers directed by Fuller.

82. *Criss Cross* (1949) Universal.

Unable to shake the spell of his ex-wife, man is induced to participate in payroll robbery planned by her new husband. Siodmak's seductive, hypnotic story of obsession and betrayal. See page 70.

83. *The Crooked Way* (1949) United Artists. *Dir* Robert Florey. *Sc* Richard H. Landau, from a radio play by Robert Monroe. *Ph* John Alton. *Mus* Louis Forbes. *Cast* John Payne, Sonny Tufts, Ellen Drew, Rhys Williams, Percy Helton, John Doucette. 87 min.

Amnesiac war veteran returns to L.A. and uncovers disturbing facts about his past. Tough, violent crime picture with good location visuals and direction.

84. *The Crooked Web* (1955) Columbia. *Dir* Nathan Juran. *Sc* Lou Breslow, from his story. *Ph* Henry Freulich. *Mus* Mischa Bakaleinikoff. *Cast* Frank Lovejoy, Mari Blanchard, Richard Denning, John Mylong, Harry Lauter. 77 min.

Restaurateur is lured back to Germany with the promise of buried war loot.

85. *Crossfire* (1947) RKO. *Dir* Edward Dmytryk. *Sc* John Paxton, from the novel *The Brick Foxhole* by Richard Brooks. *Ph* J. Roy Hunt. *Mus* Roy Webb. *Cast* Robert Young, Robert Mitchum, Robert Ryan, Gloria Grahame, Paul Kelly, Sam Levene, Steve Brodie. 85 min.

One of four army buddies is a violent racial bigot who murders two men before he is trapped by police. Tense "message picture" with a strong noir style and mood.

86. *Crossroads* (1942) MGM. *Dir* Jack Conway. *Sc* Guy Trosper, from a story by John Kafka and Howard Emmett Rogers. *Ph* Joseph Ruttenberg. *Mus* Bronislau Kaper. *Cast* William Powell, Hedy Lamarr, Claire Trevor, Basil Rathbone, Margaret Wycherly, Felix Bressart, Sig Rumann. 84 min.

French diplomat with amnesia is accused of being murderer.

87. *Cry Danger* (1951) RKO. *Dir* Robert Parrish. *Sc* William Bowers, from a story by Jerome Cady. *Ph* Joseph F. Biroc. *Mus* Emil Newman, Paul Dunlap. *Cast* Dick Powell, Rhonda Fleming, Richard Erdman, William Conrad, Regis Toomey. 79 min.

Man framed for robbery seeks those responsible. Entertaining thriller dominated by laconic tough guy Powell.

88. *A Cry in the Night* (1956) Warner Brothers. *Dir* Frank Tuttle. *Sc* David Dortort, from the novel *All Through the Night* by Whit Masterson. *Ph* John F. Seitz. *Mus* David Buttolph. *Cast* Edmond O'Brien, Brian Donlevy, Natalie Wood, Raymond Burr, Richard Anderson. 75 min.

Mentally disturbed man kidnaps young girl from lover's lane; police hunt ensues.

89. *Cry of the City* (1948) 20th Century-Fox. *Dir* Robert Siodmak. *Sc* Richard Murphy, from the novel *The Chair for Martin Rome* by Henry Edward Helseth. *Ph* Lloyd Ahern. *Mus* Alfred Newman. *Cast* Victor Mature, Richard Conte, Fred Clark, Shelley Winters, Betty Garde, Debra Paget. 96 min.

Wounded criminal is hunted by tough cop that was his childhood friend. The most realistic and conventional of Siodmak's noir films carries a script which emphasizes moral ambiguity.

90. *Cry Terror* (1958) MGM. *Dir* Andrew L. Stone. *Sc* Stone. *Ph* Walter Strenge. *Mus* Howard Jackson. *Cast* James Mason, Rod Steiger, Inger Stevens, Neville Brand, Angie Dickinson, Jack Klugman. 96 min.

Brilliant psychopath holds innocent family captive as a part of an elaborate extortion plot. Good New York City location work and suspense.

91. *Cry Tough* (1959) United Artists. *Dir* Paul Stanley. *Sc* Harry Kleiner, from the novel *Children of the Dark* by Irving Shulman. *Ph* Philip Lathrop. *Mus* Laurindo Almeida. *Cast* John Saxon, Linda Cristal, Joseph Calleia, Harry Townes, Don Gordon. 83 min.

A Puerto Rican juvenile is drawn into a life of crime, with tragic results.

92. *Cry Vengeance* (1954) Allied Artists. *Dir* Mark Stevens. *Sc* Warren Douglas and George Bricker. *Ph* William Sickner. *Mus* Paul Dunlap. *Cast* Mark Stevens, Martha Hyer, Skip Homeier, Joan Vohs. 83 min.

Embittered ex-con seeks those responsible for framing him and murdering his family.

93. *Cry Wolf* (1947) Warner Brothers. *Dir* Peter Godfrey. *Sc* Catherine Turney, from the novel by Marjorie Carleton. *Ph* Carl Guthrie. *Mus* Franz Waxman. *Cast* Errol Flynn, Barbara Stanwyck, Geraldine Brooks, Richard Basehart, Jerome Cowan, John Ridgely. 84 min.

Woman arrives at mysterious country estate claiming to be the late heir's wife. Menacing gothic noir set in contemporary New England.

94. *D.O.A.* (1950) United Artists.
One of the best noir concept films, about a dying man who hunts his own murderer. See page 88.

95. *The Damned Don't Cry* (1950) Warner Brothers. *Dir* Vincent Sherman. *Sc* Harold Medford and Jerome Weidman, from a story by Gertrude Walker. *Ph* Ted McCord. *Mus* Daniele Amfitheatrof. *Cast* Joan Crawford, David Brian, Steve Cochran, Kent Smith, Richard Egan. 103 min.

Ambitious, frustrated woman walks out on her lower-class life, claws her way to the top, and then gets caught in the middle of a vicious syndicate power struggle. Important Joan Crawford noir, with irony, excitement and a strong class theme.

96. *Danger Signal* (1945) Warner Brothers. *Dir* Robert Florey. *Sc* Adele Commandini and Graham Baker, from the novel by Phyllis Bottome. *Ph* James Wong Howe. *Mus* Adolphe Deutsch. *Cast* Faye Emerson, Zachary Scott, Dick Erdman, Rosemary DeCamp, Bruce Bennett, Mona Freeman, John Ridgely. 78 min.

Mysterious artist rents a room in middle-class household, sets two sisters against each other.

97. *Dangerous Crossing* (1953) 20th Century–Fox. *Dir* Joseph M. Newman. *Sc* Leo Townsend, from a story by John Dickson Carr. *Ph* Joseph La Shelle. *Mus* Lionel Newman. *Cast* Jeanne Crain, Michael Rennie, Casey Adams, Carl Betz, Mary Anderson. 75 min.

Woman's husband disappears on honeymoon cruise; evidence indicates he never existed.

98. *A Dangerous Profession* (1949) RKO. *Dir* Ted Tetzlaff. *Sc* Martin Rackin and Warren Duff. *Ph* Robert de Grasse. *Mus* Frederick Hollander. *Cast* George Raft, Ella Raines, Pat O'Brien, Bill Williams, Jim Backus. 79 min.

A bail bondsman is asked to help the husband of a mysterious woman he has fallen for, which leads to trouble.

99. *Dark City* (1950) Paramount.

A tough, alienated gambler is stalked by a homicidal maniac bent on avenging the death of his brother. See page 101.

100. *The Dark Corner* (1946) 20th Century–Fox. *Dir* Henry Hathaway. *Sc* Jay Dratler and Bernard Schoenfeld, from the story by Leo Rosten. *Ph* Joe MacDonald. *Mus* Cyril Mockridge. *Cast* Mark Stevens, Lucille Ball, Clifton Webb, William Bendix, Kurt Kreuger, Cathy Downs. 99 min.

A private detective is tabbed as the pawn in a haughty art dealer's murderous plot to eliminate his wife's lover. One of the most important noirs of 1946, whose emphasis is on the psychological anguish and confusion of a tough but emotionally vulnerable protagonist.

101. *The Dark Mirror* (1946) Universal. *Dir* Robert Siodmak. *Sc* Nunnally Johnson, from a story by Vladimir Pozner. *Ph* Milton Krasner. *Mus* Dimitri Tiomkin. *Cast* Olivia De Havilland, Lew Ayres, Thomas Mitchell, Richard Long, Charles Evans, Garry Owen. 85 min.

One of a pair of identical twin sisters has murdered a psychiatrist, but no one knows which. The Doppelgänger concept is here treated simply as a classic split between good and evil.

102. _Dark Passage_ (1947) Warner Brothers. _Dir_ Delmer Daves. _Sc_ Daves, from the novel by David Goodis. _Ph_ Sid Hickox. _Mus_ Franz Waxman. _Cast_ Humphrey Bogart, Lauren Bacall, Bruce Bennett, Agnes Moorehead, Tom D'Andrea, Houseley Stevenson. 106 min.

Escaped convict undergoes plastic surgery and meets a girl who helps him attempt to prove his innocence. Entertaining Bogart-Bacall thriller, notable for its subjective-camera opening and its positive resolution "outside the law."

103. _The Dark Past_ (1948) Columbia. _Dir_ Rudolph Maté. _Sc_ Philip MacDonald, Michael Blankfort, and Albert Duffy, adapted by Malvin Wald and Oscar Saul, from a play by James Warwick. _Ph_ Joseph Walker. _Mus_ George Duning. _Cast_ William Holden, Nina Foch, Lee J. Cobb, Adele Jergens, Stephen Dunne, Lois Maxwell, Steven Geray. 74 min.

Notorious killer and his gang hold up at a psychiatrist's home. Psychological concept film which attempts to analyze and explain the nightmarish roots of a killer's psychopathic behavior. (Remake of 1939 film, _Blind Alley_.)

104. _Dark Waters_ (1944) United Artists. _Dir_ André de Toth. _Sc_ Joan Harrison and Marion Cockrell, from a story by Frank and Marion Cockrell. _Ph_ Archie Stout, John Mescall. _Mus_ Miklos Rozsa. _Cast_ Merle Oberon, Franchot Tone, Thomas Mitchell, Fay Bainter, Rex Ingram, John Qualen, Elisha Cook, Jr. 90 min.

Heiress returns home after crisis at sea, begins to hear voices and strange sounds. Strong mood piece which asserts the film noir's newfound ability to transcend its own plot material through aesthetic execution and refined psychological emphasis.

105. _Dead Reckoning_ (1947) Columbia. _Dir_ John Cromwell. _Sc_ Oliver H.P. Garrett and Steve Fisher, adapted by Allen Rivkin, from a story by Gerald Adams and Sidney Biddell. _Ph_ Leo Tover. _Mus_ Marlin Skiles. _Cast_ Humphrey Bogart, Lizabeth Scott, Morris Carnovsky, Charles Cane, William Prince, Wallace Ford. 100 min.

Seeking the truth about the mysterious disappearance and death of his wartime buddy, returning veteran becomes involved with a wealthy _femme fatale_ and a crooked nightclub owner. Bogart noir with plenty of postwar menace that is narrated as a doomed romance.

106. _Deadline at Dawn_ (1946) RKO. _Dir_ Harold Clurman. _Sc_ Clifford Odets, from the novel by Cornell Woolrich. _Ph_ Nicholas Musuraca. _Mus_ Hanns Eisler. _Cast_ Susan Hayward, Paul Lukas, Bill Williams, Joseph Calleia, Osa Massen, Lola Lane, Jerome Cowan. 83 min.

Taxi dancer and cab driver try to help young sailor clear himself of impending murder charge. Atmosphere predominates as some "little people of the night" try to fight off darkness.

Deadly Is the Female see _Gun Crazy_

107. _Death of a Scoundrel_ (1956) RKO. _Dir_ Charles Martin. _Sc_ Martin. _Ph_ James Wong Howe. _Mus_ Max Steiner. _Cast_ George Sanders, Yvonne De Carlo, Zsa Zsa Gabor, Victor Jory, Nancy Gates, Coleen Gray. 119 min.

Penniless European charms a fortune out of rich and influential women.

108. *Deception* (1946) Warner Brothers. *Dir* Irving Rapper. *Sc* John Collier and Joseph Than, from a play by Louis Verneuil. *Ph* Ernest Haller. *Mus* Erich Wolfgang Korngold. *Cast* Bette Davis, Paul Henreid, Claude Rains, John Abbott, Benson Fong. 110 min.

Music teacher is caught between sensitive cellist and celebrated composer. Intelligent melodrama of "the musical world," clearly with a noirish sensibility.

109. *Decoy* (1946) Monogram. *Dir* Jack Bernhard. *Sc* Ned Young, from a story by Stanley Rubin. *Ph* L.W. O'Connell. *Mus* Edward J. Kay. *Cast* Jean Gillie, Edward Norris, Herbert Rudley, Robert Armstrong, Sheldon Leonard. 76 min.

Greedy woman devises ingenious plan to save a hoodlum from execution so that she can get her hands on a bundle he's hidden. Harsh cheapie centering on the diabolical exploits of a ruthless *femme fatale*.

110. *Deep Valley* (1947) Warner Brothers. *Dir* Jean Negulesco. *Sc* Salka Viertel and Stephen Morehouse Avery, from the novel by Dan Totheroh. *Ph* Ted McCord. *Mus* Max Steiner. *Cast* Ida Lupino, Dane Clark, Wayne Morris, Fay Bainter, Henry Hull. 104 min.

Convict on the run is given aid by a drab, unhappy mountain girl.

111. *Desperate* (1947) RKO. *Dir* Anthony Mann. *Sc* Harry Essex, from a story by Dorothy Atlas and Mann. *Ph* George E. Diskant. *Mus* Paul Sawtell. *Cast* Steve Brodie, Audrey Long, Raymond Burr, Douglas Fowley, William Challee. 73 min.

Young truck driver becomes the innocent dupe of a vicious robbery gang, tries to escape to freedom with his wife.

112. *The Desperate Hours* (1955) Paramount. *Dir* William Wyler. *Sc* Joseph Hayes, from his play and novel. *Ph* Lee Garmes. *Mus* Gail Kubik. *Cast* Humphrey Bogart, Fredric March, Arthur Kennedy, Martha Scott, Dewey Martin, Mary Murphy, Robert Middleton. 112 min.

Three escaped convicts hide out in the home of respectable department store executive, terrifying and terrorizing his family. Notable, well-executed '50s thriller that features Humphrey Bogart in his last criminal role.

113. *Destination Murder* (1950) RKO. *Dir* Edward L. Cahn. *Sc* Don Martin. *Ph* Jackson J. Rose. *Mus* Irving Gertz. *Cast* Joyce MacKenzie, Stanley Clements, Hurd Hatfield, Albert Dekker, James Flavin, John Dehner. 72 min.

Woman sets out to find her father's killer, becomes involved with racketeers and murder.

114. *Destiny* (1944) Universal. *Dir* Reginald LeBorg and (uncredited) Julien Duvivier. *Sc* Roy Chanslor and Ernest Pascal. *Ph* George Robinson, Paul Ivano. *Mus* Frank Skinner, Alexander Tausman. *Cast* Gloria Jean, Alan Curtis, Frank Craven, Grace McDonald, Frank Fenton. 65 min.

A fugitive from the law becomes the victim of several double-crosses, eventually finding refuge with a blind girl and her father at a secluded farmhouse. Little-known noirish melodrama, with dreamlike flashback plot expanded from sequence originally intended for Duvivier's *Flesh and Fantasy*.

115. _Detective Story_ (1951) Paramount.
William Wyler's study of a hardened police detective whose two separate worlds come crashing together. See page 109.

116. _Detour_ (1945) PRC.
Man is involved in two freakish accidents that make him look like a murderer. Poverty row masterwork that is the most precise elucidation of the noir theme of explicit fatalism. See page 27.

117. _Dial 1119_ (1950) MGM. _Dir_ Gerald Mayer. _Sc_ John Monks, Jr., from a story by Hugh King and Don McGuire. _Ph_ Paul C. Vogel. _Mus_ André Previn. _Cast_ Marshall Thompson, Virginia Field, Andrea King, Sam Levene, Leon Ames, Keefe Brasselle, Richard Rober, William Conrad. 74 min.
Homicidal maniac escapes from mental hospital, holds bar patrons hostage.

The Dividing Line see _The Lawless_

118. _Don't Bother to Knock_ (1952) 20th Century–Fox. _Dir_ Roy Baker. _Sc_ Daniel Taradash, from the novel _Mischief_ by Charlotte Armstrong. _Ph_ Lucien Ballard. _Mus_ Lionel Newman. _Cast_ Richard Widmark, Marilyn Monroe, Anne Bancroft, Elisha Cook, Jr., Jeanne Cagney. 76 min.
Disillusioned with his torch-singing girlfriend, a restless young man meets a beautiful but disturbed girl in the hotel room across the hall.

119. _Double Indemnity_ (1944) Paramount.
Insurance salesman and restless married woman carry out daring plan to murder her husband and collect on his "double indemnity" policy. One of the most important and influential films of the early noir period that has today become a classic of the cycle. See page 12.

120. _A Double Life_ (1948) Universal. _Dir_ George Cukor. _Sc_ Ruth Gordon and Garson Kanin. _Ph_ Milton Krasner. _Mus_ Miklos Rozsa. _Cast_ Ronald Colman, Signe Hasso, Edmond O'Brien, Shelley Winters, Ray Collins, Philip Loeb, Millard Mitchell. 103 min.
An actor's protrayal of Othello turns into the real thing. Dark, brooding melodrama with some elegant noir visuals.

121. _Drive a Crooked Road_ (1954) Columbia. _Dir_ Richard Quine. _Sc_ Blake Edwards, adapted by Quine, from a story by James Benson. _Ph_ Charles Lawton, Jr. _Mus_ Ross di Maggio. _Cast_ Mickey Rooney, Dianne Foster, Kevin McCarthy, Jack Kelly, Jerry Paris, Paul Picerni, 83 min.
Ambitious auto mechanic is induced by sultry woman to drive robbery getaway car.

122. _Edge of Doom_ (1950) RKO. _Dir_ Mark Robson. _Sc_ Philip Yordan, from the novel by Leo Brady. _Ph_ Harry Stradling. _Mus_ Hugo Friedhofer. _Cast_ Dana Andrews, Farley Granger, Joan Evans, Robert Keith, Paul Stewart, Mala Powers, Adele Jergens. 99 min.
Confused, poverty-stricken man lashes out in an ironic act of murder. The only film noir produced by Samuel Goldwyn conveys its compassionate social theme with surprising intensity.

123. *The Enforcer* (1951) Warner Brothers. *Dir* Bretaigne Windust and (uncredited) Raoul Walsh. *Sc* Martin Rackin. *Ph* Robert Burks. *Mus* David Buttolph. *Cast* Humphrey Bogart, Zero Mostel, Ted de Corsia, Everett Sloane, Roy Roberts. 88 min.

After his chief witness against the head of Murder, Inc., is killed, a determined assistant D.A. combs his files for a clue that will give him a new case. Relentless, stylized flashback narrative.

124. *Escape* (1948) 20th Century-Fox. *Dir* Joseph L. Mankiewicz. *Sc* Philip Dunne, from the play by John Galsworthy. *Ph* Frederick A. Young. *Mus* William Alwyn. *Cast* Rex Harrison, Peggy Cummins, William Hartnell, Felix Aylmer, Norman Wooland. 78 min.

Man sent to prison for accidental killing escapes and receives aid from a girl.

125. *Escape in the Fog* (1945) Columbia. *Dir* Bud Boetticher. *Sc* Aubrey Wiseberg. *Ph* George Meehan. *Cast* Nina Foch, William Wright, Otto Kruger, Konstantin Shayne. 65 min.

A nurse dreams of a murder and then meets the victim in real life.

126. *Experiment Perilous* (1944) RKO. *Dir* Jacques Tourneur. *Sc* Warren Duff, from the novel by Margaret Carpenter. *Ph* Tony Gaudio. *Mus* Roy Webb. *Cast* Hedy Lamarr, George Brent, Paul Lukas, Albert Dekker, Carl Esmond, Margaret Wycherly. 91 min.

Insanely jealous, possessive husband keeps his beautiful wife a prisoner in a secluded mansion. Victorian melodrama which reveals the perversity and violence lurking beneath a prominent household's calm, stable facade.

127. *Fall Guy* (1947) Monogram. *Dir* Reginald LeBorg. *Sc* Jerry Warner, from the story "Cocaine" by Cornell Woolrich. *Ph* Mack Stengler. *Mus* Edward J. Kay. *Cast* Clifford Penn, Teala Loring, Robert Armstrong, Virginia Dale, Elisha Cook, Jr., Douglas Fowley. 64 min.

With no memory of the night in question and few clues, a man tries to prove he did not murder an attractive woman.

128. *Fallen Angel* (1945) 20th Century-Fox. *Dir* Otto Preminger. *Sc* Harry Kleiner, from the novel by Marty Holland. *Ph* Joseph La Shelle. *Mus* David Raksin. *Cast* Dana Andrews, Alice Faye, Linda Darnell, Charles Bickford, Anne Revere, Bruce Cabot, John Carradine. 98 min.

A drifter marries for money so he can run away with another woman, but she is murdered first and he is suspected of the crime. Ambiguous characters caught in a bleak world of moral uncertainty and sexual doubt.

129. *The Fallen Sparrow* (1943) RKO. *Dir* Richard Wallace. *Sc* Warren Duff, from the novel by Dorothy B. Hughes. *Ph* Nicholas Musuraca. *Mus* Roy Webb. *Cast* John Garfield, Maureen O'Hara, Walter Slezak, Patricia Morison, Martha O'Driscoll, Bruce Edwards. 94 min.

An emotionally scarred survivor of the Spanish Civil War is pursued by both mental and physical demons. The idea of psychological torture is handled with depth and sensitivity.

130. *Fear* (1946) Monogram. *Dir* Alfred Zeisler. *Sc* Zeisler and Dennis Cooper. *Ph* Jackson Rose. *Cast* Warren William, Anne Gwynne, Peter Cookson, James Cardwell, Nestor Paiva, Francis Pierlot. 68 min.

Frustrated medical student murders his professor with ironic results. Expressionistic cheapie, apparently inspired by Dostoevsky's *Crime and Punishment*.

131. *Fear in the Night* (1947) Paramount. *Dir* Maxwell Shane. *Sc* Shane, from the story "Nightmare" by Cornell Woolrich. *Ph* Jack Greenhalgh. *Mus* Rudy Schrager. *Cast* Paul Kelly, De Forest Kelly, Ann Doran, Kay Scott, Robert Emmett Keane. 71 min.

A man dreams of committing a murder, then finds evidence that it wasn't a dream. Notable, eerie B noir adaption of an important Woolrich story.

132. *Female on the Beach* (1955) Universal. *Dir* Joseph Pevney. *Sc* Robert Hill and Richard Alan Simmons, from a play by Hill. *Ph* Charles Lang. *Mus* Joseph Gershenson. *Cast* Joan Crawford, Jeff Chandler, Jan Sterling, Cecil Kellaway, Natalie Schafer, Charles Drake. 97 min.

Woman moves into California beach house, falls for neighbor and then begins to fear that he is a murderer.

133. *The File on Thelma Jordon* (1949) Paramount.

Assistant D.A. tries to help his illicit lover beat a murder rap. Elusive, sophisticated thriller by distinguished noir director, Robert Siodmak. See page 83.

134. *The Flame* (1947) Republic. *Dir* John H. Auer. *Sc* Lawrence Kimble, from a story by Robert T. Shannon. *Ph* Reggie Lanning. *Mus* Heinz Roemheld. *Cast* John Carroll, Vera Ralston, Robert Paige, Broderick Crawford, Henry Travers, Constance Dowling. 97 min.

Stylish B noir of man inducing an ambitious nurse to marry his rich, dying brother for the bucks.

135. *Flamingo Road* (1949) Warner Brothers. *Dir* Michael Curtiz. *Sc* Robert Wilder, from the play by Robert and Sally Wilder. *Ph* Ted McCord. *Mus* Ray Heindorf. *Cast* Joan Crawford, Zachary Scott, David Brian, Sydney Greenstreet, Gladys George. 94 min.

Carnival dancer marries wealthy Southerner for money, gets caught in web of political intrigue, jealousy, and murder. Tough Joan Crawford melodrama with first-rate Warners production values.

136. *Flaxy Martin* (1949) Warner Brothers. *Dir* Richard Bare. *Sc* David Lang. *Ph* Carl Guthrie. *Mus* William Lava. *Cast* Virginia Mayo, Zachary Scott, Dorothy Malone, Tom D'Andrea, Helen Westcott, Elisha Cook, Jr. 86 min.

An honest attorney becomes involved with a crime syndicate and ends up confessing to a murder that his *femme fatale* girlfriend committed.

137. *Follow Me Quietly* (1949) RKO. *Dir* Richard Fleischer. *Sc* Lillie Hayward, from a story by Francis Rosenwald and Anthony Mann. *Ph* Robert de Grasse. *Mus* Leonid Raab. *Cast* William Lundigan, Dorothy Patrick, Jeff Corey, Nestor Paiva, Charles D. Brown. 59 min.

Police detective hunts psycho-murderer out to rid the world of scum.

138. *Footsteps in the Night* (1957) Allied Artists. *Dir* Jean Yarbrough. *Sc* Albert Band and Elwood Ullman, from a story by Band. *Ph* Harry Neumann. *Mus* Marlin Skiles. *Cast* Bill Elliott, Don Haggerty, Eleanore Tanin, Zena Marshall. 62 min.

Police detective, who works to solve the murder of a friend, believes that the wrong man has been charged.

139. *For You I Die* (1948) Film Classics. *Dir* John Reinhardt. *Sc* Robert Presnell, Sr. *Ph* William Clothier. *Mus* Paul Sawtell. *Cast* Cathy Downs, Paul Langton, Mischa Auer, Roman Bohnen. 80 min.

Forced to participate in a prison break, a convict on the run holds up at a roadside diner.

140. *Forbidden* (1954) Universal. *Dir* Rudolph Maté. *Sc* William Sackheim and Gil Doud. *Ph* William Daniels. *Mus* Frank Skinner. *Cast* Tony Curtis, Joanne Dru, Lyle Bettger, Marvin Miller, Victor Sen Yung. 85 min.

Man is hired by Chicago mobster to find a woman he once knew, traces her to Macao where numerous complications arise.

141. *Force of Evil* (1948) MGM. *Dir* Abraham Polonsky. *Sc* Polonsky and Ira Wolfert, from the novel *Tucker's People* by Wolfert. *Ph* George Barnes. *Mus* David Raksin. *Cast* John Garfield, Beatrice Pearson, Thomas Gomez, Howland Chamberlain, Roy Roberts, Marie Windsor. 88 min.

Syndicate lawyer is opposed by his brother in efforts to bring about numbers racket takeover. Important, sincere noir whose veiled attack on American capitalism did not go over well in its time.

142. *Fourteen Hours* (1951) 20th Century-Fox. *Dir* Henry Hathaway. *Sc* John Paxton, from a story by Joel Sayre. *Ph* Joe MacDonald. *Mus* Alfred Newman. *Cast* Paul Douglas, Richard Basehart, Barbara Bel Geddes, Agnes Moorehead, Robert Keith, Howard da Silva, Martin Gabel, Debra Paget, Jeffrey Hunter. 92 min.

A distraught man positions himself on the ledge of a tall building, threatening to jump. Despite an altered ending, this unheralded film is a sharp, effective indictment of the forces which produced its suicidal situation.

143. *Framed* (1947) Columbia. *Dir* Richard Wallace. *Sc* Ben Maddow, from a story by Jack Patrick. *Ph* Burnett Guffey. *Mus* Marlin Skiles. *Cast* Glenn Ford, Janis Carter, Barry Sullivan, Edgar Buchanan, Karen Morley. 82 min.

Man is seduced by woman who intends to make him the patsy in a clever embezzlement plan.

144. *Gambling House* (1951) RKO. *Dir* Ted Tetzlaff. *Sc* Marvin Borowsky and Allen Rivkin. *Ph* Harry Wild. *Mus* Roy Webb. *Cast* Victor Mature, Terry Moore, William Bendix, Zachary Charles, Cleo Moore, Ann Doran. 80 min.

A crooked gambler decides to turn on his murderous boss.

145. *The Gangster* (1947) Allied Artists. *Dir* Gordon Wiles. *Sc* Daniel Fuchs, from his novel *Low Company*. *Ph* Paul Ivano. *Mus* Louis Gruenberg.

Cast Barry Sullivan, Belita, Joan Lorring, Akim Tamiroff, Henry Morgan, John Ireland. 84 min.

A troubled gangster, who has lost all faith in people, loses his weak grip on life. Intense, highly stylized mood piece that is one of several distinguished noirs scripted by writer Daniel Fuchs.

146. *The Garment Jungle* (1957) Columbia. *Dir* Vincent Sherman and (uncredited) Robert Aldrich. *Sc* Harry Kleiner, from articles by Lester Velie. *Ph* Joseph Biroc. *Mus* Leith Stevens. *Cast* Lee J. Cobb, Kerwin Matthews, Gia Scala, Richard Boone, Robert Loggia, Joseph Wiseman. 88 min.

Young man goes to work in his father's dress manufacturing business, learns of its vindictive antilabor practices. Late noir social comment at its best, never stooping to the level of preachy rhetoric.

147. *Gaslight* (1944) MGM. *Dir* George Cukor. *Sc* Walter Reisch and John L. Balderston, from a play by Patrick Hamilton. *Ph* Joseph Ruttenberg. *Mus* Bronislau Kaper. *Cast* Ingrid Bergman, Charles Boyer, Joseph Cotten, Dame May Whitty, Angela Lansbury. 114 min.

Victorian melodrama about a ruthless English gentleman who tries to drive his young wife to insanity. Strong production values highlight this atmospheric remake of an excellent 1940 British picture.

148. *Gilda* (1946) Columbia.

Suspense thriller in which the protagonist's redemption depends on his faith in a beautiful but tarnished woman. See page 36.

149. *The Glass Alibi* (1946) Republic. *Dir* W. Lee Wilder. *Sc* Mindret Lord. *Ph* Henry Sharp. *Mus* Alexander Laszlo. *Cast* Paul Kelly, Douglas Fowley, Anne Gwynne, Maris Wrixon, Jack Conrad. 68 min.

A reporter marries a dying girl for her money, but she recovers from her illness and so he plots murder.

150. *The Glass Key* (1942) Paramount. *Dir* Stuart Heisler. *Sc* Jonathan Latimer, from the novel by Dashiell Hammett. *Ph* Theodor Sparkuhl. *Mus* Victor Young. *Cast* Brian Donlevy, Veronica Lake, Alan Ladd, Bonita Granville, Joseph Calleia, Richard Denning. 85 min.

Politician's assistant attempts to clear his boss of murder and foil the plans of a scheming racketeer. Significant early noir narrative of political corruption and aberrant violence, adapted from a Hammett novel that was filmed before, in 1935.

151. *The Glass Wall* (1953) Columbia. *Dir* Maxwell Shane. *Sc* Ivan Tors and Shane. *Ph* Joseph F. Biroc. *Mus* Leith Stevens. *Cast* Vittorio Gassmann, Gloria Grahame, Ann Robinson, Douglas Spencer, Jerry Paris. 80 min.

A European refugee becomes desperate and goes on the run when New York officials refuse him entry into the country.

152. *The Glass Web* (1953) United Artists. *Dir* Jack Arnold. *Sc* Robert Blees and Leonard Lee, from the novel by Max S. Ehrlich. *Ph* Maury Gertsman. *Mus* Joseph Gershenson. *Cast* Edward G. Robinson, John Forsythe, Kathleen Hughes, Marcia Henderson, Richard Denning, Hugh Sanders. 81 min.

Research authority for television crime show knows too much about fact-based murder story. Well-structured concept film, with good use of Robinson.

153. *The Green Glove* (1952) United Artists. *Dir* Rudolph Maté. *Sc* Charles Bennett, from his story. *Ph* Claude Renoir. *Mus* Joseph Kosma. *Cast* Glenn Ford, Geraldine Brooks, Cedric Hardwicke, George Macready, Gaby Andre. 88 min.

An ex-GI faces danger on his return to France to retrieve a priceless antique glove, which is also a religious symbol to the people.

154. *Guest in the House* (1944) United Artists. *Dir* John Brahm (Lewis Milestone and André de Toth uncredited). *Sc* Ketti Frings, from the play by Hagar Wilde and Dale Eunson. *Ph* Lee Garmes. *Mus* Werner Janssen. *Cast* Anne Baxter, Ralph Bellamy, Aline MacMahon, Ruth Warrick, Jerome Cowan. 121 min.

Dark psychological picture in which a disturbed young woman has startling effects on a happy household.

155. *The Guilty* (1947) Monogram. *Dir* John Reinhardt. *Sc* Robert R. Presnell, Sr., from the story "Two Men in a Furnished Room" by Cornell Woolrich. *Ph* Henry Sharp. *Mus* Rudy Schrager. *Cast* Bonita Granville, Don Castle, Wally Cassell, Regis Toomey, John Litel. 71 min.

Twin sisters' love for the same man leads to murder. Capable low budget sketch of a bleak urban noir landscape.

156. *Guilty Bystander* (1950) Film Classics. *Dir* Joseph Lerner. *Sc* Don Ettlinger, from the novel by Wade Miller. *Ph* Gerald Hirschfeld. *Mus* Dimitri Tiomkin. *Cast* Zachary Scott, Faye Emerson, Mary Boland, Sam Levene, J. Edward Bromberg, Kay Medford. 92 min.

Alcoholic ex-cop searches for his former wife's kidnapped son. Notable low-life settings pervade this sleazy detective thriller.

157. *Gun Crazy* [also titled **Deadly Is the Female**] (1950) United Artists. *Dir* Joseph H. Lewis. *Sc* MacKinlay Kantor and Millard Kaufman, from a story by Kantor. *Ph* Russell Harlan. *Mus* Victor Young. *Cast* Peggy Cummins, John Dall, Barry Kroeger, Morris Carnovsky, Anabel Shaw, Harry Lewis. 87 min.

A restless young couple embark on a violent, destructive life of criminal rebellion. Forerunner of *Bonnie and Clyde* that is now widely considered a key late forties noir.

158. *Hangover Square* (1945) 20th Century–Fox. *Dir* John Brahm. *Sc* Barre Lyndon, from the novel by Patrick Hamilton. *Ph* Joseph La Shelle. *Mus* Bernard Herrmann. *Cast* Laird Cregar, Linda Darnell, George Sanders, Glenn Langan, Faye Marlowe, Alan Napier. 77 min.

In *fin-de-siècle* London, the police suspect that a composer who suffers from periods of amnesia may be a murderer. Notable example of film noir's frequent interest in art and artists, whose climax takes place during the performance of the protagonist's "Concerto Macabre" (written for the film by Bernard Herrmann).

159. *The Harder They Fall* (1956) Columbia. *Dir* Mark Robson.

Sc Philip Yordan, from the novel by Budd Schulberg. *Ph* Burnett Guffey. *Mus* Hugo Friedhofer. *Cast* Humphrey Bogart, Rod Steiger, Jan Sterling, Mike Lane, Max Baer, Sr., Edward Andrews, Nehemiah Persoff. 108 min.

Unemployed sportswriter takes a job promoting fighter for the syndicate, becomes disgusted with the total corruption of big-time boxing. An appropriate last film for the weary, cancer-ridden Bogart.

160. *He Ran All the Way* (1951) United Artists. *Dir* John Berry.
Sc Guy Endore and Hugo Butler, from the novel by Sam Ross. *Ph* James Wong Howe. *Mus* Franz Waxman. *Cast* John Garfield, Shelley Winters, Wallace Ford, Selena Royle, Gladys George. 77 min.

A desperate criminal on the run holds up in the tenement home of a frightened family. Grim and powerful noir that was the last film Garfield made before his untimely death.

161. *He Walked by Night* (1948) Eagle Lion. *Dir* Alfred Werker.
(Anthony Mann uncredited). *Sc* John C. Higgins and Crane Wilbur, from a story by Wilbur. *Ph* John Alton. *Mus* Leonid Raab. *Cast* Richard Basehart, Scott Brady, Roy Roberts, Whit Bissell, Jimmy Cardwell, Jack Webb. 79 min.

Los Angeles police conduct an elaborate hunt for a cunning nocturnal psychopath. One of the coldest and blackest semidocumentary thrillers of the period, with classic noir visuals by John Alton.

162. *Hell's Half Acre* (1954) Republic. *Dir* John H. Auer. *Sc*
Steve Fisher. *Ph* John L. Russell, Jr. *Mus* R. Dale Butts. *Cast* Wendell Corey, Evelyn Keyes, Elsa Lanchester, Marie Windsor, Nancy Gates. 91 min.

Woman travels to Hawaii in search of husband lost in war, gets caught in tangled web of suspense and murder.

163. *Her Kind of Man* (1946) Warner Brothers. *Dir* Frederick de
Cordova. *Sc* Gordon Kahn and Leopold Atlas, from a story by Charles Hoffman and James V. Kern. *Ph* Carl Guthrie. *Mus* Franz Waxman. *Cast* Dane Clark, Janis Paige, Zachary Scott, Faye Emerson, George Tobias, Sheldon Leonard. 78 min.

Nightclub singer is caught between big-time gangster and tough Broadway columnist.

164. *The Hidden Room* [British title, **Obsession**] (1949) Eagle
Lion. *Dir* Edward Dmytryk. *Sc* Alec Coppel, from his play. *Ph* C. Pennington Richards. *Mus* Nino Rota. *Cast* Robert Newton, Sally Gray, Phil Brown, Naunton Wayne. 98 min.

A jealous husband has an elaborate, gruesome murder planned for his wife's paramour. British produced thriller, directed by an American noir veteran.

165. *High Sierra* (1941) Warner Brothers. *Dir* Raoul Walsh. *Sc*
John Huston and W.R. Burnett, from the novel by Burnett. *Ph* Tony Gaudio. *Mus* Adolf Deutsch. *Cast* Humphrey Bogart, Ida Lupino, Alan Curtis, Arthur Kennedy, Joan Leslie, Henry Hull, Barton MacLane. 100 min.

A tired middle-aged criminal agrees to pull one last job, but everything goes wrong. The doomed thirties gangster is here transformed into a more existential noir protagonist, pursued doggedly by his inescapable fate.

166. High Tide (1947) Monogram. *Dir* John Reinhardt. *Sc* Robert Presnell, Sr. *Ph* Henry Sharp. *Mus* Rudy Schrager. *Cast* Lee Tracy, Don Castle, Julie Bishop, Anabel Shaw, Regis Toomey. 70 min.

Newspaperman is caught in the middle of a ruthless city power struggle.

167. The High Wall (1947) MGM. *Dir* Curtis Bernhardt. *Sc* Sydney Boehm and Lester Cole, from the novel and play by Alan R. Clark and Bradbury Foote. *Ph* Paul Vogel. *Mus* Bronislau Kaper. *Cast* Robert Taylor, Audrey Totter, Herbert Marshall, Dorothy Patrick, H.B. Warner, Warner Anderson. 100 min.

War veteran that has periodic blackouts is arrested for murdering his wife, gets himself committed to an asylum to buy time. Stylish, representative late forties noir thriller.

168. Highway Dragnet (1954) Allied Artists. *Dir* Nathan Juran. *Sc* U.S. Anderson and Roger Corman. *Ph* John Martin. *Mus* Edward J. Kay. *Cast* Richard Conte, Joan Bennett, Wanda Hendrix, Reed Hadley, Mary Beth Hughes. 71 min.

Suspicious-acting woman gives ride to ex-marine on the run from a false murder charge.

169. Highway 301 (1950) Warner Brothers. *Dir* Andrew L. Stone. *Sc* Stone. *Ph* Carl Guthrie. *Mus* William Lava. *Cast* Steve Cochran, Virginia Grey, Wally Cassell, Robert Webber, Richard Egan. 83 min.

Daring robbery gang pulls several lucrative jobs and terrorizes the countryside before meeting violent end. Tough semidocumentary style crime film with Steve Cochran as a vicious gangleader.

170. His Kind of Woman (1951) RKO. *Dir* John Farrow. *Sc* Frank Fenton and Jack Leonard, from a story by Gerald Drayson Adams. *Ph* Harry J. Wild. *Mus* Leigh Harline. *Cast* Robert Mitchum, Jane Russell, Vincent Price, Tim Holt, Charles McGraw, Raymond Burr. 120 min.

Rough, tough gambler takes a lucrative but mysterious job in Mexico, tangling with a gold-digger and a racketeer. Odd noir entertainment that has a lot of depth and meaning for a film that often verges on self-parody.

171. The Hitch-Hiker (1953) RKO. *Dir* Ida Lupino. *Sc* Collier Young and Lupino, adapted by Robert Joseph, from a story by Daniel Mainwaring. *Ph* Nicholas Musuraca. *Mus* Leith Stevens. *Cast* Edmond O'Brien, Frank Lovejoy, William Talman, Jose Torvay. 71 min.

Two businessmen on a fishing trip to Mexico are held captive by psychokiller. "Paranoid thriller" notable for being the only film noir directed by a woman.

172. Hollow Triumph [also titled The Scar] (1948) Eagle Lion. *Dir* Steve Sekely. *Sc* Daniel Fuchs, from the novel by Murray Forbes. *Ph* John Alton. *Mus* Sol Kaplan. *Cast* Paul Henreid, Joan Bennett, Eduard Franz, Leslie Brooks, John Qualen. 82 min.

Harsh tale of an alienated criminal's attempt to impersonate his psychiatrist-double. Important fatalistic noir, with classy visuals and a very fine script that features a creative doppelgänger theme.

173. *Hollywood Story* (1951) Universal. *Dir* William Castle. *Sc* Frederick Kohner and Fred Brady. *Ph* Carl Guthrie. *Mus* Joseph Gershenson. *Cast* Richard Conte, Julia Adams, Richard Egan, Henry Hull, Fred Clark, Jim Backus. 77 min.

Producer plans movie about unsolved 1929 murder of a Hollywood director.

174. *The Hoodlum* (1951) United Artists. *Dir* Max Nosseck. *Sc* Sam Neuman and Nat Tanchuck. *Ph* Clark Ramsey. *Mus* Darrell Calker. *Cast* Lawrence Tierney, Allene Roberts, Marjorie Riordan, Lisa Golm. 61 min.

Ex-con plans bank robbery implicating his brother.

175. *Hoodlum Empire* (1952) Republic. *Dir* Joseph Kane. *Sc* Bruce Manning and Bob Considine, from a story by Considine. *Ph* Reggie Lanning. *Mus* Nathan Scott. *Cast* Brian Donlevy, Claire Trevor, Forrest Tucker, Vera Ralston, Luther Adler. 98 min.

An army veteran breaks with the crime syndicate he belonged to before the war, but they continue to use his name for their payoff operations.

176. *House by the River* (1950) Republic. *Dir* Fritz Lang. *Sc* Mel Dinelli, from the novel by A.P. Herbert. *Ph* Edward Cronjager. *Mus* George Antheil. *Cast* Louis Hayward, Jane Wyatt, Lee Bowman, Dorothy Patrick, Ann Shoemaker. 88 min.

Desperate writer will do anything to cover up accidental killing. One of Fritz Lang's least known and blackest noirs.

177. *House of Strangers* (1949) 20th Century-Fox. *Dir* Joseph L. Mankiewicz. *Sc* Philip Yordan, from the novel *I'll Never Go There Again* by Jerome Weidman. *Ph* Milton Krasner. *Mus* Daniele Amfitheatrof. *Cast* Edward G. Robinson, Susan Hayward, Richard Conte, Luther Adler, Debra Paget, Hope Emerson. 101 min.

Ruthless banker sets four sons at odds; well-directed psycho melodrama.

178. *The House on 92nd Street* (1945) 20th Century-Fox. *Dir* Henry Hathaway. *Sc* Barre Lyndon, Charles G. Booth and John Monks, Jr., from a story by Booth. *Ph* Norbert Brodine. *Mus* David Buttolph. *Cast* William Eythe, Lloyd Nolan, Signe Hasso, Gene Lockhart, Leo G. Carroll. 89 min.

With the help of a student turned undercover agent, the F.B.I. breaks up a Nazi espionage ring. The first film noir produced by Louis de Rochemont, credited as a pioneer of the semidocumentary style police thriller.

179. *House on Telegraph Hill* (1951) 20th Century-Fox. *Dir* Robert Wise. *Sc* Elick Moll and Frank Partos, from the novel *The Frightened Child* by Dana Lyon. *Ph* Lucien Ballard. *Mus* Sol Kaplan. *Cast* Richard Basehart, Valentina Cortesa, William Lundigan, Fay Baker. 92 min.

World War II refugee assumes the identity of a dead friend so that she can live with a wealthy family in San Francisco.

180. *Human Desire* (1954) Columbia. *Dir* Fritz Lang. *Sc* Alfred Hayes, from the novel *La Bête Humaine* by Emile Zola. *Ph* Burnett Guffey. *Mus* Daniele Amfitheatrof. *Cast* Glenn Ford, Gloria Grahame, Broderick Crawford, Edgar Buchanan, Kathleen Case. 90 min.

A sultry *femme fatale* tries to induce a young railroad engineer to kill her unwanted, alcoholic husband. Interesting Americanized remake of Jean Renoir's classic of French poetic realism, *La Bête Humaine* (1938).

181. *The Human Jungle* (1954) Allied Artists. *Dir* Joseph M. Newman. *Sc* William Sackheim and Daniel Fuchs. *Ph* Ellis Carter. *Mus* Hans J. Salter. *Cast* Gary Merrill, Jan Sterling, Paula Raymond, Emile Meyer, Regis Toomey, Chuck Connors. 82 min.

Ambitious cop tries to clean up dirtiest precinct in the city.

182. *Humoresque* (1947) Warner Brothers. *Dir* Jean Negulesco. *Sc* Clifford Odets and Zachary Gold, from a story by Fannie Hurst. *Ph* Ernest Haller. *Mus* Franz Waxman. *Cast* Joan Crawford, John Garfield, Oscar Levant, J. Carrol Naish, Tom D'Andrea, Craig Stevens, Paul Cavanagh. 125 min.

A promising young violinist becomes involved with a moody patroness of the arts. An apparently tame subject is given a powerful noir treatment, most evidenced by the casting of Garfield and Crawford as two very substantial characters who face conflict head on.

183. *Hunt the Man Down* (1950) RKO. *Dir* George Archainbaud. *Sc* De Vallon Scott. *Ph* Nicholas Musuraca. *Mus* Paul Sawtell. *Cast* Gig Young, Lynn Roberts, Mary Anderson, Willard Parker, Gerald Mohr, Cleo Moore. 68 min.

Public defender tracks down seven people associated with a twelve-year-old crime.

184. *The Hunted* (1948) Allied Artists. *Dir* Jack Bernhard. *Sc* Steve Fisher. *Ph* Harry Neumann. *Mus* Edward J. Kay. *Cast* Preston Foster, Belita, Pierre Watkin, Edna Holland. 85 min.

A policeman sends his girlfriend to prison, won't leave her alone when she gets out.

185. *I Confess* (1953) Warner Brothers. *Dir* Alfred Hitchcock. *Sc* George Tabori and William Archibald, from a play by Paul Anthelme. *Ph* Robert Burks. *Mus* Dimitri Tiomkin. *Cast* Montgomery Clift, Anne Baxter, Karl Malden, Brian Aherne, O.E. Hasse. 95 min.

A young priest hears the confession of a murder for which he is then himself accused. Underrated, meaningful Hitchcock concept film.

186. *I, Jane Doe* (1948) Republic. *Dir* John H. Auer. *Sc* Lawrence Kimble, from an adaption by Decla Dunning. *Ph* Reggie Lanning. *Mus* Heinz Roemheld. *Cast* Ruth Hussey, John Carroll, Vera Ralston, Gene Lockhart, John Howard. 85 min.

French war bride murders two-timing husband, then refuses to divulge her true identity at the trial.

I Married a Communist see *The Woman on Pier 13*

187. *I, the Jury* (1953) United Artists. *Dir* Harry Essex. *Sc* Essex, from the novel by Mickey Spillane. *Ph* John Alton. *Mus* Franz Waxman. *Cast* Biff Elliot, Preston Foster, Peggie Castle, Alan Reed, Elisha Cook, Jr. 88 min.

Private eye Mike Hammer goes after the murderer of his best friend. Crude, violent film which matches the tone of Spillane's novel.

188. *I Wake Up Screaming* (1941) 20th Century-Fox. *Dir* H. Bruce Humberstone. *Sc* Dwight Taylor, from the novel by Steve Fisher. *Ph* Edward Cronjager. *Mus* Cyril J. Mockridge. *Cast* Betty Grable, Victor Mature, Carole Landis, Laird Cregar, William Gargan, Alan Mowbray, Allyn Joslyn, Elisha Cook, Jr. 82 min.

Innocent promoter, accused of murdering an actress he "discovered," escapes from jail to search for real culprit. Stylish, influential early-noir thriller.

189. *I Walk Alone* (1948) Paramount. *Dir* Byron Haskin. *Sc* Charles Schnee, adapted by Robert Smith and John Bright, from a play by Theodore Reeves. *Ph* Leo Tover. *Mus* Victor Young. *Cast* Burt Lancaster, Lizabeth Scott, Kirk Douglas, Wendell Corey, Kristine Miller, Marc Lawrence, Mike Mazurki. 98 min.

Embittered ex-con wants his share of former partner's nightclub operation, but the partner has other ideas. First-class crime film in which a bewildered protagonist returns (from prison instead of war) to a decadent, alien American society.

190. *I Want to Live* (1958) United Artists. *Dir* Robert Wise. *Sc* Nelson Gidding, based on articles by Ed Montgomery and letters of Barbara Graham. *Ph* Lionel Lindon. *Mus* John Mandel. *Cast* Susan Hayward, Simon Oakland, Virginia Vincent, Theodore Bikel. 120 min.

Powerful drama, based on a true story, in which a woman is sent to the gas chamber for a murder she may not have committed.

191. *I Was a Communist for the F.B.I.* (1951) Warner Brothers. *Dir* Gordon Douglas. *Sc* Crane Wilbur, from a story by Matt Cvetic and Pete Martin. *Ph* Edwin DuPar. *Cast* Frank Lovejoy, Dorothy Hart, Philip Carey, Dick Webb, James Millican. 84 min.

Pittsburgh steel worker infiltrates a Communist part cell. "Red scare" melodrama with some strong noir elements.

192. *I Wouldn't Be in Your Shoes* (1948) Monogram. *Dir* William Nigh. *Sc* Steve Fisher, from the novel by Cornell Woolrich. *Ph* Mack Stengler. *Mus* Edward J. Kay. *Cast* Don Castle, Elyse Knox, Regis Toomey, Charles D. Brown. 70 min.

Police detective helps a woman clear her husband of murder, with ironic results.

193. *Illegal* (1955) Warner Brothers. *Dir* Lewis Allen. *Sc* W.R. Burnett, James R. Webb, from the play by Frank J. Collins. *Ph* Peverell Marley. *Mus* Max Steiner. *Cast* Edward G. Robinson, Nina Foch, Hugh Marlowe, De Forest Kelley, Albert Dekker, Jayne Mansfield. 88 min.

Former D.A. becomes defense attorney deeply involved in complex murder case. Noir remake of *The Mouthpiece* (1933).

194. *Illegal Entry* (1949) Universal. *Dir* Frederick de Cordova. *Sc* Joel Malone, adapted by Art Cohn from a story by Ben Bengal, Herbert Kline and

Dan Moore. *Ph* William Daniels. *Mus* Milton Schwarzwald. *Cast* Howard Duff, Marta Toren, George Brent, Gar Moore, Tom Tully. 84 min.
Undercover agents attack Mexican border smuggling operation.

195. *Impact* (1949) United Artists. *Dir* Arthur Lubin. *Sc* Dorothy Reid and Jay Dratler. *Ph* Ernest Laszlo. *Mus* Michel Michelet. *Cast* Brian Donlevy, Ella Raines, Helen Walker, Charles Coburn. 111 min.
After his wife and her lover try to kill him, a successful businessman decides to start a new life in obscurity.

196. *In a Lonely Place* (1950) Columbia.
Important Bogart noir that is a dark romance about the existential angst of a Hollywood screenwriter. See page 93.

197. *Incident* (1948) Monogram. *Dir* William Beaudine. *Sc* Fred Niblo, Jr. and Sam Roeca, from a story by Harry Lewis. *Ph* Marcel Le Picard. *Mus* Edward J. Kay. *Cast* Warren Douglas, Jane Frazee, Joyce Compton, Robert Osterloh, Anthony Caruso. 68 min.
Man is mistaken for hoodlum and beaten up, leading him into sordid web of violence and danger.

198. *Inside Job* (1946) Universal. *Dir* Jean Yarbrough. *Sc* George Bricker and Jerry Warner, from a story by Tod Browning and Garrett Fort. *Ph* Maury Gertsman. *Mus* Frank Skinner. *Cast* Preston Foster, Alan Curtis, Ann Rutherford, Jimmy Moss. 65 min.
Ex-con has choice of losing job or participating in robbery.

199. *Iron Man* (1951) Universal. *Dir* Joseph Pevney. *Sc* George Zuckerman and Borden Chase, from a story by W.R. Burnett. *Ph* Carl Guthrie. *Mus* Joseph Gershenson. *Cast* Jeff Chandler, Evelyn Keyes, Stephen McNally, Joyce Holden, Rock Hudson, Jim Backus. 82 min.
Tough coal miner thinks fight game will bring him all he's ever wanted.

200. *Ivy* (1947) Universal. *Dir* Sam Wood. *Sc* Charles Bennett, from the novel *The Story of Ivy* by Marie Belloc-Lowndes. *Ph* Russell Metty. *Mus* Daniele Amfitheatrof. *Cast* Joan Fontaine, Patric Knowles, Herbert Marshall, Sir Cedric Hardwicke, Richard Ney, Lucile Watson. 99 min.
When an ambitious, conniving woman poisons her husband, her lover is charged with the crime. Classy portrait of one of the cycle's ultimate Victorian "black widows."

201. *Jealousy* (1945) Republic. *Dir* Gustav Machaty. *Sc* Arnold Phillips and Machaty, from a story by Dalton Trumbo. *Ph* Henry Sharp. *Mus* Hanns Eisler. *Cast* John Loder, Jane Randolph, Karen Moore, Nils Asther, Hugo Haas. 71 min.
A successful alcoholic writer is murdered and his loyal wife is accused.

202. *Jennifer* (1953) Allied Artists. *Dir* Joel Newton. *Sc* Harold Buchman and Maurice Rapf, from a story by Jane Eberle. *Ph* James Wong Howe. *Mus* Ernest Gold. *Cast* Ida Lupino, Howard Duff, Robert Nichols, Mary Shipp, Ned Glass. 73 min.

A woman down on her luck takes a job as caretaker of a mysterious Southern California mansion. Unique, meaningful "woman's thriller."

203. *Jeopardy* (1953) MGM. *Dir* John Sturges. *Sc* Mel Dinelli and Maurice Zimm. *Ph* Victor Milner. *Mus* Dimitri Tiomkin. *Cast* Barbara Stanwyck, Barry Sullivan, Ralph Meeker, Lee Aaker. 69 min.

Desperately trying to find help for her injured husband, woman becomes the prisoner of an escaped killer. Taut thriller which takes woman-in-distress concept to one of its most frenzied extremes.

204. *Jigsaw* (1949) United Artists. *Dir* Fletcher Markle. *Sc* Markle and Vincent McConnor, from a story by John Roeburt. *Ph* Don Malkames. *Mus* Robert W. Stringer. *Cast* Franchot Tone, Jean Wallace, Myron McCormick, Marc Lawrence, Betty Harper. 70 min.

Assistant D.A. investigates a series of murders, with photograph of beautiful woman his only clue.

205. *Johnny Angel* (1945) RKO. *Dir* Edwin L. Marin. *Sc* Steve Fisher, adapted by Frank Gruber, from the novel *Mr. Angel Comes Aboard* by Charles Gordon Booth. *Ph* Harry J. Wild. *Mus* Leigh Harline. *Cast* George Raft, Claire Trevor, Signe Hasso, Lowell Gilmore, Hoagy Carmichael, Marvin Miller. 76 min.

Merchant marine captain searches New Orleans for clues to the mysterious death of his father. Stylish Raft vehicle, strong on mood and atmosphere.

206. *Johnny O'Clock* (1947) Columbia. *Dir* Robert Rossen. *Sc* Rossen, from a story by Milton Holmes. *Ph* Burnett Guffey. *Mus* George Duning. *Cast* Dick Powell, Evelyn Keyes, Lee J. Cobb, Ellen Drew, Nina Foch, Thomas Gomez. 95 min.

Co-owner of casino is caught between police, hoodlum partner and several women. Hard-boiled thriller that was Robert Rossen's first directorial effort.

207. *Johnny Stool Pigeon* (1949) Universal. *Dir* William Castle. *Sc* Robert L. Richards, from a story by Henry Jordan. *Ph* Maury Gertsman. *Mus* Milton Schwarzwald. *Cast* Howard Duff, Dan Duryea, Shelley Winters, Tony Curtis, John McIntire. 76 min.

Narcotics agent induces convict to help him infiltrate dope smuggling ring.

208. *Journey into Fear* (1943) RKO. *Dir* Norman Foster (Orson Welles, uncredited). *Sc* Joseph Cotten and Orson Welles, from the novel by Eric Ambler. *Ph* Karl Struss. *Mus* Roy Webb. *Cast* Joseph Cotten, Dolores Del Rio, Orson Welles, Ruth Warrick, Agnes Moorehead, Everett Sloane, 71 min.

Naval engineer flees Nazi agents aboard a steamship filled with suspicious characters. Marginal early noir with good feeling of paranoia and some moderate visual flair.

209. *Julie* (1956) MGM. *Dir* Andrew L. Stone. *Sc* Stone. *Ph* Fred Jackman, Jr. *Mus* Leith Stevens. *Cast* Doris Day, Louis Jourdan, Barry Sullivan, Frank Lovejoy, Jack Kelly. 99 min.

Woman discovers her husband is maniac that killed his first wife and may kill again.

210. *Kansas City Confidential* (1952) United Artists. *Dir* Phil Karlson. *Sc* George Bruce and Harry Essex, from a story by Harold R. Greene and Rowland Brown. *Ph* George E. Diskant. *Mus* Paul Sawtell. *Cast* John Payne, Coleen Gray, Preston Foster, Jack Elam, Neville Brand, Lee Van Cleef. 98 min.

Ex-con seeks revenge for being made the patsy in a diabolical armored car robbery. Gritty, violent crime drama with an engaging trio of bad guys.

211. *Key Largo* (1948) Warner Brothers. *Dir* John Huston. *Sc* Richard Brooks and Huston, from the play by Maxwell Anderson. *Ph* Karl Freund. *Mus* Max Steiner. *Cast* Humphrey Bogart, Edward G. Robinson, Lauren Bacall, Lionel Barrymore, Claire Trevor, Thomas Gomez. 100 min.

A vicious gangster holds a group of people captive in a Florida Keys hotel during a storm. Though still a borderline entry, the recognition of this film as a noir indicates that the sensibility was more far-reaching than many have thus far acknowledged.

212. *Key Witness* (1947) Columbia. *Dir* D. Ross Lederman. *Sc* Edward Bock, adapted by Bock and Raymond L. Schrock, from a story by J. Donald Wilson. *Ph* Philip Tannura. *Mus* Mischa Bakaleinikoff. *Cast* John Beal, Trudy Marshall, Jimmy Lloyd, Helen Mowry, Wilton Graff. 67 min.

Man runs away to avoid suspicion of murder, ends up in more trouble.

213. *The Killer Is Loose* (1956) United Artists. *Dir* Bud Boetticher. *Sc* Harold Medford, from a story by John and Ward Hawkins. *Ph* Lucien Ballard. *Mus* Lionel Newman. *Cast* Joseph Cotten, Rhonda Fleming, Wendell Corey, Alan Hale, Jr., Michael Pate, John Larch. 73 min.

Mentally unbalanced convict blames police detective for his wife's death, escapes prison bent on violent revenge.

214. *The Killer That Stalked New York* (1950) Columbia. *Dir* Earl McEvoy. *Sc* Harry Essex, from a story by Milton Lehman. *Ph* Joseph Biroc. *Mus* Hans J. Salter. *Cast* Evelyn Keyes, Charles Korvin, William Bishop, Dorothy Malone, Lola Albright, Carl Benton Reid, Art Smith, Whit Bissell. 79 min.

Two-timing husband directs wife in shrewd diamond smuggling plan, but he doesn't know that she has contracted smallpox. Little-known B noir that effectively extends an idea first postulated by *Panic in the Streets*.

215. *The Killers* (1946) Universal.
Hemingway's classic hard-boiled short story is depicted and extended with stylistic intensity. See page 39.

216. *Killer's Kiss* (1955) United Artists. *Dir* Stanley Kubrick. *Sc* Kubrick. *Ph* Kubrick. *Mus* Gerald Fried. *Cast* Frank Silvera, Jamie Smith, Irene Kane, Jerry Jarret. 67 min.

Second-rate boxer and nightclub dancer plan to leave the city together; club owner has other ideas. Dark, violent early cheapie by Kubrick, with some interesting visuals.

217. *The Killing* (1956) United Artists.
Important, creative late-noir heist film by Stanley Kubrick. See page 117.

218. *Kiss Me Deadly* (1955) United Artists. *Dir* Robert Aldrich *Sc* A.I. Bezzerides, from the novel by Mickey Spillane. *Ph* Ernest Laszlo. *Mus* Frank DeVol. *Cast* Ralph Meeker, Albert Dekker, Paul Stewart, Maxine Cooper, Gaby Rodgers, Nick Dennis, Cloris Leachman, Jack Lambert, Jack Elam. 105 min.

A self-centered, brutish Mike Hammer follows a series of leads in search of "the great whatsit." The ultimate noir detective film, which never ceases to amaze.

219. *Kiss of Death* (1947) 20th Century-Fox. *Dir* Henry Hathaway. *Sc* Ben Hecht and Charles Lederer, from the novel by Eleazar Lipsky. *Ph* Norbert Brodine. *Mus* David Buttolph. *Cast* Victor Mature, Brian Donlevy, Coleen Gray, Richard Widmark, Karl Malden, Taylor Holmes, Mildred Dunnock. 98 min.

Well-known noir depicting the many forces which make it difficult for a man to escape his criminal past. Often remembered for Widmark's graphic portrayal of a vicious, giggling psycho-killer.

220. *Kiss the Blood Off My Hands* (1948) Universal. *Dir* Norman Foster. *Sc* Leonardo Bercovici, adapted by Ben Maddow and Walter Bernstein, from the novel by Gerald Butler. *Ph* Russell Metty. *Mus* Miklos Rozsa. *Cast* Joan Fontaine, Burt Lancaster, Robert Newton, Lewis Russell. 79 min.

Embittered war veteran accidentally kills pub owner in a fight, flees from the police and receives aid from a shy young nurse. Intelligent, sensitive treatment of the fugitive-on-the-run theme.

221. *Kiss Tomorrow Goodbye* (1950) Warner Brothers.

Cagney's harsh, violent follow-up to *White Heat* is an adaption of the Horace McCoy novel that tells the story of a rat in a rat's world. See page 97.

222. *Knock on Any Door* (1949) Columbia. *Dir* Nicholas Ray. *Sc* Daniel Taradash and John Monks, Jr., from the novel by William Motley. *Ph* Burnett Guffey. *Mus* George Antheil. *Cast* Humphrey Bogart, John Derek, George Macready, Allene Roberts, Susan Perry. 100 min.

A rebellious youth with a depressed slum background is put on trial for murder, defended by an understanding attorney. This film's didactic social consciousness exists uneasily beside its moderately noirish tone and plot.

223. *Ladies in Retirement* (1941) Columbia. *Dir* Charles Vidor. *Sc* Garrett Fort and Reginald Denham, from the play by Denham and Edward Percy. *Ph* George Barnes. *Mus* Ernst Toch. *Cast* Ida Lupino, Louis Hayward, Evelyn Keyes, Elsa Lanchester, Edith Barrett, Isobel Elsom. 92 min.

Stark, little-known early noir in which a housekeeper murders her employer to protect a pair of dotty sisters.

224. *The Lady from Shanghai* (1948) Columbia. *Dir* Orson Welles. *Sc* Welles, from the novel *Before I Die* by Sherwood King. *Ph* Charles Lawton, Jr. *Mus* Heinz Roemheld. *Cast* Rita Hayworth, Orson Welles, Everett Sloane, Glenn Anders, Ted de Corsia, Erskine Sanford, 86 min.

Irish seaman is hooked by deadly *femme fatale*, gets caught in the middle of a confusing murder scheme. Witty, bizarre, hallucinatory Welles thriller.

225. *Lady in the Lake* (1947) MGM. *Dir* Robert Montgomery. *Sc*

Steve Fisher, from the novel by Raymond Chandler. *Ph* Paul C. Vogel. *Mus* David Snell. *Cast* Robert Montgomery, Lloyd Nolan, Audrey Totter, Tom Tully, Leon Ames, Jayne Meadows. 105 min.

Detective Philip Marlowe is hired to find the missing publisher of a crime magazine, and then becomes involved in a typically confusing series of plot twists and turnarounds. This film is shot almost entirely with a subjective, "point-of-view" camera, which helps to make it one of the most unusual and humorous of all hard-boiled noirs.

226. *A Lady Without Passport* (1950) MGM. *Dir* Joseph H. Lewis. *Sc* Howard Dimsdale, adapted by Cyril Hume, from a story by Lawrence Taylor. *Ph* Paul C. Vogel. *Mus* David Raksin. *Cast* Hedy Lamarr, John Hodiak, James Craig, George Macready, Steven Geray. 72 min.

Immigration agent goes undercover in Cuba, induces beautiful alien to help him get the goods on a smuggling racket.

227. *Larceny* (1948) Universal. *Dir* George Sherman. *Sc* Herbert F. Margolis, Louis Morheim and William Bowers, from the novel *The Velvet Fleece* by Lois Eby and John Fleming. *Ph* Irving Glassberg. *Mus* Leith Stevens. *Cast* John Payne, Joan Caulfield, Dan Duryea, Shelley Winters, Dorothy Hart, Richard Rober. 89 min.

Con man talks grieving war widow into signing over large sum of money for a phony memorial to her late husband.

228. *The Last Mile* (1959) United Artists. *Dir* Howard W. Koch. *Sc* Milton Subotsky, Seton I. Miller, from a play by John Wexley. *Ph* Joseph Brun. *Mus* Van Alexander. *Cast* Mickey Rooney, Alan Bunce, Frank Conroy, Clifford David, Harry Millard, Ford Rainey. 81 min.

Inmates on death row can't take the wait, try to bust out. Explosive remake of a 1932 film with the same title.

229. *Laura* (1944) 20th Century–Fox.

Glistening adaption of the popular suspense novel about a detective's obsession with a beautiful girl who he thinks has been murdered. See page 21.

230. *The Lawless* [British title, **The Dividing Line**] (1950) Paramount. *Dir* Joseph Losey. *Sc* Geoffrey Homes (Daniel Mainwaring), from his novel *The Voice of Stephen Wilder*. *Ph* J. Roy Hunt. *Mus* Mahlon Merrick. *Cast* Macdonald Carey, Gail Russell, Lalo Rios, Lee Patrick, John Hoyt, John Sands, Martha Hyer. 83 min.

Racial tensions explode when Mexican youth hits a policeman, leading to vicious rumors of rape and murder. Disturbing, violent and cynical view of a small Southern California town.

231. *The Letter* (1940) Warner Brothers. *Dir* William Wyler. *Sc* Howard Koch, from the story by W. Somerset Maugham. *Ph* Tony Gaudio. *Mus* Max Steiner. *Cast* Bette Davis, Herbert Marshall, James Stephenson, Frieda Inescort, Gale Sondergaard. 95 min.

Plantation wife kills her illicit lover in a jealous rage, then fabricates a clever lie to maintain her innocence. Notable example of the 1940 outburst of noir style in a mainstream Hollywood production.

232. *Lightning Strikes Twice* (1951) Warner Brothers. *Dir* King Vidor. *Sc* Lenore Coffee, from the novel *A Man Without Friends* by Margaret Echard. *Ph* Sid Hickox. *Mus* Max Steiner. *Cast* Richard Todd, Ruth Roman, Zachary Scott, Mercedes McCambridge, Frank Conroy, Darryl Hickman. 91 min.

A man acquitted of murdering his wife returns home to face lingering suspicions. Forceful film in which Vidor subordinated himself to the Warners noir style, with great success.

233. *The Lineup* (1958) Columbia. *Dir* Don Siegel. *Sc* Sterling Silliphant. *Ph* Hal Mohr. *Mus* Mischa Bakaleinikoff. *Cast* Eli Wallach, Robert Keith, Warner Anderson, Richard Jaeckel, Emile Meyer. 85 min.

Two icy professional killers attempt to track down several packages of heroin that were unwittingly smuggled into the country by innocent travelers. Important example of a "new," late fifties noir vision, with strong direction by Don Siegel.

234. *Loan Shark* (1952) Lippert. *Dir* Seymour Friedman. *Sc* Martin Rackin and Eugene Ling, from a story by Rackin. *Ph* Joseph Biroc. *Cast* George Raft, Dorothy Hart, Paul Stewart, Helen Wescott, John Hoyt. 79 min.

Ex-con avenges his brother's death by infiltrating vicious loan racket.

235. *The Locket* (1946) RKO. *Dir* John Brahm. *Sc* Sheridan Gibney. *Ph* Nicholas Musuraca. *Mus* Roy Webb. *Cast* Laraine Day, Brian Aherne, Robert Mitchum, Gene Raymond, Sharyn Moffett, Ricardo Cortez. 85 min.

Draws the viewer into a disorienting (but perfectly intelligible) vortex of flashbacks within flashbacks that relate the story of a disturbed woman's acquisitive destructiveness.

236. *The Lodger* (1944) 20th Century-Fox. *Dir* John Brahm. *Sc* Barre Lyndon, from the book by Marie Belloc-Lowndes. *Ph* Lucien Ballard. *Mus* Hugo Friedhofer. *Cast* Laird Cregar, Merle Oberon, George Sanders, Cedric Hardwicke, Sara Allgood. 84 min.

Mysterious "pathologist" roams the streets of London at night looking for young actresses to kill. Handsome production of famous Victorian murder story based on the "Jack the Ripper" killings.

237. *The Long Night* (1947) RKO. *Dir* Anatole Litvak. *Sc* John Wexley, from the story by Jacques Viot. *Ph* Sol Polito. *Mus* Dimitri Tiomkin. *Cast* Henry Fonda, Barbara Bel Geddes, Vincent Price, Ann Dvorak, Moroni Olsen, Elisha Cook, Jr., Queenie Smith. 101 min.

A brooding, tormented killer locks himself in his dingy tenement room, with police and a girl trying to talk him into surrendering. As in the case of *Human Desire*, this remake of the French masterpiece *Le Jour Se Lève* (Carné, 1939) retains the mood but not the complete fatalism of its predecessor.

238. *The Long Wait* (1954) United Artists. *Dir* Victor Saville. *Sc* Alan Green and Lesser Samuels, from the novel by Mickey Spillane. *Ph* Franz Planer. *Mus* Mario Castenuova-Tedesco. *Cast* Anthony Quinn, Charles Coburn, Gene Evans, Peggie Castle, Mary Ellen Kay, Barry Kelley. 94 min.

Harsh, violent story of amnesia victim's efforts to clear himself of a mysterious murder charge. Spillane's most noirish novel is given appropriate enhancement.

239. _Loophole_ (1954) Allied Artists. _Dir_ Harold D. Schuster. _Sc_ Warren Douglas, from a story by George Bricker and Dwight Babcock. _Ph_ William Sickner. _Mus_ Paul Dunlap. _Cast_ Barry Sullivan, Charles McGraw, Dorothy Malone, Don Haggerty, Mary Beth Hughes, Don Beddoe. 79 min.

Bank teller is hounded by inexorable bonding company investigator, who refuses to believe that he is innocent of a $50,000 embezzlement.

240. _Love from a Stranger_ (1947) Eagle Lion. _Dir_ Richard Whorf. _Sc_ Philip MacDonald, from a play by Frank Vosper and a story by Agatha Christie. _Ph_ Tony Gaudio. _Mus_ Hans J. Salter. _Cast_ Sylvia Sidney, John Hodiak, Isobel Elsom, Ernest Cossart. 81 min.

Based on the same idea as Hitchcock's _Suspicion_, that a woman fears her new husband will murder her.

241. _Lured_ [also titled **Personal Column**] (1947) United Artists. _Dir_ Douglas Sirk. _Sc_ Leo Rosten, from a story by Jacques Campaneez, Ernest Neuville and Simon Gantillon. _Ph_ William Daniels. _Mus_ Michel Michelet. _Cast_ George Sanders, Lucille Ball, Charles Coburn, Boris Karloff, Sir Cedric Hardwicke, Alan Mowbray, George Zucco, Joseph Calleia. 102 min.

A girl turns detective to find a missing friend, ends up as bait for a maniac killer.

242. _M_ (1951) Columbia. _Dir_ Joseph Losey. _Sc_ Norman Raine and Leo Katcher, based on the 1931 screenplay by Thea Von Harbou. _Ph_ Ernest Laszlo. _Mus_ Michel Michelet. _Cast_ David Wayne, Howard da Silva, Martin Gable, Luther Adler, Steve Brodie, Karen Morley, Glenn Anders. 87 min.

Compulsive child killer is hunted by both police and the underworld. Faithful noir remake of Lang's German Expressionist masterpiece.

243. _Macao_ (1952) RKO. _Dir_ Josef von Sternberg and (uncredited) Nicholas Ray. _Sc_ Bernard C. Schoenfeld and Stanley Rubin, from a story by Bob Williams. _Ph_ Harry J. Wild. _Mus_ Anthony Collins. _Cast_ Robert Mitchum, Jane Russell, William Bendix, Thomas Gomez, Gloria Grahame, Brad Dexter. 81 min.

Ex-GI, on the lam from a minor criminal charge in the states, gets his identity crossed with a detective attempting to nab a Macao racketeer. Violent, exotic RKO entertainment which was orginally filmed by von Sternberg and then largely reshot by Ray.

244. _The Macomber Affair_ (1947) United Artists. _Dir_ Zoltan Korda. _Sc_ Casey Robinson, adapted by Seymour Bennett and Frank Arnold from a story by Ernest Hemingway. _Ph_ Karl Struss. _Mus_ Miklos Rozsa. _Cast_ Gregory Peck, Joan Bennett, Robert Preston, Reginald Denny, Carl Harbord. 89 min.

Tragedy results when safari guide is caught between corrosive woman and her weak husband. Popular Hemingway story is given stylish noir treatment.

245. _Make Haste to Live_ (1954) Republic. _Dir_ William A. Seiter.

Sc Warren Duff. *Ph* John L. Russell. *Mus* Elmer Bernstein. *Cast* Dorothy McGuire, Stephen McNally, Mary Murphy, Edgar Buchanan, John Howard. 90 min.

After 18 year prison term, man threatens to destroy estranged wife's peaceful, secure new existence.

246. *The Maltese Falcon* (1941) Warner Brothers.

After the murder of his partner, Sam Spade becomes involved with a group of shifty characters engaged in a deadly race to find a priceless antique bird. Humphrey Bogart gives a memorable performance in the first and best noir detective film of the 1940s, adapted from Dashiell Hammett's classic. See page 7.

247. *The Man I Love* (1946) Warner Brothers.

Eloquent noir "woman's film", starring Ida Lupino as a gutsy postwar torch singer. See page 48.

248. *Man in the Attic* (1953) 20th Century-Fox. *Dir* Hugo Fregonese. *Sc* Barre Lyndon, Robert Presnell, Jr., from the novel *The Lodger* by Marie Belloc-Lowndes. *Ph* Leo Tover. *Mus* Lionel Newman. *Cast* Jack Palance, Constance Smith, Byron Palmer, Francis Bavier, Rhys Williams. 82 min.

Third film adaption and second noir version of *The Lodger*, with good performance by Jack Palance.

249. *Man in the Dark* (1953) Columbia. *Dir* Lew Landers. *Sc* George Bricker and Jack Leonard, adapted by William Sackheim, from a story by Tom Van Dycke and Henry Altimus. *Ph* Floyd Crosby. *Mus* Ross di Maggio. *Cast* Edmond O'Brien, Audrey Totter, Ruth Warren, Ted de Corsia, Horace McMahon. 70 min.

Convict submits to brain operation intended to eliminate his criminal motivation; he's paroled, loses his memory, and is accosted by old gang members. Unique twist on the amnesia plot, originally screened in 3-D.

250. *Man in the Net* (1959) United Artists. *Dir* Michael Curtiz. *Sc* Reginald Rose, from a story by Patrick Quentin. *Ph* John F. Seitz. *Mus* Hans J. Salter. *Cast* Alan Ladd, Carolyn Jones, Diane Brewster, John Lupton, Charles McGraw. 97 min.

Commerical artist trys desperately to clear himself of his wife's murder.

251. *The Man Is Armed* (1956) Republic. *Dir* Franklin Adreon. *Sc* Richard Landau and Robert C. Dennis, from a story by Don Martin. *Ph* Bud Thackery. *Mus* R. Dale Butts. *Cast* Dane Clark, William Talman, May Wynn, Robert Horton, Barton MacLane. 70 min.

Man is tricked by former boss into helping him pull a robbery, which leads to murder.

252. *The Man Who Cheated Himself* (1951) 20th Century-Fox. *Dir* Felix Feist. *Sc* Seton I. Miller and Phillip MacDonald, from a story by Miller. *Ph* Russell Harlan. *Mus* Louis Forbes. *Cast* Lee J. Cobb, John Dall, Jane Wyatt, Lisa Howard. 81 min.

Tough cop helps his lover cover up the shooting of her wealthy husband. Mainstream noir, primarily distinguished by its acting and San Francisco visuals.

253. *The Man with My Face* (1951) United Artists. *Dir* Edward J. Montagne. *Sc* Samuel W. Taylor, T.J. McGowan, Vincent Bogert and Edward J. Montagne, from the novel by Taylor. *Ph* Fred Jackman, Jr. *Mus* Samuel G. Engel. *Cast* Barry Nelson, Lynn Ainley, John Harvey, Carole Matthews, Jack Warden, 86 min.

Accountant arrives home, finds a man who looks just like him taking over his life. Potent, noir Doppelgänger theme taken to its ultimate extreme.

254. *Manhandled* (1949) Paramount. *Dir* Lewis R. Foster. *Sc* Foster and Whitman Chambers, from a story by L.S. Goldsmith. *Ph* Ernest Laszlo. *Mus* Darrell Calker. *Cast* Dorothy Lamour, Dan Duryea, Sterling Hayden, Irene Hervey, Alan Napier, Art Smith. 97 min.

A wealthy man recounts a disturbing dream to his psychiatrist, which sets into motion a complex narrative of violence, theft and murder.

255. *The Mask of Diljon* (1946) PRC. *Dir* Lew Landers. *Sc* Arthur St. Claire, Griffin Jay, from a story by St. Claire. *Ph* Jack Greenhalgh. *Mus* Karl Hajos. *Cast* Erich Von Stroheim, Jeanne Bates, William Wright, Edward Van Sloan. 73 min.

Von Stroheim plays a former vaudeville magician whose power-crazed interest in hypnotism leads to madness and murder.

256. *The Mask of Dimitrios* (1944) Warner Brothers. *Dir* Jean Negulesco. *Sc* Frank Gruber, from the novel *A Coffin for Dimitrios* by Eric Ambler. *Ph* Arthur Edeson. *Mus* Adolph Deutsch. *Cast* Sydney Greenstreet, Zachary Scott, Faye Emerson, Peter Lorre, George Tobias, Victor Francen, Steven Geray, Eduardo Ciannelli, Florence Bates. 95 min.

Mystery writer becomes obsessed with piecing together the story of a notorious phantom criminal. Classy adaption of a formidable British suspense novel, representative of a significant link between Warners and the early development of noir stylistics.

257. *Mildred Pierce* (1945) Warner Brothers. *Dir* Michael Curtiz. *Sc* Ranald MacDougall, from the novel by James M. Cain. *Ph* Ernest Haller. *Mus* Max Steiner. *Cast* Joan Crawford, Jack Carson, Zachary Scott, Eve Arden, Ann Blyth, Bruce Bennett, Moroni Olsen. 111 min.

Under suspicion of murder, a world-weary woman gives police an account of her past. Significant, popular film which masterfully intensifies the style of James M. Cain's antisuccess story.

258. *Ministry of Fear* (1944) Paramount. *Dir* Fritz Lang. *Sc* Seton I. Miller, from the novel by Graham Greene. *Ph* Henry Sharp. *Mus* Victor Young. *Cast* Ray Milland, Marjorie Reynolds, Carl Esmond, Hillary Brooke, Dan Duryea, Alan Napier. 86 min.

Just after being released from a mental institution, a man is plunged into a bizarre, confusing adventure in which he is caught between Nazi spies and police. Lang's first film noir was a powerful addition to the developing nightmare concept which was to become one of the most important ideas behind the cycle.

259. *Mr. Arkadin* [British title, **Confidential Report**] (1955) M&A Alexander. *Dir* Orson Welles. *Sc* Welles, from his novel. *Ph* Jean Bourgoin. *Mus*

Paul Misraki. *Cast* Orson Welles, Paola Mori, Robert Arden, Akim Tamiroff, Michael Redgrave, Patricia Medina, Mischa Auer. 100 min.

American adventurer becomes involved with a mysterious European financier and his daughter, soon being hired to uncover this imposing gentleman's allegedly unknown past. Pulpish, melodramatic story (somewhat reminiscent of *Citizen Kane*), in which the corrupting force of high places is unveiled with an exotic, almost surreal intensity.

260. *The Mob* (1951) Columbia. *Dir* Robert Parrish. *Sc* William Bowers, from the novel *Waterfront* by Ferguson Findley. *Ph* Joseph Walker. *Mus* George Duning. *Cast* Broderick Crawford, Betty Buehler, Richard Kiley, Matt Crowley, Neville Brand, Ernest Borgnine. 87 min.

Two tough undercover cops infiltrate vicious waterfront mob. About as close as noir ever came to resurrecting the 1930s gangster film.

261. *Moonrise* (1948) Republic. *Dir* Frank Borzage. *Sc* Charles Haas, from the novel by Theodore Strauss. *Ph* John L. Russell. *Mus* William Lava. *Cast* Dane Clark, Gail Russell, Ethel Barrymore, Allyn Joslyn, Rex Ingram, Henry Morgan. 90 min.

Self-defense killing aggravates young man's nightmarish fear that he is the victim of "bad blood." One of the most significant and powerful redemptive noirs, in which director Borzage successfully merges his distinctive spiritual viewpoint with noir-oriented psychology and style.

262. *Moontide* (1942) 20th Century-Fox. *Dir* Archie Mayo and (uncredited) Fritz Lang. *Sc* John O'Hara, from the novel by Willard Robertson. *Ph* Charles Clarke. *Mus* Cyril Mockridge, Alfred Newman. *Cast* Jean Gabin, Ida Lupino, Thomas Mitchell, Claude Rains, Jerome Cowan, Helen Reynolds, Ralph Byrd, Sen Yung. 94 min.

Moody, atmospheric story of seaman's involvement with suicidal girl. Little-known early noir, inspired by Gabin's films of French poetic realism.

263. *Moss Rose* (1947) 20th Century-Fox. *Dir* Gregory Ratoff. *Sc* Jules Furthman and Tom Reed, adapted by Niven Busch, from the novel by Joseph Shearing. *Ph* Joe MacDonald. *Mus* David Buttolph. *Cast* Peggy Cummins, Victor Mature, Ethel Barrymore, Vincent Price, Margo Woode, George Zucco, Patricia Medina, Rhys Williams. 82 min.

Ambitious young woman blackmails country gentleman suspected of murder. Atmospheric Victorian thriller with some good characterizations.

264. *Murder by Contract* (1958) Columbia. *Dir* Irving Lerner. *Sc* Ben Simcoe. *Ph* Lucien Ballard. *Mus* Perry Botkin. *Cast* Vince Edwards, Phillip Pine, Herschel Bernardi, Caprice Toriel. 81 min.

A hired killer stalks his victim, then becomes one himself.

265. *Murder Is My Beat* (1955) Allied Artists. *Dir* Edgar G. Ulmer. *Sc* Aubrey Wiseberg, from a story by Wiseberg and Martin Field. *Ph* Harold E. Wellman. *Mus* Albert Glasser. *Cast* Paul Langton, Barbara Payton, Robert Shayne, Selena Royle, Roy Gordon. 77 min.

On the way to prison, woman sees the man she was convicted of murdering. Stylish, crafted B film which was Ulmer's last noir.

266. *Murder My Sweet* (1944) RKO. *Dir* Edward Dmytryk. *Sc* John Paxton, from the novel *Farewell, My Lovely* by Raymond Chandler. *Ph* Harry J. Wild. *Mus* Roy Webb. *Cast* Dick Powell, Claire Trevor, Ann Shirley, Otto Kruger, Mike Mazurki. 95 min.

Private eye Philip Marlowe goes through a series of confusing and dangerous adventures which culminate in the unmasking of a murderous *femme fatale*. The first full-fledged noir version of a Raymond Chandler detective novel.

267. *My Name Is Julia Ross* (1945) Columbia. *Dir* Joseph H. Lewis. *Sc* Muriel Roy Bolton, from the novel *The Woman in Red* by Anthony Gilbert. *Ph* Burnett Guffey. *Mus* Mischa Bakaleinikoff. *Cast* Nina Foch, Dame May Whitty, George Macready, Roland Varno, Anita Bolster. 64 min.

Hired as private secretary by wealthy old matron and her son, young woman wakes up from a deep sleep to be told that she is the son's mentally disturbed wife. Technically adept woman-in-distress thriller, set in England.

268. *Mystery Street* (1950) MGM. *Dir* John Sturges. *Sc* Sydney Boehm and Richard Brooks, from a story by Leonard Spigelgass. *Ph* John Alton. *Mus* Rudolph G. Kopp. *Cast* Ricardo Montalban, Sally Forrest, Bruce Bennett, Elsa Lanchester, Marshall Thompson, Jan Sterling. 94 min.

Cape Cod architect murders cheap bar hostess; three months later police discover the body and attempt to solve the crime. Effectively combines elements of *policier* and noir melodrama.

269. *The Naked Alibi* (1954) Universal. *Dir* Jerry Hopper. *Sc* Lawrence Roman, from a story by J. Robert Bren and Gladys Atwater. *Ph* Russell Metty. *Mus* Joseph Gershenson. *Cast* Sterling Hayden, Gloria Grahame, Gene Barry, Marcia Henderson, Casey Adams. 85 min.

Dismissed from the force for pressuring a murder suspect, tough cop tries to vindicate himself by trailing the man in question to Mexico.

270. *The Naked City* (1948) Universal. *Dir* Jules Dassin. *Sc* Albert Maltz and Malvin Wald, from a story by Wald. *Ph* William Daniels. *Mus* Miklos Rozsa, Frank Skinner. *Cast* Barry Fitzgerald, Howard Duff, Dorothy Hart, Don Taylor, Ted de Corsia. 96 min.

Two police detectives comb New York for the murderers of a beautiful young woman. Well-known *policier* with strong location work and a powerful climactic chase scene.

271. *The Naked Street* (1955) United Artists. *Dir* Maxwell Shane. *Sc* Shane and Leo Katcher. *Ph* Floyd Crosby. *Mus* Emil Newman. *Cast* Farley Granger, Anthony Quinn, Anne Bancroft, Peter Graves, Jerry Paris, Whit Bissell. 84 min.

Tough racketeer pulls strings to get his sister's punk boyfriend out of the death house.

272. *The Narrow Margin* (1952) RKO. *Dir* Richard Fleischer. *Sc* Earl Felton, from a story by Martin Goldsmith and Jack Leonard. *Ph* George E. Diskant. *Cast* Charles McGraw, Marie Windsor, Jacqueline White, Gordon Gebert. 71 min.

Los Angeles cop sheperds "hot" grand jury witness on perilous cross-country train trip. Nothing is what it seems in this tight-knit B thriller with a well-deserved reputation.

273. *New York Confidential* (1955) Warner Brothers. *Dir* Russell Rouse. *Sc* Clarence Greene and Rouse, suggested by the book by Jack Lait and Lee Mortimer. *Ph* Edward Fitzgerald. *Mus* Joseph Mullendore. *Cast* Broderick Crawford, Richard Conte, Marilyn Maxwell, Anne Bancroft, J. Carrol Naish, Onslow Stevens. 87 min.

Efficient syndicate assassin is ordered to kill his best friend in the organization. Stark, fast-moving exposé thriller with good performance by Conte.

274. *Night and the City* (1950) 20th Century-Fox. *Dir* Jules Dassin. *Sc* Jo Eisinger, from the novel by Gerald Kersh. *Ph* Max Greene. *Mus* Franz Waxman. *Cast* Richard Widmark, Gene Tierney, Googie Withers, Hugh Marlowe, Francis L. Sullivan, Herbert Lom, Mike Mazurki. 95 min.

Cheap hustler's underhanded scheme for becoming big wrestling promoter backfires, and he is marked for death by London's underworld chief. Intense, relentless story of one of the cycle's most memorable doomed protagonists.

275. *Night Editor* (1946) Columbia. *Dir* Henry Levin. *Sc* Hal Smith, from a radio program by Hal Burdick and a story by Scott Littleton. *Ph* Burnett Guffey, Philip Tannura. *Mus* Mischa Bakaleinikoff. *Cast* William Gargan, Janis Carter, Jeff Donnell, Coulter Irwin. 66 min.

Police detective can't report killing he has witnessed because it would involve a scandalous disclosure of his illicit affair with a socialite.

276. *The Night Has a Thousand Eyes* (1948) Paramount. *Dir* John Farrow. *Sc* Barre Lyndon and Jonathan Latimer, from the novel by Cornell Woolrich. *Ph* John F. Seitz. *Mus* Victor Young. *Cast* Edward G. Robinson, Gail Russell, John Lund, Virginia Bruce, William Demarest. 81 min.

Fortune teller's discovery of genuine clairvoyance brings him only torment and guilt. Noir theme of implacable fate is perfectly suited to this dark tale of occult power.

277. *The Night Holds Terror* (1955) Columbia. *Dir* Andrew L. Stone. *Sc* Stone. *Ph* Fred Jackman, Jr. *Mus* Lucien Cailliet. *Cast* Jack Kelly, Hildy Parks, Vince Edwards, John Cassavetes, David Cross. 85 min.

Three desperate criminals hold a terrified family hostage. Notable addition to a series of suspense thrillers made in the fifties by Andrew Stone and his wife.

278. *The Night Runner* (1957) Universal. *Dir* Abner Biberman. *Sc* Gene Levitt, from a story by Owen Cameron. *Ph* George Robinson. *Mus* Joseph Gershenson. *Cast* Ray Danton, Colleen Miller, Willis Bouchey, Merry Anders. 79 min.

Mental hospital outpatient is pushed over the edge by his girlfriend's taunting father. Interesting B thriller that anticipates *Psycho* in setting and theme.

279. *Night Without Sleep* (1952) 20th Century-Fox. *Dir* Roy Ward Baker. *Sc* Frank Partos and Elick Moll, from the novel by Moll. *Ph* Lucien Ballard. *Mus* Cyril Mockridge. *Cast* Linda Darnell, Gary Merrill, Hildegarde Neff, Joyce MacKenzie, June Vincent, Hugh Beaumont. 77 min.

Alcholic songwriter reconstructs the events of a previous evening's binge, fearing that he committed a murder. Dark, brooding flashback melodrama.

280. *Nightfall* (1957) Columbia. *Dir* Jacques Tourneur. *Sc* Stirling Silliphant, from the novel by David Goodis. *Ph* Burnett Guffey. *Mus* George Duning. *Cast* Aldo Ray, Brian Keith, Anne Bancroft, Jocelyn Brando, James Gregory. 80 min.

Commercial artist is hunted by police for a killing he didn't do and crooks for stolen money he doesn't have. Paranoid thriller which seems to be Tourneur's return to some of the territory he explored in *Out of the Past*.

281. *Nightmare* (1956) United Artists. *Dir* Maxwell Shane. *Sc* Shane, from the story by Cornell Woolrich. *Ph* Joseph Biroc. *Mus* Herschel Burke Gilbert. *Cast* Edward G. Robinson, Kevin McCarthy, Connie Russell, Virginia Christine, Rhys Williams. 89 min.

New Orleans musician discovers evidence that his dream of committing a bizarre murder actually took place. Atmospheric remake of *Fear in the Night*, Shane's 1947 filmization of Woolrich's classic story.

282. *Nightmare Alley* (1947) 20th Century–Fox. *Dir* Edmund Goulding. *Sc* Jules Furthman, from the novel by William Lindsay Gresham. *Ph* Lee Garmes. *Mus* Cyril Mockridge. *Cast* Tyrone Power, Joan Blondell, Coleen Gray, Helen Walker, Taylor Holmes, Mike Mazurki. 110 min.

Ambitious carnival worker makes it big as a fake spiritualist, is exposed and sinks to the lowest level of human existence. Popular melodrama which clearly demonstrates the noir sensibility's all-pervasive Hollywood influence by 1947.

283. *99 River Street* (1953) United Artists. *Dir* Phil Karlson. *Sc* Robert Smith, from a story by George Zuckerman. *Ph* Franz Planer. *Mus* Emil Newman, Arthur Lange. *Cast* John Payne, Evelyn Keyes, Brad Dexter, Frank Faylen, Peggie Castle, Jack Lambert. 83 min.

Embittered ex-boxer is framed for his wife's murder by her jewel thief lover. Possibly the best of a series of violent, well-executed noirs made in the early fifties by Phil Karlson.

284. *No Escape* [also titled **City on a Hunt**] (1953) United Artists. *Dir* Charles Bennett. *Sc* Bennett. *Ph* Ben Kline. *Mus* Bert Shefter. *Cast* Lew Ayres, Majorie Steele, Sonny Tufts, Lewis Martin, Gertrude Michael. 76 min.

A couple suspected of murder follow a trail of clues which lead them to the real culprit.

285. *No Man of Her Own* (1950) Paramount. *Dir* Mitchell Leisen. *Sc* Sally Benson, Catherine Turney (and Leisen uncredited), from the novel *I Married a Dead Man* by Cornell Woolrich. *Ph* Daniel L. Fapp. *Mus* Hugo Friedhofer. *Cast* Barbara Stanwyck, John Lund, Jane Cowl, Phyllis Thaxter, Lyle Bettger, Richard Denning, Milburn Stone. 98 min.

Unmarried woman goes along with a case of mistaken identity so that her newborn child can have a decent life; dangerous complications soon arise. Fervent, suspenseful woman's noir that actually seems to elevate its Woolrich source material.

286. No Questions Asked (1951) MGM. *Dir* Harold F. Kress. *Sc* Sidney Sheldon, from a story by Berne Giler. *Ph* Harold Lipstein. *Mus* Leith Stevens. *Cast* Barry Sullivan, Arlene Dahl, George Murphy, Jean Hagen, Richard Anderson, Moroni Olsen. 80 min.

To please a greedy woman, lawyer handles negotiations between big-time criminals and insurance companies willing to buy back stolen merchandise.

287. No Way Out (1950) 20th Century-Fox. *Dir* Joseph L. Mankiewicz. *Sc* Mankiewicz and Lesser Samuels. *Ph* Milton Krasner. *Mus* Alfred Newman. *Cast* Richard Widmark, Linda Darnell, Stephen McNally, Sidney Poitier, Henry Bellaver, Stanley Ridges, Ruby Dee, Ossie Davis. 106 min.

When a black doctor fails to save his dying brother, a vindictive hoodlum incites a race riot. Tense narrative of racial bigotry and mob violence.

288. Nobody Lives Forever (1946) Warner Brothers. *Dir* Jean Negulesco. *Sc* W.R. Burnett. *Ph* Arthur Edeson. *Mus* Adolph Deutsch. *Cast* John Garfield, Geraldine Fitzgerald, Walter Brennan, Faye Emerson, George Coulouris, George Tobias. 100 min.

An ex-GI returns from the war and attempts to reattain his previous status as a big-time hustler. Crisp hard-boiled melodrama that is the first of a series of important Garfield noirs.

289. Nocturne (1946) RKO. *Dir* Edwin L. Marin. *Sc* Jonathan Latimer, from a story by Frank Fenton and Rowland Brown. *Ph* Harry J. Wild. *Mus* Leigh Harline. *Cast* George Raft, Lynn Bari, Virginia Huston, Joseph Pevney, Myrna Dell. 87 min.

Police detective puts his job on the line to prove that a songwriter's death was murder. Pungent film of questing protagonist driven to expose a truth defined, in effect, as an amalgam of noir settings and characters.

290. Nora Prentiss (1947) Warner Brothers. *Dir* Vincent Sherman. *Sc* Richard Nash, from a story by Paul Webster and Jack Sobell. *Ph* James Wong Howe. *Mus* Franz Waxman. *Cast* Ann Sheridan, Kent Smith, Bruce Bennett, Robert Alda, Rosemary DeCamp, John Ridgely. 111 min.

Successful doctor fakes his own death and tries to start a new life with a nightclub singer. Dark, well-plotted woman's noir with some excellent visuals.

291. Notorious (1946) RKO. *Dir* Alfred Hitchcock. *Sc* Ben Hecht. *Ph* Ted Tetzlaff. *Mus* Roy Webb. *Cast* Cary Grant, Ingrid Bergman, Claude Rains, Louis Calhern. 101 min.

The daughter of a Nazi spy accompanies a government agent on a dangerous espionage mission in South America. Hitchcock romantic thriller that shows a distinct noir bent in character and theme.

Obsession see *The Hidden Room*

292. Odds Against Tomorrow (1959) United Artists. *Dir* Robert Wise. *Sc* John O. Killens and Nelson Gidding, from the novel by William P. McGivern. *Ph* Joseph Brun. *Mus* John Lewis. *Cast* Harry Belafonte, Robert Ryan, Gloria Grahame, Shelley Winters, Ed Begley. 96 min.

Three desperate losers hope a small-town bank robbery will turn their luck around. Fatalistic heist film with poetic visual style that has been called "the last noir."

293. On Dangerous Ground (1952) RKO. *Dir* Nicholas Ray. *Sc* A.I. Bezzerides, adapted by Bezzerides and Nicholas Ray, from the novel *Mad With Much Heart* by Gerald Butler. *Ph* George E. Diskant. *Mus* Bernard Herrmann. *Cast* Robert Ryan, Ida Lupino, Ward Bond, Charles Kemper, Ed Begley. 82 min.

Alienated noir protagonist at the end of his rope travels a hazardous road which leads him out of the urban darkness and into a light not concealed by congenital blindness. The actual story line (about a big city cop on an out-of-town murder case) is much less descriptive of this notable film noir.

294. Once a Thief (1950) United Artists. *Dir* W. Lee Wilder. *Sc* Richard S. Conway, from a story by Max Colpet and Hans Wilhelm. *Ph* William Clothier. *Mus* Michel Michelet. *Cast* June Havoc, Cesar Romero, Marie McDonald, Lon Chaney, Jr., Iris Adrian. 88 min.

A woman down on her luck meets a first-class heel.

295. One Way Street (1950) Universal. *Dir* Hugo Fregonese. *Sc* Lawrence Kimble. *Ph* Maury Gertsman. *Mus* Frank Skinner. *Cast* James Mason, Marta Toren, Dan Duryea, William Conrad, Jack Elam. 79 min.

Doctor involved with mobsters steals gangleader's girlfriend and $200,000, then tries to start a new life in Mexico. Grim, fatalistic noir with some good performances.

296. The Other Woman (1954) 20th Century–Fox. *Dir* Hugo Haas. *Sc* Haas. *Ph* Eddie Fitzgerald. *Mus* Ernest Gold. *Cast* Hugo Haas, Cleo Moore, Lance Fuller, Lucille Barkley, John Qualen. 81 min.

Émigré director is blackmailed by actress he refuses to cast in a movie.

297. Out of the Fog (1941) Warner Brothers. *Dir* Anatole Litvak. *Sc* Robert Rossen, Jerry Wald, and Richard Macaulay, from a play by Irwin Shaw. *Ph* James Wong Howe. *Cast* Ida Lupino, John Garfield, Thomas Mitchell, Eddie Albert, John Qualen, George Tobias, Jerome Cowan. 86 min.

Small-time racketeer falls for a girl while trying to extort money from her father. Offbeat Warners character study that was Garfield's first noir.

298. Out of the Past (1947) RKO.
Private detective runs off with a girl he's hired to track down, then spends the rest of his life trying to escape the consequences. One of the most important films of the cycle, with many representative noir qualities and more than one hidden secret. See page 65.

299. Outside the Wall (1950) Universal. *Dir* Crane Wilbur. *Sc* Wilbur, from a story by Henry Edward Helseth. *Ph* Irving Glassberg. *Mus* Milton Schwarzwald. *Cast* Richard Basehart, Marilyn Maxwell, Signe Hasso, Dorothy Hart, Joseph Pevney, John Hoyt, Henry Morgan. 80 min.

An ex-con gets a job at a sanitarium, which leads to involvement with a criminal patient and his greedy wife.

300. *Panic in the Streets* (1950) 20th Century-Fox. *Dir* Elia Kazan. *Sc* Richard Murphy, adapted by Daniel Fuchs, from a story by Edna and Edward Anhalt. *Ph* Joe MacDonald. *Mus* Alfred Newman. *Cast* Richard Widmark, Paul Douglas, Barbara Bel Geddes, Jack Palance, Zero Mostel. 96 min.

New Orleans public health doctor helps police search for a pair of murderers that carry bubonic plague. Unique film which combines dark noir menace with realistic portrayal of a public servant's everyday life.

301. *The Paradine Case* (1947) United Artists. *Dir* Alfred Hitchcock. *Sc* David O. Selznick, adapted by Alma Reville, from the novel by Robert Hitchens. *Ph* Lee Garmes. *Mus* Franz Waxman. *Cast* Gregory Peck, Charles Laughton, Ann Todd, Charles Coburn, Ethel Barrymore, Alida Valli, Louis Jourdan, Leo G. Carroll. 125 min.

Prominent attorney falls in love with mysterious woman that is accused of poisoning her blind husband. Classy, atypical Hitchcock melodrama with strong noir mood.

302. *Parole, Inc.* (1948) Eagle Lion. *Dir* Alfred Zeisler. *Sc* Royal Cole, from a story by Sherman T. Lowe and Cole. *Ph* Gilbert Warrenton. *Mus* Alexander Laszlo. *Cast* Michael O'Shea, Turhan Bey, Evelyn Ankers, Virginia Lee, Lyle Talbot. 71 min.

Low budget exposé thriller of corruption being uncovered in the parole system.

303. *The People Against O'Hara* (1951) MGM. *Dir* John Sturges. *Sc* John Monks, Jr., from the novel by Eleazar Lipsky. *Ph* John Alton. *Mus* Carmen Dragon. *Cast* Spencer Tracy, Pat O'Brien, Diana Lynn, John Hodiak, Eduardo Ciannelli, James Arness. 102 min.

Alcoholic lawyer tries to bribe witness in murder trial, loses the case and then sets out to find the real killer on his own. Well-made MGM noir with nice visuals and strong performance by Spencer Tracy.

Personal Column see *Lured*

304. *Phantom Lady* (1944) Universal. *Dir* Robert Siodmak. *Sc* Bernard C. Schoenfeld, from the novel by Cornell Woolrich. *Ph* Woody Bredell. *Mus* Hans J. Salter. *Cast* Franchot Tone, Ella Raines, Alan Curtis, Aurora, Thomas Gomez, Elisha Cook, Jr. 87 min.

A man's faithful secretary probes the dark and dangerous cityscape in a determined effort to obtain evidence that her boss did not murder his wife. In this, Robert Siodmak's first film noir, the stylistic contours of German Expressionism become a revelation which informs the American suspense thriller.

305. *The Phenix City Story* (1955) Allied Artists. *Dir* Phil Karlson. *Sc* Crane Wilbur and Daniel Mainwaring. *Ph* Harry Neumann. *Mus* Harry Sukman. *Cast* John McIntire, Richard Kiley, Kathryn Grant, Edward Andrews, John Larch. 100 min.

A young lawyer returns from the service to find that his home town has turned into a corrupt, vice-ridden jungle. Seedy, violent crime drama with strong '50s noir look that was based on a true story.

306. Pickup on South Street (1953) 20th Century-Fox. *Dir* Sam Fuller. *Sc* Fuller, from a story by Dwight Taylor. *Ph* Joe MacDonald. *Mus* Leigh Harline. *Cast* Richard Widmark, Jean Peters, Thelma Ritter, Richard Kiley, Murvyn Vye. 83 min.

Tough pickpocket lifts a purse that contains valuable classified microfilm, gets caught between police, Communist spies and a girl that refuses to believe her boyfriend is a traitor. Much-discussed noir with good visuals and thematic depth which transcends its apparent political subject.

307. The Pitfall (1948) United Artists. *Dir* André de Toth. *Sc* Karl Kamb, from the novel by Jay Dratler. *Ph* Harry J. Wild. *Mus* Louis Forbes. *Cast* Dick Powell, Lizabeth Scott, Jane Wyatt, Raymond Burr, John Litel, Byron Barr. 86 min.

Family man becomes bored with his routine existence, resulting in affair with shady woman and murder. Disquieting noir thriller which doesn't seem entirely able to reaffirm the middle-class values its protagonist disregards.

308. A Place in the Sun (1951) Paramount. *Dir* George Stevens. *Sc* Michael Wilson and Harry Brown, from the novel *An American Tragedy* by Theodore Dreiser and the Patrick Kearney play adapted from the novel. *Ph* William C. Mellor. *Mus* Franz Waxman. *Cast* Montgomery Clift, Elizabeth Taylor, Shelley Winters, Anne Revere, Raymond Burr, Keefe Brasselle. 122 min.

A young man makes a tragic, ill-fated attempt to break from his lower-class background. Dark, romantic adaption of Dreiser's classic novel.

309. Playgirl (1954) Universal. *Dir* Joseph Pevney. *Sc* Robert Blees, from a story by Ray Buffum. *Ph* Carl Guthrie. *Mus* Joseph Gershenson. *Cast* Shelley Winters, Barry Sullivan, Gregg Palmer, Richard Long, Kent Taylor. 85 min.

Beautiful girl from the sticks finds success and grave peril in the big city.

310. Please Murder Me (1956) Distributors Corporation of America. *Dir* Peter Godfrey. *Sc* Al C. Ward and Donald Hyde. *Ph* Allen Stensvold. *Cast* Angela Lansbury, Raymond Burr, Dick Foran, John Dehner, Lamont Johnson. 78 min.

Brilliant attorney risks all to defend a murderess with whom he is in love.

311. Plunder Road (1957) 20th Century-Fox. *Dir* Hubert Cornfield. *Sc* Steven Ritch and Jack Charney, from a story by Ritch. *Ph* Ernest Haller. *Mus* Irving Gertz. *Cast* Gene Raymond, Jeanne Cooper, Wayne Morris, Elisha Cook, Jr., Stafford Repp. 82 min.

Five men carry out an elaborate plan to rob a San Francisco bound train of a million dollars in gold bullion. Crafted low budget heist film infused with deterministic fatalism.

312. Port of New York (1949) Eagle Lion. *Dir* Laslo Benedek. *Sc* Eugene Ling, adapted by Leo Townsend, from a story by Arthur A. Ross and Bert Murray. *Ph* George E. Diskant. *Mus* Sol Kaplan. *Cast* Scott Brady, Richard Rober, K.T. Stevens, Yul Brynner, Arthur Blake. 82 min.

Two treasury agents attempt to infiltrate murderous waterfront narcotics ring. Violent *policier* with atmospheric location visuals.

313. *Possessed* (1947) Warner Brothers. *Dir* Curtis Bernhardt. *Sc* Sylvia Richards and Ranald MacDougall, from the novelette *One Man's Secret* by Rita Weiman. *Ph* Joseph Valentine. *Mus* Franz Waxman. *Cast* Joan Crawford, Van Heflin, Raymond Massey, Geraldine Brooks, Stanley Ridges. 108 min.

Under sodium pentothal, a disturbed woman tells how unrequited love led to suicide, murder and her complete mental breakdown. One of the most significant noir psychological pictures, the total emphasis of which is on communicating the subjective experience of its bewildered, schizophrenic protagonist.

314. *The Postman Always Rings Twice* (1946) MGM. *Dir* Tay Garnett. *Sc* Harry Ruskin and Niven Busch, from the novel by James M. Cain. *Ph* Sidney Wagner. *Mus* George Bassman. *Cast* Lana Turner, John Garfield, Cecil Kellaway, Hume Cronyn, Leon Ames, Audrey Totter. 113 min.

A drifter gets a job at a roadside diner, falls for the proprietor's sultry young wife and together they plot murder. Classic noir version of James M. Cain's famous novel of insatiable, misguided love.

315. *The Pretender* (1947) Republic. *Dir* W. Lee Wilder. *Sc* Don Martin. *Ph* John Alton. *Mus* Paul Dessau. *Cast* Albert Dekker, Catherine Craig, Charles Drake, Alan Carney, Linda Sterling. 69 min.

Crooked investment broker hires gangster to murder his rival for the affections of a heiress, but the plan backfires. Quality B thriller with strong noir vision that is also notable in being the first noir by the cycle's master cinematographer, John Alton.

316. *The Price of Fear* (1956) Universal. *Dir* Abner Biberman. *Sc* Robert Tallman, from a story by Dick Irving. *Ph* Irving Glassberg. *Mus* Joseph Gershenson. *Cast* Merle Oberon, Lex Barker, Charles Drake, Gia Scala, Warren Stevens. 79 min.

A career woman will go to any extreme to cover up a hit-and-run accident.

317. *Private Hell 36* (1954) Filmakers. *Dir* Don Siegel. *Sc* Collier Young and Ida Lupino. *Ph* Burnett Guffey. *Mus* Leith Stevens. *Cast* Ida Lupino, Steve Cochran, Howard Duff, Dean Jagger, Dorothy Malone. 81 min.

Temptation becomes too much for two police detectives who recover a suitcase full of stolen money. Straightforward image of noirish dissolution, prone to heavy moralizing.

318. *The Prowler* (1951) United Artists. *Dir* Joseph Losey. *Sc* Hugo Butler, from a story by Robert Thoeren and Hans Wilhelm. *Ph* Arthur Miller. *Mus* Lyn Murray. *Cast* Van Heflin, Evelyn Keyes, John Maxwell, Katherine Warren, Emerson Tracy. 92 min.

After seducing a neglected suburban housewife, an unscrupulous cop concocts a plan to kill her wealthy husband and make it look like an accident. First-rate thriller with noir protagonist corrupted by American materialist values.

319. *Pushover* (1954) Columbia. *Dir* Richard Quine. *Sc* Roy Huggins, based on two novels, *The Night Watcher* by Thomas Walsh and *Rafferty* by William S. Ballinger. *Ph* Lester H. White. *Mus* Arthur Morton. *Cast* Fred MacMurray, Kim Novak, Phil Carey, Dorothy Malone, E.G. Marshall, Allen Mourse. 88 min.

Police detective falls for a robber's girlfriend that is under his surveillance, ends up committing murder. Nocturnal B noir with MacMurray in a role that invites comparisons with *Double Indemnity*.

320. *Queen Bee* (1955) Columbia. *Dir* Ranald MacDougall. *Sc* MacDougall, from the novel by Edna Lee. *Ph* Charles Lang. *Mus* George Duning. *Cast* Joan Crawford, Barry Sullivan, Betsy Palmer, John Ireland, Lucy Marlow. 95 min.

Vitriolic late noir about a consummate witch, played, as no one else could, by Joan Crawford.

321. *Quicksand* (1950) United Artists. *Dir* Irving Pichel. *Sc* Robert Smith. *Ph* Lionel Lindon. *Mus* Louis Gruenberg. *Cast* Mickey Rooney, Jeanne Cagney, Peter Lorre, Taylor Holmes, Art Smith. 79 min.

Garage mechanic needs money, falls gradually into criminal life.

322. *Race Street* (1948) RKO. *Dir* Edwin L. Marin. *Sc* Martin Rackin, from a story by Maurice Davis. *Ph* J. Roy Hunt. *Mus* Roy Webb. *Cast* George Raft, William Bendix, Marilyn Maxwell, Frank Faylen, Henry Morgan, Gale Robbins. 79 min.

San Francisco bookie takes on an extortion ring that has murdered his lifelong friend.

323. *The Racket* (1951) RKO. *Dir* John Cromwell. *Sc* William Wister Haines and W.R. Burnett, from the play by Bartlett Cormack. *Ph* George E. Diskant. *Mus* Constantin Bakaleinikoff. *Cast* Robert Mitchum, Lizabeth Scott, Robert Ryan, William Talman, Ray Collins, William Conrad, Robert Hutton. 88 min.

Honest police captain and ruthless mobster are caught in the middle of a sordid and violent city power struggle. One of the most significant noirs dealing with organized crime and government corruption — complex, articulate and well directed. (Remake of 1928 film with the same title.)

324. *Rage in Heaven* (1941) MGM. *Dir* W.S. Van Dyke. *Sc* Christopher Isherwood and Robert Thoeren, from the novel by James Hilton. *Ph* Oliver T. Marsh. *Mus* Bronislau Kaper. *Cast* Robert Montgomery, Ingrid Bergman, George Sanders, Lucile Watson, Oscar Homolka, Philip Merivale. 82 min.

Grim, little-known early noir of mentally disturbed industrialist who marries unknowing secretary.

325. *The Raging Tide* (1951) Universal. *Dir* George Sherman. *Sc* Ernest K. Gann, from his novel *Fiddler's Green*. *Ph* Russell Metty. *Mus* Frank Skinner. *Cast* Richard Conte, Shelley Winters, Stephen McNally, Charles Bickford, Alex Nicol, John McIntire. 93 min.

Prevented from leaving San Francisco by police roadblocks, a killer plays for time working on a small fishing boat.

326. *Railroaded* (1947) PRC. *Dir* Anthony Mann. *Sc* John C. Higgins, from a story by Gertrude Walker. *Ph* Guy Roe. *Mus* Alvin Levin. *Cast* John Ireland, Sheila Ryan, Hugh Beaumont, Jane Randolph, Ed Kelly. 71 min.

Police detective tries to prove that the brother of his girlfriend did not commit murder. Compact, violent cheapie with strong noir settings and mood.

327. *Raw Deal* (1948) Eagle Lion. *Dir* Anthony Mann. *Sc* Leopold Atlas and John C. Higgins, from a story by Arnold B. Armstrong and Audrey Ashley. *Ph* John Alton. *Mus* Paul Sawtell. *Cast* Dennis O'Keefe, Claire Trevor, Marsha Hunt, John Ireland, Raymond Burr. 79 min.

Prison escapee gets caught between two women on his way to confront crime boss that had him framed. Tough, stylish film that is undoubtedly one of Mann's best noirs.

328. *Rebecca* (1940) United Artists. *Dir* Alfred Hitchcock. *Sc* Robert E. Sherwood and Joan Harrison, from the novel by Daphne du Maurier. *Ph* George Barnes. *Mus* Franz Waxman. *Cast* Laurence Olivier, Joan Fontaine, George Sanders, Judith Anderson, Nigel Bruce. 130 min.

A young woman marries a British nobleman who is obsessed with his deceased former wife. Hitchcock's first American film helped to establish a link between the newborn noir sensibility and gothic literature.

329. *The Reckless Moment* (1949) Columbia.

A woman fights a desperate battle to protect her family from scandal and tradgey. Classy, meaningful woman's thriller by Max Ophuls. See page 80.

330. *The Red House* (1947) United Artists. *Dir* Delmar Daves. *Sc* Daves, from the novel by George Agnew Chamberlain. *Ph* Bert Glennon. *Mus* Miklos Rozsa. *Cast* Edward G. Robinson, Judith Anderson, Lon McCallister, Allene Roberts, Rory Calhoun, Julie London, Ona Munson. 100 min.

Middle-aged farmer goes to extreme lengths to protect the dark secret associated with a deserted house on his property. Murky psychological thriller with resonant settings and an emotive Rozsa score.

331. *Red Light* (1949) United Artists. *Dir* Roy Del Ruth. *Sc* George Callahan. *Ph* Bert Glennon. *Mus* Dimitri Tiomkin. *Cast* George Raft, Virginia Mayo, Gene Lockhart, Barton MacLane, Henry Morgan, Raymond Burr, Arthur Franz. 84 min.

When his priest brother is murdered, a trucking company owner decides to take the law into his own hands. Unusual revenge thriller with an overt religious theme.

332. *Ride the Pink Horse* (1947) Universal. *Dir* Robert Montgomery. *Sc* Ben Hecht and Charles Lederer, from the novel by Dorothy B. Hughes. *Ph* Russell Metty. *Mus* Frank Skinner. *Cast* Robert Montgomery, Thomas Gomez, Wanda Hendrix, Rita Conde, Iris Flores, Andrea King, Art Smith, Fred Clark. 101 min.

Embittered veteran arrives in small Mexican town bent on revenge. Oft-mentioned noir adaption of significant hard-boiled suspense novel.

333. *Riot in Cell Block 11* (1954) Allied Artists. *Dir* Don Siegel. *Sc* Richard Collins. *Ph* Russell Harlan. *Mus* Herschel Burke Gilbert. *Cast* Neville Brand, Emile Meyer, Frank Faylen, Leo Gordon, Robert Osterloh. 80 min.

What happens when the inmates of a California penal institution are pushed too far. Tough, highly realistic prison film that doesn't mess around.

334. *Road House* (1948) 20th Century-Fox. *Dir* Jean Negulesco. *Sc* Edward Chodorov, from a story by Margaret Gruen and Oscar Saul. *Ph* Joseph La Shelle. *Mus* Cyril Mockridge. *Cast* Ida Lupino, Cornel Wilde, Celeste Holm, Richard Widmark, O.Z. Whitehead. 95 min.

Competing for the affections of a blues singer, unbalanced road house owner has his general manager framed from robbery. Interesting melodrama that has a crisp forties look and slowly builds to a noirish climax.

335. *Roadblock* (1951) RKO. *Dir* Harold Daniels. *Sc* Steve Fisher and George Bricker, from a story by Richard Landau and Geoffrey Homes (Daniel Mainwaring). *Ph* Nicholas Musuraca. *Mus* Paul Sawtell. *Cast* Charles McGraw, Joan Dixon, Lowell Gilmore, Louis Jean Heydt. 73 min.

Trying to please his ambitious girlfriend, insurance investigator gets himself involved in a robbery. Well-paced, fatalistic noir thriller with good performance by McGraw.

336. *Rogue Cop* (1954) MGM. *Dir* Roy Rowland. *Sc* Sydney Boehm, from the novel by William P. McGivern. *Ph* John F. Seitz. *Mus* Jeff Alexander. *Cast* Robert Taylor, Janet Leigh, George Raft, Steve Forrest, Anne Francis. 87 min.

Cop on the take vows to avenge the brutal killing of his younger brother.

337. *Rope of Sand* (1949) Paramount. *Dir* William Dieterle. *Sc* Walter Doniger. *Ph* Charles B. Lang. *Mus* Franz Waxman. *Cast* Burt Lancaster, Paul Henreid, Claude Rains, Peter Lorre, Corinne Calvet, Sam Jaffe, John Bromfield. 104 min.

Man returns to North African diamond country bent on stealing gems he was wrongly accused of taking several years earlier.

338. *Ruby Gentry* (1952) 20th Century-Fox. *Dir* King Vidor. *Sc* Silvia Richards, from a story by Arthur Fitz-Richard. *Ph* Russell Harlan. *Mus* Heinz Roemheld. *Cast* Jennifer Jones, Charlton Heston, Karl Malden, Tom Tully, James Anderson. 82 min.

A high-spirited girl from the wrong side of the tracks marries for money and position when her true love rejects her for the same. Unlikely combination of film noir and the implicit vitalism of King Vidor.

339. *Ruthless* (1948) Eagle Lion. *Dir* Edgar G. Ulmer. *Sc* S.K. Lauren and Gordon Kahn, from the novel *Prelude to Night* by Dayton Stoddart. *Ph* Bert Glennon. *Mus* Werner Janssen. *Cast* Zachary Scott, Louis Hayward, Sydney Greenstreet, Diana Lynn, Lucille Bremer, Martha Vickers, Raymond Burr. 104 min.

Man tells his girlfriend the story of a powerful financier that was his childhood pal. One of the most elegant and fascinating of all B noirs, that has been called Ulmer's *Citizen Kane*.

340. *Scandal Sheet* (1952) Columbia. *Dir* Phil Karlson. *Sc* Ted Sherdeman, Eugene Ling and James Poe, from the novel *The Dark Page* by

Samuel Fuller. *Ph* Burnett Guffey. *Mus* George Duning. *Cast* John Derek, Donna Reed, Broderick Crawford, Rosemary DeCamp, Henry O'Neill, Henry Morgan. 82 min.

Unscrupulous newspaper editor is driven to murder his wife; star reporter investigates the crime. Exposé of yellow journalism that is primarily a character study.

The Scar see *Hollow Triumph*

341. *The Scarf* (1951) United Artists. *Dir* E.A. Dupont. *Sc* Dupont, from the novel *The Dungeon* by I.G. Goldsmith and Edwin Rolfe (Dupont). *Ph* Franz Planer. *Mus* Herschel Burke Gilbert. *Cast* John Ireland, Mercedes McCambridge, Emlyn Williams, James Barton, Lloyd Gough. 93 min.

Man escapes from insane asylum, tries to convince crusty hermit, drifting saloon singer and himself that he is not a murderer. Little-known, offbeat noir that is probably German expatriate Dupont's most stylish and meaningful American film.

342. *Scarlet Street* (1945) Universal.

Sultry woman's boyfriend has her hook middle-aged clerk for his money, leading first to ironic and then tragic complications. Second of a pair of closely related middle class nightmares directed by Fritz Lang. (Remake of Jean Renoir's 1931 French film, *La Chienne*.) See page 30.

343. *Scene of the Crime* (1949) MGM. *Dir* Roy Rowland. *Sc* Charles Schnee, from a story by John Bartlow Martin. *Ph* Paul C. Vogel. *Mus* André Previn. *Cast* Van Johnson, Gloria De Haven, Tom Drake, Arlene Dahl, Leon Ames, John McIntire. 94 min.

Police detective investigates the case of a former partner that was murdered under circumstances which implicated him in a crooked payoff operation. Strong police drama with effective noir tone.

344. *Screaming Mimi* (1958) Columbia. *Dir* Gerd Oswald. *Sc* Robert Blees, from the novel by Fredric Brown. *Ph* Burnett Guffey. *Mus* Mischa Bakaleinikoff. *Cast* Anita Ekberg, Phil Carey, Gypsy Rose Lee, Harry Townes, Linda Cherney. 79 min.

Mentally disturbed dancer and her manager are linked to a series of murders.

345. *The Second Woman* (1951) United Artists. *Dir* James V. Kern. *Sc* Robert Smith and Mort Briskin. *Ph* Hal Mohr. *Mus* Nat Finston. *Cast* Robert Young, Betsy Drake, John Sutton, Florence Bates, Morris Carnovsky, Henry O'Neill. 91 min.

Successful architect, who feels responsible for his fiancee's accidental death, begins to doubt his own sanity. Somber noir melodrama with evocative postwar California setting.

346. *Secret Beyond the Door* (1948) Universal. *Dir* Fritz Lang. *Sc* Sylvia Richards, from a story by Rufus King. *Ph* Stanley Cortez. *Mus* Miklos Rozsa. *Cast* Joan Bennett, Michael Redgrave, Anne Revere, Natalie Schaefer, Paul Cavanagh. 98 min.

Woman marries successful architect, soon discovering that he is mentally unbalanced and may have murdered his first wife.

347. *The Secret Fury* (1950) RKO. *Dir* Mel Ferrer. *Sc* Lionel Houser, from a story by Jack R. Leonard and James O'Hanlon. *Ph* Leo Tover. *Mus* Roy Webb. *Cast* Claudette Colbert, Robert Ryan, Paul Kelly, Jane Cowl, Philip Ober. 85 min.

Instead of getting married, bride-to-be ends up in asylum charged with murder.

348. *The Sellout* (1952) MGM. *Dir* Gerald Mayer. *Sc* Charles Palmer, from a story by Matthew Rapf. *Ph* Paul C. Vogel. *Mus* David Buttolph. *Cast* Walter Pidgeon, John Hodiak, Audrey Totter, Paula Raymond, Thomas Gomez, Cameron Mitchell, Karl Malden, Everett Sloane. 83 min.

Crusading newpaper editor goes up against corrupt local sheriff.

349. *The Set-Up* (1949) RKO. *Dir* Robert Wise. *Sc* Art Cohn, from the poem by Joseph Moncure March. *Ph* Milton Krasner. *Mus* Constantin Bakaleinikoff. *Cast* Robert Ryan, Audrey Totter, George Tobias, Alan Baxter, Wallace Ford, James Edwards, Percy Helton, Darryl Hickman. 72 min.

A weary small-time fighter refuses to take a dive. The best boxing film of the cycle, that is a significant, expressive work by any standards.

350. *711 Ocean Drive* (1950) Columbia. *Dir* Joseph M. Newman. *Sc* Richard English and Francis Swan. *Ph* Franz Planer. *Mus* Sol Kaplan. *Cast* Edmond O'Brien, Joanne Dru, Don Porter, Sammy White, Dorothy Patrick, Barry Kelley, Otto Kruger. 102 min.

Former telephone repairman uses his technical knowledge to get strong foothold in syndicate gambling operation. One of O'Brien's better noirs, with a "powerful" climax at the Hoover Dam.

351. *The Seventh Victim* (1943) RKO. *Dir* Mark Robson. *Sc* Charles O'Neal, DeWitt Bodeen. *Ph* Nicholas Musuraca. *Mus* Roy Webb. *Cast* Tom Conway, Kim Hunter, Jean Brooks, Hugh Beaumont, Erford Gage, Isabel Jewell, Evelyn Brent. 71 min.

A young woman searches throughout the night for her disturbed sister, who has defected from a mysterious secret society. Though it belongs technically to the famous Val Lewton–produced "horror cycle," *The Seventh Victim* also deserves classification as a significant early noir.

352. *Shadow of a Doubt* (1943) Universal. *Dir* Alfred Hitchcock. *Sc* Thornton Wilder, Sally Benson and Alma Reville, from a story by Gordon McDonell. *Ph* Joseph Valentine. *Mus* Dimitri Tiomkin. *Cast* Teresa Wright, Joseph Cotten, MacDonald Carey, Henry Travers, Patricia Collinge, Hume Cronyn, Wallace Ford. 108 min.

A young woman suspects that her mysterious visiting uncle may be a murderer. Hitchcock's first full-fledged noir portrays a peaceful small American town that is menaced by that dark, ominous shadow which (in a sense deftly intimated) may plague us all.

353. *Shadow of a Woman* (1946) Warner Brothers. *Dir* Joseph

Santley. *Sc* Whitman Chambers and Graham Baker, from the novel *He Fell Down Dead* by Virginia Perdue. *Ph* Bert Glennon. *Mus* Adolph Deutsch. *Cast* Helmut Dantine, Andrea King, William Prince, John Alvin, Becky Brown, Dick Erdman. 78 min.

Woman on the verge of a breakdown marries a man she hardly knows, putting her in the path of fear and danger.

354. *Shadow of Fear* [original title, **Before I Wake**] (1956) United Artists. *Dir* Albert S. Rogell. *Sc* Robert Westerby, from the novel *Before I Wake* by Hal Debrett. *Ph* Jack Asher. *Mus* Leonard Salzedo. *Cast* Mona Freeman, Jean Kent, Maxwell Reed, Hugh Miller, Gretchen Franklin. 76 min.

Young woman returns from America after her father's death, soon realizes that her stepmother killed him and is planning the same for her. British-produced thriller with American star and director.

355. *Shadow on the Wall* (1950) MGM. *Dir* Pat Jackson. *Sc* William Ludwig, from the novel *Devil in the Doll's House* by Hannah Lees and Lawrence P. Bachmann. *Ph* Ray June. *Mus* André Previn. *Cast* Ann Sothern, Zachary Scott, Gigi Pereau, Nancy Davis, John McIntire, Barbara Billingsley. 84 min.

A six-year-old girl goes into shock after witnessing the murder of her mother; psychiatrist tries to break through to the truth.

356. *Shadow on the Window* (1957) Columbia. *Dir* William Asher. *Sc* Leo Townsend and David P. Harmon, from a story by John and Ward Hawkins. *Ph* Kit Carson. *Mus* George Duning. *Cast* Phil Carey, Betty Garrett, John Barrymore, Jr., Corey Allen, Jerry Mathers. 73 min.

Three criminals burglarize a farmhouse, kill the wealthy owner and hold his secretary hostage.

357. *Shakedown* (1950) Universal. *Dir* Joseph Pevney. *Sc* Alfred Lewis Levitt and Martin Goldsmith, from a story by Nat Dallinger and Don Martin. *Ph* Irving Glassberg. *Mus* Joseph Gershenson. *Cast* Howard Duff, Brian Donlevy, Peggy Dow, Lawrence Tierney, Bruce Bennett, Anne Vernon. 80 min.

Unscrupulous photographer gets involved with racketeers and murder.

358. *The Shanghai Gesture* (1941) United Artists. *Dir* Josef von Sternberg. *Sc* von Sternberg, Karl Vollmoeller, Geza Herczeg, and Jules Furthman, from the play by John Colton. *Ph* Paul Ivano. *Mus* Richard Hageman. *Cast* Gene Tierney, Walter Huston, Victor Mature, Ona Munson, Phyllis Brooks, Maria Ouspenskaya, Albert Basserman. 106 min.

British financier discovers that his long-lost daughter has become the victim of a decadent Shanghai gambling den. Significant early noir that prefigures postwar images of moral and spiritual dissolution.

359. *Shed No Tears* (1948) Eagle Lion. *Dir* Jean Yarbrough. *Sc* Brown Holmes and Virginia Cook, from the novel by Don Martin. *Ph* Frank Redman. *Mus* Ralph Stanley. *Cast* Wallace Ford, June Vincent, Robert Scott, Johnstone White. 70 min.

Man fakes his own death to collect insurance, then learns wife plans to double-cross him.

360. *Shield for Murder* (1954) United Artists. *Dir* Edmond O'Brien and Howard W. Koch. *Sc* Richard Alan Simmons and John C. Higgins, adapted by Simmons from the novel by William P. McGivern. *Ph* Gordon Avil. *Mus* Paul Dunlap. *Cast* Edmond O'Brien, Marla English, John Agar, Emile Meyer, Carolyn Jones, Claude Akins. 80 min.

When bookie refuses to make his regular payoff, crooked cop murders him and convinces his superiors that the killing was in the line of duty.

361. *Shock* (1946) 20th Century–Fox. *Dir* Alfred Werker. *Sc* Eugene Ling, from a story by Albert DeMond. *Ph* Glen MacWilliams, Joe MacDonald *Mus* David Buttolph. *Cast* Vincent Price. Lynn Bari, Frank Latimore, Anabel Shaw, Reed Hadley. 70 min.

A woman witnesses an act of murder, goes into shock and is "treated" by a psychiatrist who committed the crime. One of those formative noir thrillers which can't help but recall German Expressionism in plot, tone and style.

362. *Shockproof* (1949) Columbia. *Dir* Douglas Sirk. *Sc* Helen Deutsch and Samuel Fuller, from a story by Fuller. *Ph* Charles Lawton. *Mus* George Duning. *Cast* Cornel Wilde, Patricia Knight, John Baragrey, Esther Minciotti, Howard St. John. 79 min.

A woman and her parole officer fall in love; he leaves his job and is drawn into her furtive criminal life. Sirk's most personal, complex and provocative noir, despite a studio-imposed "happy ending."

363. *Shoot to Kill* (1947) Screen Guild. *Dir* William Berke. *Sc* Edwin Westrate. *Ph* Benjamin Kline. *Mus* Darrell Calker. *Cast* Russell Wade, Susan Walters, Edmund MacDonald, Douglas Blackley. 64 min.

Woman becomes involved with crooked D.A. who framed her aspiring husband.

364. *Short Cut to Hell* (1957) Paramount. *Dir* James Cagney. *Sc* Ted Berkman, Ralph Blau and W.R. Burnett, from the novel *This Gun for Hire* by Grahame Greene. *Ph* Haskell Boggs. *Mus* Irvin Talbot. *Cast* Robert Ivers, Georgann Johnson, William Bishop, Peter Baldwin, Murvyn Vye, Yvette Vickers. 87 min.

Syndicate assassin realizes he's been double-crossed. Updated, low budget remake of *This Gun for Hire*.

365. *Side Street* (1950) MGM. *Dir* Anthony Mann. *Sc* Sydney Boehm. *Ph* Joseph Ruttenberg. *Mus* Lennie Hayton. *Cast* Farley Granger, Cathy O'Donnell, James Craig, Paul Kelly, Jean Hagen, Paul Harvey, Charles McGraw. 83 min.

Mailman's inadvertent act of theft snowballs into a nightmarish web of danger and guilt, from which he tries desperately to escape.

366. *The Sign of the Ram* (1948) Columbia. *Dir* John Sturges. *Sc* Charles Bennett, from the novel by Margaret Ferguson. *Ph* Burnett Guffey. *Mus* Hans J. Salter. *Cast* Susan Peters, Alexander Knox, Phyllis Thaxter, Peggy Ann Garner, Ron Randell. 88 min.

A crippled woman dominates and manipulates all those around her.

367. *Singapore* (1947) Universal. *Dir* John Brahm. *Sc* Seton I. Miller and Robert Thoeren, from a story by Miller. *Ph* Maury Gertsman. *Mus* Daniele Amfitheatrof. *Cast* Fred MacMurray, Ava Gardner, Roland Culver, Richard Hadyn, Spring Byington, Thomas Gomez. 79 min.

American adventurer returns to Singapore for pearls he had hidden during the war, encounters his former girlfriend who he thought was dead. Nicely integrated elements of noir style and plot.

368. *Sirocco* (1951) Columbia. *Dir* Curtis Bernhardt. *Sc* A.I. Bezzerides and Hans Jacoby, from the novel by Joseph Kessel. *Ph* Burnett Guffey. *Mus* George Antheil. *Cast* Humphrey Bogart, Marta Toren, Lee J. Cobb, Everett Sloane, Gerald Mohr, Zero Mostel. 98 min.

Mercenary gun runner gets caught in the middle of 1925 middle east rebellion. Somber little film with good use of Bogart's screen persona.

369. *Sleep, My Love* (1948) United Artists. *Dir* Douglas Sirk. *Sc* St. Clair McKelway and Leo Rosten, from the novel by Rosten. *Ph* Joseph Valentine. *Mus* Rudy Schrager. *Cast* Claudette Colbert, Robert Cummings, Don Ameche, Rita Johnson, George Coulouris, Hazel Brooks. 97 min.

Man hatches cunning plot to drive his socialite wife to suicide. Noirish lady-in-distress narrative with some good details.

370. *The Sleeping City* (1950) Universal. *Dir* George Sherman. *Sc* Jo Eisinger. *Ph* William Miller. *Mus* Frank Skinner. *Cast* Richard Conte, Coleen Gray, Peggy Dow, John Alexander, Alex Nicol. 85 min.

Police detective investigates murder by posing as an intern at a large metropolitan hospital. Forceful melodrama in which another "sacred American institution" has its unspoiled image shattered by the all-pervasive noir vision.

371. *The Sleeping Tiger* (1954) Astor. *Dir* Joseph Losey (credited to Victor Hanbury). *Sc* Harold Buchman and Carl Foreman, from the novel by Maurice Moisewisch. *Ph* Harry Waxman. *Mus* Malcolm Arnold. *Cast* Dirk Bogarde, Alexis Smith, Alexander Knox, Hugh Griffith, Patricia McCarron. 89 min.

Psychiatrist brings criminal home for study, arousing the interest of his bored middle-class wife. This film noir (which still seems largely in the American tradition) marks the beginning of Joseph Losey's distinguished British career.

372. *The Sniper* (1952) Columbia. *Dir* Edward Dmytryk. *Sc* Harry Brown, from a story by Edna and Edward Anhalt. *Ph* Burnett Guffey. *Mus* George Antheil. *Cast* Adolphe Menjou, Arthur Franz, Gerald Mohr, Marie Windsor, Richard Kiley, Frank Faylen. 87 min.

A disturbed young man is compelled to shoot women from rooftops throughout the city. Intense, believable portrait of a psychopath's torment.

373. *So Dark the Night* (1946) Columbia. *Dir* Joseph H. Lewis. *Sc* Martin Berkeley and Dwight Babcock, from a story by Aubrey Wisberg. *Ph* Burnett Guffey. *Mus* Hugo Friedhofer. *Cast* Steven Geray, Micheline Cheirel, Eugene Borden, Ann Codee, Egon Brecher. 70 min.

Parisian police detective on vacation in small country village falls in love with young girl, who then becomes the first of several murder victims. Tasteful B film which treats ironic murder theme with significance and depth.

374. *So Evil My Love* (1949) Paramount. *Dir* Lewis Allen. *Sc* Leonard Spigelgass and Ronald Millar, from the novel *For Her to See* by Joseph Shearing. *Ph* Max Greene. *Mus* Victor Young, William Alwyn. *Cast* Ann Todd, Ray Milland, Geraldine Fitzgerald, Moira Lister, Raymond Huntley, Leo G. Carroll. 109 min.

Spinsterish woman falls for unregenerate artist that leads her into a dark web of blackmail and murder. Victorian melodrama that witnesses the complete transformation of its straight-laced female protagonist into an unflinching murderess.

375. *Somewhere in the Night* (1946) 20th Century-Fox. *Dir* Joseph L. Mankiewicz. *Sc* Mankiewicz and Howard Dimsdale, adapted by Lee Strasberg from a story by Marvin Borowsky. *Ph* Norbert Brodine. *Mus* David Buttolph. *Cast* John Hodiak, Nancy Guild, Lloyd Nolan, Richard Conte, Josephine Hutchinson, Fritz Kortner, Sheldon Leonard. 110 min.

While searching for his true identity, amnesiac war veteran gets tangled up with the murderous thieves of precious Nazi war booty. Quintessential postwar amnesia film.

376. *Sorry, Wrong Number* (1948) Paramount. *Dir* Anatole Litvak. *Sc* Lucille Fletcher, from her radio play. *Ph* Sol Polito. *Mus* Franz Waxman. *Cast* Barbara Stanwyck, Burt Lancaster, Ann Richards, Wendell Corey, Ed Begley, Leif Erickson, William Conrad, John Bromfield. 90 min.

An invalid heiress hears a murder plan through crossed telephone wires, gradually realizes that she's to be the victim. One of those auspicious meldings of high noir style and content that depicts a grim, hysterical situation with maximum levels of narrative depth, credibility and suspense.

The Sound of Fury see Try and Get Me

377. *Southside 1-1000* (1950) Allied Artists. *Dir* Boris Ingster. *Sc* Leo Townsend and Ingster, from a story by Milton M. Raison and Bert C. Brown. *Ph* Russell Harlan. *Mus* Paul Sawtell. *Cast* Don DeFore, Andrea King, George Tobias, Barry Kelley, Morris Ankrum. 73 min.

T-man goes undercover to track down the source of high quality counterfeit bills.

378. *Specter of the Rose* (1946) Republic. *Dir* Ben Hecht. *Sc* Hecht. *Ph* Lee Garmes. *Mus* George Antheil. *Cast* Judith Anderson, Michael Chekhov, Ivan Kirov, Viola Essen, Lionel Stander, Charles (Red) Marshall. 90 min.

Brilliant ballet dancer teeters on the brink of insanity. Engaging, bizarre Hecht melodrama with noirish cutting edge.

379. *Spellbound* (1945) United Artists. *Dir* Alfred Hitchcock. *Sc* Ben Hecht, adapted by Angus MacPhail, from the novel *The House of Dr. Edwards* by Francis Beeding. *Ph* George Barnes. *Mus* Miklos Rozsa. *Cast* Ingrid Bergman, Gregory Peck, Leo G. Carroll, Michael Chekhov, Rhonda Fleming, John Emery, Norman Lloyd, Steven Geray. 111 min.

A victim of psychological shock who fears that he is a murderer is given aid by a female psychiatrist. The first Hollywood film to embrace overt Freudianism also owes a debt to German Expressionism (*The Cabinet of Dr. Caligari*) and Salvador Dali (for contributing an impressive surrealist dream sequence).

380. *The Spider* (1945) 20th Century-Fox. *Dir* Robert D. Webb. *Sc* Jo Eisinger and W. Scott Darling, from a story by Charles Fulton Oursler and Lowell Brentano. *Ph* Glen MacWilliams. *Mus* David Buttolph. *Cast* Richard Conte, Faye Marlowe, Kurt Kreuger, John Harvey, Martin Kosleck. 61 min.

A private detective is pursued by both police and a mysterious killer.

381. *The Spiral Staircase* (1946) RKO. *Dir* Robert Siodmak. *Sc* Mel Dinelli, from the novel *Some Must Watch* by Ethel Lena White. *Ph* Nicholas Musuraca. *Mus* Roy Webb. *Cast* Dorothy McGuire, George Brent, Ethel Barrymore, Kent Smith, Rhonda Fleming, Gordon Oliver, Elsa Lanchester, Rhys Williams. 83 min.

Mute servant becomes the target of psycho-killer that preys on handicapped women. Eerie gothic thriller, strong on mood, suspense and resonance.

382. *Stage Fright* (1950) Warner Brothers. *Dir* Alfred Hitchcock. *Sc* Whitfield Cook, adapted by Alma Reville, from two stories by Selwyn Jepson. *Ph* Wilkie Cooper. *Mus* Leighton Lucas. *Cast* Marlene Dietrich, Jane Wyman, Michael Wilding, Richard Todd, Alastair Sim, Sybil Thorndike. 110 min.

Trusting young woman is befriended by a man sought for murder. Clever, deceptive Hitchcock thriller with controversial flashback sequence.

383. *The Steel Jungle* (1956) Warner Brothers. *Dir* Walter Doniger. *Sc* Doniger. *Ph* J. Peverell Marley. *Mus* David Buttolph. *Cast* Perry Lopez, Beverly Garland, Walter Abel, Ted de Corsia, Ken Tobey, Leo Gordon. 86 min.

Prison drama in which a man is encouraged to betray his boss, who is a racketeer.

384. *The Steel Trap* (1952) 20th Century- Fox. *Dir* Andrew L. Stone. *Sc* Stone. *Ph* Ernest Laszlo. *Mus* Dimitri Tiomkin. *Cast* Joseph Cotten, Teresa Wright, Jonathan Hale, Walter Sande, Tom Powers. 85 min.

Tense, realistic thriller of banker's attempt at robbing the vault without detection.

385. *Step Down to Terror* (1959) Universal. *Dir* Harry Keller. *Sc* Mel Dinelli, Czenzi Ormonde, and Chris Cooper, from a story by Gordon McDonell. *Mus* Joseph Gershenson. *Ph* Russell Metty. *Cast* Charles Drake, Colleen Miller, Rod Taylor, Josephine Hutchinson, Jocelyn Brando. 75 min.

A son returns home to his family for ominous reasons. Low budget remake of *Shadow of a Doubt*.

386. *Storm Fear* (1956) United Artists. *Dir* Cornel Wilde. *Sc* Horton Foote, from the novel by Clinton Seeley. *Ph* Joseph La Shelle. *Mus* Elmer Bernstein. *Cast* Cornel Wilde, Jean Wallace, Dan Duryea, Lee Grant, David Stollery, Dennis Weaver, Steven Hill. 88 min.

Wounded bank robber takes refuge at New England farmhouse of his brother, dredging up tensions and guilt from the past.

387. *Storm Warning*. (1950) Warner Brothers. *Dir* Stuart Heisler. *Sc* Daniel Fuchs and Richard Brooks, from a story by Fuchs. *Ph* Eugene Ritchie. *Mus* Daniele Amfitheatrof. *Cast* Ginger Rogers, Ronald Reagan, Doris Day, Steve Cochran, Hugh Sanders, Stuart Randall, Sean McClory. 93 min.

A woman stops in a small southern town to visit her sister, gets caught in the middle of a Ku Klux Klan reign of terror. Forceful, neglected Warners thriller, whose problem subject is attacked within a total, integrated noir context.

388. *The Strange Affair of Uncle Harry* [also titled **Uncle Harry**] (1945) Universal. *Dir* Robert Siodmak. *Sc* Stephen Longstreet, adapted by Keith Winter, from the play by Thomas Job. *Ph* Paul Ivano. *Mus* Hans J. Salter. *Cast* George Sanders, Geraldine Fitzgerald. Ella Raines, Sara Allgood, Moyna MacGill, Samuel S. Hinds. 80 min.

Middle-aged bachelor has marriage plans spoiled by one of the two spinsterish sisters he lives with, causing him to take drastic action. Siodmak's version of the repressed bourgeois nightmare.

389. *Strange Bargain* (1949) RKO. *Dir* Will Price. *Sc* Lillie Hayward, from a story by J.H. Wallis. *Ph* Harry Wild. *Mus* Frederick Hollander. *Cast* Martha Scott, Jeffrey Lynn, Henry Morgan, Katherine Emery, Henry O'Neill, Walter Sande. 68 min.

A bookkeeper in need of money agrees against his own better judgment to help a wealthy man carry out an elaborate suicide plan.

390. *Strange Fascination* (1952) Columbia. *Dir* Hugo Haas. *Sc* Haas. *Ph* Paul Ivano. *Mus* Vaclav Divina. *Cast* Cleo Moore, Hugo Haas, Mona Barrie, Rick Vallin, Karen Sharpe. 80 min.

A beautiful *femme fatale* ruins a pianist's life.

391. *Strange Illusion* (1945) PRC. *Dir* Edgar G. Ulmer. *Sc* Adele Commandini, from a story by Fritz Rotter. *Ph* Philip Tannura. *Mus* Leo Erdody. *Cast* James Lydon, Warren William, Sally Eilers, Regis Toomey. 84 min.

Adolescent believes that his widowed mother's suitor may have murdered his father. Stylish cheapie by the recognized master of stylish cheapies.

392. *Strange Impersonation* (1946) Republic. *Dir* Anthony Mann. *Sc* Mindret Lord, from a story by Anne Wigton and Louis Herman. *Ph* Robert W. Pittack. *Mus* Alexander Laszlo. *Cast* Brenda Marshall, William Gargan, Hillary Brooke, George Chandler, H.B. Warner. 68 min.

A disfigured woman scientist undergoes plastic surgery and then assumes the identity of a dead blackmailer.

393. *The Strange Love of Martha Ivers* (1946) Paramount. *Dir* Lewis Milestone. *Sc* Robert Rossen, from a story by Jack Patrick. *Ph* Victor Milner. *Mus* Miklos Rozsa. *Cast* Barbara Stanwyck, Van Heflin, Lizabeth Scott, Kirk Douglas, Judith Anderson, Roman Bohnen, Darryl Hickman. 115 min.

Man is waylaid by chance in old home town, meets a girl down on her luck and a turbulent couple with whom he shares a dark childhood secret. Significant noir melodrama focusing on provocative, intermingling relationships of neurotic love, guilt and fear.

394. *Strange Triangle* (1946) 20th Century-Fox. *Dir* Ray McCarey. *Sc* Mortimer Braus, adapted by Charles G. Booth, from a story by Jack Andrews. *Ph* Harry Jackson. *Mus* David Buttolph. *Cast* Signe Hasso, Preston Foster, Anabel Shaw, John Shepperd, Roy Roberts. 65 min.

A bank examiner becomes involved with a couple planning embezzlement, which then leads to murder.

395. *The Strange Woman* (1946) United Artists. *Dir* Edgar G. Ulmer. *Sc* Herb Meadow, from the novel by Ben Ames Williams. *Ph* Lucien Andriot. *Mus* Carmen Dragon. *Cast* Hedy Lamarr, George Sanders, Louis Hayward, Gene Lockhart, Hillary Brooke, Rhys Williams. 100 min.

Ambitious, predatory woman destroys several men on her way to the top of New England society.

396. *The Stranger* (1946) RKO. *Dir* Orson Welles. *Sc* Anthony Veiller (with Orson Welles and John Huston, uncredited), from a story by Victor Trivas. *Ph* Russell Metty. *Mus* Bronislau Kaper. *Cast* Edward G. Robinson, Loretta Young, Orson Welles, Philip Merivale, Billy House, Richard Long. 95 min.

A diabolical Nazi war criminal is traced by a government agent to a peaceful New England college town. The lesser of Welles' two forties noir films is still distinguished by its sense of grotesquerie and disturbing portrayal of a barely detectable menace.

397. *Stranger on the Prowl* (1953) United Artists. *Dir* Joseph Losey (under the pseudonyn Andrea Forzano). *Sc* Ben Barzman, from a story by Noel Calef. *Ph* Henri Alekan. *Mus* G.C. Sonzogno. *Cast* Paul Muni, Joan Lorring, Vittorio Manunta, Aldo Silvani. 82 min. (originally 180 min. cut to 100 for British release).

Disillusioned vagrant accidentally kills shop owner, is joined by rebellious youngster in his flight from apprehension. International production, filmed in Italy during the Hollywood blacklisting debacle.

398. *The Stranger on the Third Floor* (1940) RKO. *Dir* Boris Ingster. *Sc* Frank Partos. *Ph* Nicholas Musuraca. *Mus* Roy Webb. *Cast* Peter Lorre, John McGuire, Margaret Tallichet, Charles Waldron, Elisha Cook, Jr. 64 min.

After his testimony convicts a man of murder, a newspaper reporter is gnawed by fear and guilt. Often referred to as the first true or total film noir, *Stranger on the Third Floor* is, among other things, replete with provocative nightmare images.

399. *Strangers in the Night* (1944) Republic. *Dir* Anthony Mann. *Sc* Bryant Ford, Paul Gangelin, from the story by Philip MacDonald. *Ph* Reggie Lanning. *Mus* Morton Scott. *Cast* William Terry, Virginia Grey, Helene Thimig, Edith Barrett. 56 min.

Unbalanced woman invents a daughter, and is pushed over the brink when her phantom's pen pal soldier returns home. Eerie low budget melodrama evincing several early noir elements of plot and style.

400. *Strangers on a Train* (1951) Warner Brothers. *Dir* Alfred Hitchcock. *Sc* Raymond Chandler and Czenzi Ormonde, adapted by Whitfield

Cook, from the novel by Patricia Highsmith. *Ph* Robert Burks. *Mus* Dimitri Tiomkin. *Cast* Farley Granger, Ruth Roman, Robert Walker, Leo G. Carroll, Laura Elliott, Patricia Hitchcock. 101 min.

Two men meet on a train, one of them suggesting that they exchange convenient murders. Ultimate example of Hitchcock's famous transfer-of-guilt theme, with plenty of suspense and an outstanding "attractive villain" role by Robert Walker.

401. *Street of Chance* (1942) Paramount. *Dir* Jack Hively. *Sc*
Garrett Fort, from the novel *The Black Curtain* by Cornell Woolrich. *Ph* Theodor Sparkul. *Mus* David Buttolph. *Cast* Burgess Meredith, Claire Trevor, Louise Platt, Sheldon Leonard, Frieda Inescort, Jerome Cowan. 74 min.

A man has an accident at work, returns home and is told by his wife that he has been missing for a year. The original noir amnesia story, which was also the first adaption of a Cornell Woolrich novel.

402. *The Street with No Name* (1948) 20th Century-Fox. *Dir*
William Keighley. *Sc* Harry Kleiner. *Ph* Joe MacDonald. *Mus* Lionel Newman. *Cast* Mark Stevens, Richard Widmark, Lloyd Nolan, Barbara Lawrence, Ed Begley, Donald Buka, Joseph Pevney, John McIntire. 91 min.

F.B.I. agent goes undercover to get the goods on a death-dealing robbery gang. Semidocumentary thriller with noir style to spare.

403. *The Strip* (1951) MGM. *Dir* Leslie Kardos. *Sc* Allen Rivkin. *Ph*
Robert Surtees. *Mus* Georgie Stoll. *Cast* Mickey Rooney, Sally Forrest, William Demarest, James Craig. 84 min.

Jazz drummer and aspiring actress become involved with racketeers, ending in violent tragedy. Los Angeles jazz scene nicely woven into tough noir plot.

404. *Sudden Danger* (1955) United Artists. *Dir* Hubert Cornfield.
Sc Dan and Elwood Ullman. *Ph* Ellsworth Fredricks. *Mus* Marlin Skiles. *Cast* Bill Elliott, Tom Drake, Beverly Garland, Dayton Lummis, Lucien Littlefield, Minerva Urecal, Lyle Talbot. 85 min.

A blind man has his sight restored through an operation, then sets out to clear himself of a murder charge.

405. *Sudden Fear* (1952) RKO. *Dir* David Miller. *Sc* Lenore Coffee
and Robert Smith, from the novel by Edna Sherry. *Ph* Charles B. Lang, Jr. *Mus* Elmer Bernstein. *Cast* Joan Crawford, Jack Palance, Gloria Grahame, Bruce Bennett, Virginia Huston. 110 min.

Heiress/playwright marries an ambitious actor she has rejected for one of her plays, soon realizes that he plans to kill her. Undoubtedly one of the most stylish and refined woman-in-distress noirs.

406. *Suddenly* (1954) United Artists. *Dir* Lewis Allen. *Sc* Richard
Sale. *Ph* Charles Clarke. *Mus* David Raksin. *Cast* Frank Sinatra, Sterling Hayden, James Gleason, Nancy Gates. 77 min.

Three gunmen, who have been hired to assassinate the President, hold a family hostage while waiting for their target. Interesting B film which focuses on psychopathic killer well-portrayed against type by Frank Sinatra.

407. *The Sun Sets at Dawn* (1950) Eagle Lion. *Dir* Paul H. Sloane. *Sc* Sloane, from his story. *Ph* Lionel Lindon. *Mus* Leith Stevens. *Cast* Philip Shawn, Sally Parr, Howard St. John, King Donovan, Percy Helton. 71 min.

Flashbacks relate how man on death row was falsely convicted of murder.

408. *Sunset Boulevard* (1950) Paramount. *Dir* Billy Wilder. *Sc* Charles Brackett, Wilder, and D.M. Marshman, Jr. *Ph* John F. Seitz. *Mus* Franz Waxman. *Cast* William Holden, Gloria Swanson, Erich von Stroheim, Nancy Olson, Fred Clark, Jack Webb. 115 min.

A mercenary Hollywood writer tells how involvement with an aging silent film star led to his own murder. Film noir looks at the phenomena of its source, filtered most appropriately through the sardonic wit and cynicism of Billy Wilder.

409. *The Suspect* (1945) Universal. *Dir* Robert Siodmak. *Sc* Bertram Millhouser, adapted by Arthur T. Horman, from the novel *This Way Out* by James Ronald. *Ph* Paul Ivano. *Mus* Frank Skinner. *Cast* Charles Laughton, Ella Raines, Henry Daniell, Rosalind Ivan, Dean Harens, Stanley Ridges. 85 min.

Middle-aged tobacconist dreams of a new life with a beautiful young girl, is driven to murder his shrewish wife. Masterful Victorian melodrama that disturbs by generating quite a lot of sympathy for its doomed protagonist.

410. *Suspense* (1946) Monogram. *Dir* Frank Tuttle. *Sc* Phillip Yordan. *Ph* Karl Struss. *Mus* Daniele Amfitheatrof. *Cast* Barry Sullivan, Belita, Albert Dekker, Eugene Pallette, Bonita Granville. 101 min.

Promoter's illicit involvement with star of ice show leads to deception and murder. Strange film, with expressive sets and visuals, that was one of Monogram's only A productions.

411. *Suspicion* (1941) RKO. *Dir* Alfred Hitchcock. *Sc* Samson Raphaelson, Joan Harrison and Alma Reville, from the novel *Before the Fact* by Francis Iles. *Ph* Harry Stradling. *Mus* Franz Waxman. *Cast* Joan Fontaine, Cary Grant, Nigel Bruce, Sir Cedric Hardwicke, Dame May Whitty, Isabel Jeans, Leo G. Carroll. 99 min.

A woman begins to suspect that her new husband is planning to kill her. Important early psychological picture that was a prototype of the "woman-in-distress" thriller.

412. *Sweet Smell of Success* (1957) United Artists. *Dir* Alexander MacKendrick. *Sc* Clifford Odets, adapted by Ernest Lehman, from his story. *Ph* James Wong Howe. *Mus* Elmer Bernstein. *Cast* Burt Lancaster, Tony Curtis, Susan Harrison, Martin Milner, Sam Levene, Emile Meyer. 96 min.

Ruthless Broadway columnist has young jazz musician, who's courting his sister, smeared as a dope addict and Communist sympathizer. One of the most powerful and important late noirs, with poetic Odets dialogue, striking performances and visuals.

413. *The System* (1953) Warner Brothers. *Dir* Lewis Seiler. *Sc* Jo Eisinger, from a story by Edith and Samuel Grafton. *Ph* Edwin Dupar. *Mus* David Buttolph. *Cast* Frank Lovejoy, Joan Weldon, Robert Arthur, Paul Picerni, Don Beddoe, Jerome Cowan. 90 min.

Honest bookmaker learns the hard way that his line of work is a lot more dangerous and destructive than he thought.

414. *T-Men* (1948) Eagle Lion. *Dir* Anthony Mann. *Sc* John C. Higgins (and Mann uncredited), from a story by Virginia Kellogg. *Ph* John Alton. *Mus* Paul Sawtell. *Cast* Dennis O'Keefe, Alfred Ryder, Mary Meade, Wallace Ford, Art Smith, Charles McGraw, June Lockhart. 92 min.

Two treasury agents pose as small-time hoods in an effort to infiltrate counterfeiting ring. One of the most significant noir *policiers*, with dynamic visuals and provocative direction that combine to deflect the script's conventional law-and-order stance.

415. *Take One False Step* (1949) Universal. *Dir* Chester Erskine. *Sc* Irwin Shaw and Erskine, from a story by Irwin and David Shaw. *Ph* Franz Planer. *Mus* Walter Scharf. *Cast* William Powell, Shelley Winters, Marsha Hunt, Dorothy Hart, James Gleason, Sheldon Leonard. 94 min.

Married college professor agrees to have a drink with old girlfriend; the next day he's being hunted for her murder.

416. *Talk About a Stranger* (1952) MGM. *Dir* David Bradley. *Sc* Margaret Fitts, from a story by Charlotte Armstrong. *Ph* John Alton. *Mus* David Buttolph. *Cast* George Murphy, Nancy Davis, Billy Gray, Lewis Stone, Kurt Kasznar. 65 min.

Young boy is convinced that a new neighbor has poisoned his dog. Atypical film with good visuals that encourages the viewer to identify with a paranoid juvenile.

417. *The Tattooed Stranger* (1950) RKO. *Dir* Edward J. Montagne. *Sc* Phil Reisman, Jr. *Ph* William Steiner. *Mus* Alan Schulman. *Cast* John Miles, Patricia White, Walter Kinsella, Frank Tweddell. 64 min.

A rookie detective heads up the investigation of a series of brutal murders. Cheapie *policier* set in New York City.

418. *Temptation* (1946) Universal. *Dir* Irving Pichel. *Sc* Robert Thoeren, from the novel *Bella Donna* by Robert Hitchens, and the play by James Bernard Fagen. *Ph* Lucien Ballard. *Mus* Daniele Amfitheatrof. *Cast* Merle Oberon, Paul Lukas, George Brent, Charles Korvin, Lenore Ulric, Arnold Moss. 92 min.

Victorian melodrama, set in Egypt, of refined woman whose illicit affair leads to murder. Well-mounted portrait of an ambiguous *femme fatale*.

419. *Tension* (1949) MGM. *Dir* John Berry. *Sc* Allen Rivkin, from a story by John Klorer. *Ph* Harry Stradling. *Mus* André Previn. *Cast* Richard Basehart, Audrey Totter, Cyd Charisse, Barry Sullivan, Lloyd Gough, William Conrad. 95 min.

Meek druggist devises elaborate plan for murdering his two-timing spouse. Top-rate, cynical murder thriller.

420. *Terror at Midnight* (1956) Republic. *Dir* Franklin Adreon. *Sc* John K. Butler, from a story by Butler and Irving Shulman. *Ph* Bud Thackery.

Mus R. Dale Butts. *Cast* Scott Brady, Joan Vohs, Frank Faylen, John Dehner, Virginia Gregg. 70 min.
Police detective's girlfriend is involved in accident and blackmailed.

Thelma Jordon see *The File on Thelma Jordon*

421. *They Drive by Night* (1940) Warner Brothers. *Dir* Raoul Walsh. *Sc* Jerry Wald and Richard Macaulay, from the novel *The Long Haul* by A.I. Bezzerides. *Ph* Arthur Edeson. *Mus* Adolph Deutsch. *Cast* George Raft, Humphrey Bogart, Ann Sheridan, Ida Lupino, Alan Hale, Gale Page, Roscoe Karns. 93 min.
Two independent truck drivers struggle to stay in business and alive. Raoul Walsh classic with clearly visible elements of an early noir sensibility.

422. *They Live by Night* [British title, The Twisted Road] (1949) RKO. *Dir* Nicholas Ray. *Sc* Charles Schnee, adapted by Ray from the novel *Thieves Like Us* by Edward Anderson. *Ph* George E. Diskant. *Mus* Leigh Harline. *Cast* Cathy O'Donnell, Farley Granger, Howard da Silva, Jay C. Flippen, Helen Craig. 95 min.
A young criminal falls in love with an innocent girl, and together they make a desperate attempt to start a new life. Nicholas Ray's first film is an extremely emotional depiction of two human beings "who were never properly introduced to the world."

423. *They Won't Believe Me* (1947) RKO. *Dir* Irving Pichel. *Sc* Jonathan Latimer, from a story by Gordon McDonell. *Ph* Harry J. Wild. *Mus* Roy Webb. *Cast* Robert Young, Susan Hayward, Jane Greer, Rita Johnson, Tom Powers, Don Beddoe. 95 min.
A man's involvement with several women leads to an ironic murder charge. Notable, lesser-known film noir with a strong sense of sexual malaise.

424. *The Thief* (1952) United Artists. *Dir* Russell Rouse. *Sc* Clarence Greene and Rouse. *Ph* Sam Leavitt. *Mus* Herschel Burke Gilbert. *Cast* Ray Milland, Martin Gabel, Rita Gam, Harry Bronson. 87 min.
Scientist who sells secrets to the Communists becomes "hot" and prepares to leave the country. Unique film, very strong on mood and suspense, that runs its entire length without a word uttered.

425. *Thieves' Highway* (1949) 20th Century-Fox. *Dir* Jules Dassin. *Sc* A.I. Bezzerides, from his novel *Thieves' Market*. *Ph* Norbert Brodine. *Mus* Alfred Newman. *Cast* Richard Conte, Valentina Cortesa, Lee J. Cobb, Barbara Lawrence, Jack Oakie, Millard Mitchell, Joseph Pevney, Morris Carnovsky. 94 min.
Ex-GI truck driver becomes involved with sultry refugee while battling crooked fruit wholesaler. Robust, violent proletarian melodrama.

426. *The Thirteenth Letter* (1951) 20th Century-Fox. *Dir* Otto Preminger. *Sc* Howard Koch, from a story and screenplay by Louis Chavance. *Ph* Joseph La Shelle. *Mus* Alex North. *Cast* Linda Darnell, Charles Boyer, Michael Rennie, Constance Smith, Francoise Rosay, 88 min.
Mysterious poison pen letters shatter the tranquility of a small Canadian

village. Suspenseful remake of the French noir masterpiece, *Le Corbeau* (Clouzot, 1943).

427. *This Gun for Hire* (1942) Paramount. *Dir* Frank Tuttle. *Sc* Albert Maltz and W.R. Burnett, from the novel by Grahame Greene. *Ph* John F. Seitz. *Mus* David Buttolph. *Cast* Alan Ladd, Veronica Lake, Robert Preston, Laird Cregar, Tully Marshall. 80 min.

Hired killer is paid for a job with "hot" money, goes after his employer with police in pursuit. Important, meaningful early noir which links the cycle with British suspense novels of that period.

428. *This Side of the Law* (1950) Warner Brothers. *Dir* Richard Bare. *Sc* Russell Hughes, suggested by a Richard Sale story. *Ph* Carl Guthrie. *Mus* William Lava. *Cast* Viveca Lindfors, Kent Smith, Janis Paige, Robert Douglas, Monte Blue. 74 min.

Man is hired by crooked lawyer to impersonate wealthy client whom he strongly resembles.

429. *This Woman Is Dangerous* (1952) Warner Brothers. *Dir* Felix Feist. *Sc* Geoffrey Homes (Daniel Mainwaring), and George Worthing Yates, from a story by Bernard Girard. *Ph* Ted McCord. *Mus* David Buttolph. *Cast* Joan Crawford, Dennis Morgan, David Brian, Richard Webb, Phil Carey, Sherry Jackson. 97 min.

Tough lady criminal falls for surgeon attempting to restore her failing eyesight, but the past won't let her go without a fight. Interesting, well-paced Warners B thriller.

430. *The Threat* (1949) RKO. *Dir* Felix Feist. *Sc* Hugh King and Dick Irving, from a story by King. *Ph* Harry Wild. *Mus* Paul Sawtell. *Cast* Michael O'Shea, Virginia Grey, Charles McGraw, Julie Bishop. 66 min.

Vengeful killer escapes from prison, kidnaps three who helped jail him.

431. *Three Steps North* (1951) United Artists. *Dir* W. Lee Wilder. *Sc* Lester Fuller, from a story by Robert Harari. *Ph* Aldo Giordani. *Mus* Roman Vlad. *Cast* Lloyd Bridges, Lea Padovani, Aldo Fabrizi, William C. Tubbs. 85 min.

An ex-soldier returns to Italy to recover black market loot he had buried there during the war.

432. *Three Strangers* (1946) Warner Brothers. *Dir* Jean Negulesco. *Sc* John Huston and Howard Koch. *Ph* Arthur Edeson. *Mus* Adolph Deutsch. *Cast* Sydney Greenstreet, Geraldine Fitzgerald, Peter Lorre, Joan Lorring, Robert Shayne, Marjorie Riordan. 92 min.

Three strangers attempt to follow old Chinese superstition by sharing a sweepstakes ticket under prescribed conditions, resulting in tragedy for all concerned. Nicely structured parable of greed and fate.

433. *Tight Spot* (1955) Columbia. *Dir* Phil Karlson. *Sc* William Bowers, from a novel by Leonard Kantor. *Ph* Burnett Guffey. *Mus* George Duning. *Cast* Ginger Rogers, Edward G. Robinson, Brian Keith, Lorne Greene. 97 min.

Clever, ironic narrative of female convict being taken from prison and guarded by tough cop so she can testify against her former boyfriend.

434. *Timetable* (1956) United Artists. *Dir* Mark Stevens. *Sc* Aben Kandel, from a story by Robert Angus. *Ph* Charles Van Enger. *Mus* Walter Scharf. *Cast* Mark Stevens, King Calder, Felicia Farr, Marianne Stewart, Wesley Addy. 79 min.

Insurance investigator is assigned to train robbery he masterminded.

435. *To the Ends of the Earth* (1948) Columbia. *Dir* Robert Stevenson. *Sc* Jay Richard Kennedy. *Ph* Burnett Guffey. *Mus* George Duning. *Cast* Dick Powell, Signe Hasso, Ludwig Donath, Vladimir Sokoloff, Edgar Barrier. 109 min.

Government agent relentlessly pursues narcotics smuggling ring. One of the more extreme law-and-order films of the cycle.

436. *Tomorrow Is Another Day* (1951) Warner Brothers. *Dir* Felix Feist. *Sc* Art Cohn and Guy Endore. *Ph* Robert Burks. *Mus* Daniele Amfitheatrof. *Cast* Steve Cochran, Ruth Roman, Lurene Tuttle, Ray Teal, Morris Ankrum. 90 min.

Ex-con thinks he has killed dime-a-dance girl's old boyfriend, runs away with her to try and start a new life.

437. *Too Late for Tears* (1949) United Artists. *Dir* Byron Haskin. *Sc* Roy Huggins, from his novel. *Ph* William Mellor. *Mus* R. Dale Butts. *Cast* Lizabeth Scott, Don DeFore, Dan Duryea, Arthur Kennedy, Kristine Miller. 98 min.

Married couple have bag full of stolen money mistakenly thrown into their car; wife is driven mad with greed. Notable, well-directed film in which Lizabeth Scott plays a restless housewife who will stop at nothing to get what she wants.

438. *Touch of Evil* (1958) Universal. *Dir* Orson Welles. *Sc* Welles, from the novel *Badge of Evil* by Whit Masterson. *Ph* Russell Metty. *Mus* Henry Mancini. *Cast* Charlton Heston, Janet Leigh, Orson Welles, Joseph Calleia, Akim Tamiroff, Marlene Dietrich, Ray Collins, Dennis Weaver, Mercedes McCambridge. 95 min.

With the reluctant cooperation of an American police captain, a Mexican narcotics detective investigates the bombing death of a local millionaire at a small border town. Welles' baroque low-life thriller is loaded down with remarkable features, from stunning visual expressionism and the seediest Mexican settings imaginable to harshly stated characterizations and powerful dramatic ironies, all of which combine to create a very significant image of noir corruption and decay.

439. *Trapped* (1949) Eagle Lion. *Dir* Richard Fleischer. *Sc* Earl Felton and George Zuckerman. *Ph* Guy Roe. *Mus* Sol Kaplan. *Cast* Lloyd Bridges, John Hoyt, Barbara Payton, James Todd. 78 min.

T-men allow a prisoner to escape from jail, hoping he will lead them to a counterfeiting gang.

440. *Try and Get Me* [also titled **The Sound of Fury**] (1950) United Artists. *Dir* Cyril Endfield. *Sc* Jo Pagano, from his novel *The Condemned*. *Ph*

Guy Roe. *Mus* Hugo Friedhofer. *Cast* Frank Lovejoy, Lloyd Bridges, Kathleen Ryan, Richard Carlson, Katherine Locke, Adele Jergens, Art Smith. 85 min.

Unemployed veteran becomes involved with small-time hoodlum, soon graduating from gas station robberies to kidnapping and murder. A film of gut-wrenching harshness, high style and total intensity that is easily one of the most cynical and impressive entries of the cycle.

441. The Turning Point (1952) Paramount. *Dir* William Dieterle.
Sc Warren Duff, from a story by Horace McCoy. *Ph* Lionel Lindon. *Mus* Irvin Talbot. *Cast* William Holden, Edmond O'Brien, Alexis Smith, Tom Tully, Ed Begley, Ray Teal, Ted de Corsia, Neville Brand. 85 min.

While aiding special crime committee, investigative reporter discovers that the chairman's father is on the syndicate payroll. Tense, dramatic exposé film with some strong performances.

442. Twist of Fate [original title, The Beautiful Stranger] (1954)
United Artists. *Dir* David Miller. *Sc* Robert Westerby and Carl Nystrom, from a story by Rip Von Ronkel and David Miller. *Ph* Robert Day, Ted Scaife. *Mus* Malcolm Arnold. *Cast* Ginger Rogers, Jacques Bergerac, Herbert Lom, Stanley Baker. 89 min.

An American actress learns that her fiancé is a dangerous criminal. British produced and set on the French Riviera.

The Twisted Road see They Live by Night

443. The Two Mrs. Carrolls (1947) Warner Brothers. *Dir* Peter
Godfrey. *Sc* Thomas Job, from the play by Martin Vale. *Ph* Peverell Marley. *Mus* Franz Waxman. *Cast* Humphrey Bogart, Barbara Stanwyck, Alexis Smith, Nigel Bruce, Isobel Elsom. 99 min.

Woman realizes her artist husband intends to murder her as he did his first wife, after he has finished painting her portrait. A kind of modern gothic woman-in-distress thriller, with good performances by the principals and an audacious Waxman score.

444. Two O'Clock Courage (1945) RKO. *Dir* Anthony Mann.
Sc Robert E. Kent, from the novel *Two in the Dark* by Gelett Burgess. *Ph* Jack MacKenzie. *Mus* Roy Webb. *Cast* Tom Conway, Ann Rutherford, Richard Lane, Lester Matthews. 66 min.

Amnesiac accused of murder searches for the truth with the help of a girl.

445. Two of a Kind (1951) Columbia. *Dir* Henry Levin. *Sc*
Lawrence Kimble and Gordon Kahn, from the novelette *Lefty Farrell* by James Edward Grant. *Ph* Burnett Guffey. *Mus* George Duning. *Cast* Edmond O'Brien, Lizabeth Scott, Terry Moore, Alexander Knox, Robert Anderson. 75 min.

Con man impersonates long-lost son of wealthy couple.

446. Two Smart People (1946) MGM. *Dir* Jules Dassin. *Sc* Ethel
Hill and Leslie Charteris, from a story by Ralph Wheelwright and Allan Kenward. *Ph* Karl Freund. *Mus* George Bassman. *Cast* Lucille Ball, John Hodiak, Lloyd Nolan, Hugo Haas, Elisha Cook, Jr., Vladimir Sokoloff. 93 min.

Two rival swindlers fall for each other while one is en route to jail.

Uncle Harry see *The Strange Affair of Uncle Harry*

447. *Under the Gun* (1950) Universal. *Dir* Ted Tetzlaff. *Sc* George Zuckerman, from a story by Daniel B. Ullman. *Ph* Henry Freulich. *Mus* Joseph Gershenson. *Cast* Richard Conte, Audrey Totter, John McIntire, Sam Jaffe, Shepperd Strudwick, Royal Dano. 84 min.

Racketeer fights his way to the top of a vicious prison farm jungle.

448. *The Undercover Man* (1949) Columbia. *Dir* Joseph H. Lewis. *Sc* Sydney Boehm, based on an article by Frank J. Wilson and a screen story by Jack Rubin. *Ph* Burnett Guffey. *Mus* George Duning. *Cast* Glenn Ford, Nina Foch, James Whitmore, Barry Kelley, Howard St. John. 85 min.

Federal undercover agent faces extreme danger in attempting to obtain evidence against mob leader. Semidocumentary with some good scenes and suspense.

449. *Undercurrent* (1946) MGM.

Woman unwittingly caught between two mysterious brothers. See page 45.

450. *Undertow* (1949) Universal. *Dir* William Castle. *Sc* Arthur T. Horman and Lee Loeb, from a story by Horman. *Ph* Irving Glassberg. *Mus* Milton Schwarzwald. *Cast* Scott Brady, John Russell, Dorothy Hart, Peggy Dow, Bruce Bennett, Rock Hudson. 70 min.

Menacing story of returning war veteran framed for underworld murder, racing against time to prove his innocence.

451. *The Underworld Story* [also titled **The Whipped**] (1950) United Artists. *Dir* Cy Endfield. *Sc* Henry Blankfort, adapted by Endfield, from the novel *The Big Story* by Craig Rice. *Ph* Stanley Cortez. *Mus* David Rose. *Cast* Dan Duryea, Herbert Marshall, Gale Storm, Howard da Silva, Michael O'Shea, Mary Anderson. 90 min.

Dark, effective little film of a hardened reporter's involvement with a corrupt newspaper publisher.

452. *The Unfaithful* (1947) Warner Brothers. *Dir* Vincent Sherman. *Sc* David Goodis, from his own story. *Ph* Ernest Haller. *Mus* Max Steiner. *Cast* Ann Sheridan, Lew Ayres, Zachary Scott, Eve Arden, Steven Geray, John Hoyt. 109 min.

Woman is not telling the truth about the death of an intruder. Involved narrative depicting the nightmarish results of a wife's indiscretion.

453. *Union Station* (1950) Paramount. *Dir* Rudolph Maté. *Sc* Sydney Boehm, from a story by Thomas Walsh. *Ph* Daniel L. Fapp. *Mus* Irvin Talbot. *Cast* William Holden, Nancy Olson, Barry Fitzgerald, Lyle Bettger, Jan Sterling. 80 min.

Desperate loser kidnaps blind girl at Los Angeles Union Station; police close in. As in *He Walked by Night*, the vengeful, relentless police hunt epitomizes (unintentionally?) the dehumanization of life in a large metropolitan city.

454. *The Unknown Man* (1951) MGM. *Dir* Richard Thorpe. *Sc* Ronald Millar and George Froeschel. *Ph* William Mellor. *Mus* Conrad Salinger.

Cast Walter Pidgeon, Ann Harding, Barry Sullivan, Keefe Brasselle, Lewis Stone, Edward Franz. 88 min.

Orderly world of a prominent lawyer collapses when he learns that a man he has successfully defended is not innocent of murder. Well-plotted film with several ironic twists.

455. *The Unseen* (1945) Paramount. *Dir* Lewis Allen. *Sc* Hagar Wilde and Raymond Chandler, adapted by Wilde and Ken Englund, from the novel *Her Heart in Her Throat* by Ethel Lina White. *Ph* John F. Seitz. *Mus* Ernst Toch. *Cast* Joel McCrea, Gail Russell, Herbert Marshall, Phyllis Brooks, Isobel Elsom. 81 min.

Young woman takes a job as governess in a mysterious house whose master may or may not be a murderer. Narrative conventions of the "old house thriller" given a refined, intelligent noir treatment.

456. *The Unsuspected* (1947) Warner Brothers.

Brilliant radio personality and his beautiful ward stand in the center of a complex murder case. One of the most stylish and meaningful mysteries of the cycle. See page 58.

457. *Valerie* (1957) United Artists. *Dir* Gerd Oswald. *Sc* Leonard Heideman and Emmett Murphy. *Ph* Ernest Laszlo. *Mus* Albert Glasser. *Cast* Sterling Hayden, Anita Ekberg, Anthony Steel, Peter Walker, Malcolm Atterbury. 84 min.

Flashbacks give conflicting accounts of a married couple's murder; wounded daughter vows to set things straight.

458. *The Velvet Touch* (1948) RKO. *Dir* John Gage. *Sc* Leo Rosten, adapted by Walter N. Reilly, from a story by William Mercer and Annabel Ross. *Ph* Joseph Walker. *Mus* Leigh Harline. *Cast* Rosalind Russell, Leo Genn, Claire Trevor, Sydney Greenstreet, Leon Ames, Frank McHugh. 97 min.

Famous stage actress inadvertently murders her producer, then tries to elude discovery. Dark, ironic noir of theater life, which seems somewhat inspired by *A Double Life*.

459. *The Verdict* (1946) Warner Brothers. *Dir* Don Siegel. *Sc* Peter Milne, from the novel *The Big Bow Mystery* by Israel Zangwill. *Ph* Ernest Haller. *Mus* Frederick Hollander. *Cast* Sydney Greenstreet, Peter Lorre, George Coulouris, Joan Lorring, Rosalind Ivan. 86 min.

Former Scotland Yard inspector tries to prove a friend is innocent of murder. Atmospheric Victorian crime picture with some good irony and a nice twist ending.

460. *Vicki* (1953) 20th Century-Fox. *Dir* Harry Horner. *Sc* Dwight Taylor, from the novel *I Wake Up Screaming* by Steve Fisher. *Ph* Milton Krasner. *Mus* Leigh Harline. *Cast* Jeanne Crain, Jean Peters, Elliott Reid, Richard Boone, Casey Adams, Carl Betz, Aaron Spelling. 85 min.

Police detective becomes obsessed with investigating the murder of an ambitious young model. Second adaption of Steve Fisher's classic suspense novel, which uses a complex flashback structure to portray a stark noir world of selfishness and twisted dreams.

461. *Voice in the Wind* (1944) United Artists. *Dir* Arthur Ripley. *Sc* Fredrick Torberg, from a story by Ripley. *Ph* Dick Fryer. *Mus* Michel Michelet. *Cast* Francis Lederer, Sigrid Gurie, J. Edward Bromberg, J. Carroll Naish, Alexander Granach. 85 min.

Former concert pianist, victim of Nazi torture, pursues a melancholic existence on the island of Guadalupe. Notable, little-known B noir that is grim, romantic and arty.

462. *Walk Softly, Stranger* (1950) RKO. *Dir* Robert Stevenson. *Sc* Frank Fenton, from a story by Manny Seff and Paul Yawitz. *Ph* Harry Wild. *Mus* Frederick Hollander. *Cast* Joseph Cotten, Valli, Spring Byington, Paul Stewart, Jack Parr. 81 min.

Petty crook holds up in small Ohio town, becomes involved with bitter girl confined to a wheelchair.

463. *The Web* (1947) Universal. *Dir* Michael Gordon. *Sc* William Bowers and Bernard Millhauser, from a story by Harry Kurnitz. *Ph* Irving Glassberg. *Mus* Hans J. Salter. *Cast* Edmond O'Brien, Ella Raines, Vincent Price, William Bendix, John Abbott. 87 min.

Ambitious young lawyer, who has been hired to protect a wealthy industrialist, becomes the patsy in a cunning murder scheme. Intelligent hard-boiled melodrama in which an aggressive protagonist is easily manipulated by a smooth arch-villain while falling in love with a classy, no-nonsense dame.

464. *The Well* (1951) United Artists. *Dir* Russell Rouse. *Sc* Rouse and Clarence Greene. *Ph* Ernest Laszlo. *Mus* Dimitri Tiomkin. *Cast* Richard Rober, Barry Kelley, Henry Morgan, Christine Larson, Maidie Norman. 85 min.

Racial tensions reach the boiling point when a black child is trapped in an abandoned well. Tough, inspired social commentary with good suspense.

465. *When Strangers Marry* (1944) Monogram. *Dir* William Castle. *Sc* Philip Yordan and Dennis J. Cooper, from a story by George V. Moscov. *Ph* Ira Morgan. *Mus* Dimitri Tiomkin. *Cast* Dean Jagger, Kim Hunter, Robert Mitchum, Neil Hamilton. 67 min.

Woman's new husband is prime murder suspect, and she fears that he is guilty of the crime. Early B noir that demonstrates how unpredictable and effective the woman-in-distress format can be.

466. *Where Danger Lives* (1950) RKO. *Dir* John Farrow. *Sc* Charles Bennett, from a story by Leo Rosten. *Ph* Nicholas Musuraca. *Mus* Roy Webb. *Cast* Robert Mitchum, Faith Domergue, Claude Rains, Maureen O'Sullivan, Jack Kelly. 84 min.

Young doctor gets involved with sultry married woman, runs away with her thinking he has killed the husband. Mitchum gives another strong performance as the victim of a *femme fatale*.

467. *Where the Sidewalk Ends* (1950) 20th Century-fox. *Dir* Otto Preminger. *Sc* Ben Hecht, adapted by Victor Trivas, Frank P. Rosenberg and Robert E. Kent from the novel *Night Cry* by William L. Stuart. *Ph* Joseph La Shelle. *Mus* Cyril Mockridge. *Cast* Dana Andrews, Gene Tierney, Gary Merrill, Bert Freed, Tom Tully, Karl Malden, Craig Stevens, Ruth Donnelly. 95 min.

Tough police officer accidentally kills robbery suspect, then tries to frame a mobster for the crime. Significant portrait of a confused and misguided noir cop.

468. *While the City Sleeps* (1956) RKO. *Dir* Fritz Lang. *Sc* Casey Robinson, from the novel *The Bloody Spur* by Charles Einstein. *Ph* Ernest Laszlo. *Mus* Herschel Burke Gilbert. *Cast* Dana Andrews, Rhonda Fleming, Sally Forrest, Thomas Mitchell, Vincent Price, Howard Duff, Ida Lupino, George Sanders, John Barrymore, Jr. 100 min.

Newspaper owner offers big promotion to member of his staff who can catch psycho-murderer. Offbeat thriller which is one of the most original and provocative noir newspaper films.

469. *Whiplash* (1948) Warner Brothers. *Dir* Lewis Seiler. *Sc* Maurice Geraghty, adapted by Gordon Kahn, from a story by Kenneth Earl. *Ph* Peverell Marley. *Mus* Franz Waxman. *Cast* Dane Clark, Alexis Smith, Zachary Scott, Eve Arden, Jeffrey Lynn. 91 min.

A struggling artist has an affair with an attractive married woman and is induced by her husband to become a boxer.

The Whipped see *The Underworld Story*

470. *Whirlpool* (1949) 20th Century–Fox. *Dir* Otto Preminger. *Sc* Ben Hecht (under the pseudonym Lester Bartow) and Andrew Solt, from the novel *Me Thinks the Lady* by Guy Endore. *Ph* Arthur Miller. *Mus* David Raksin. *Cast* Gene Tierney, Richard Conte, Jose Ferrer, Charles Bickford, Eduard Franz, Constance Collier. 97 min.

Disturbed woman becomes the pawn of a charlatan hypnotist in clever murder plan. Suspenseful melodrama which treats the noir theme of psychological manipulation with depth and significance.

471. *Whispering City* (1947) Eagle Lion. *Dir* Fedor Ozep. *Sc* Rian James and Leonard Lee, from a story by George Zuckerman and Michael Lennox. *Ph* Guy Roe. *Mus* Andre Mathiew. *Cast* Helmut Dantine, Mary Anderson, Paul Lukas, Mimi d'Estee. 98 min.

Female reporter's murder investigation leads her to uncover the sordid past of a prominent attorney. The first of a number of well-made noirs produced by Eagle Lion, a short-lived company that was formerly Producers Releasing Corporation.

472. *Whispering Footsteps* (1943) Republic. *Dir* Howard Bretherton. *Sc* Gertrude Walker and Dane Lussier. *Ph* Jack Marta. *Mus* Morton Scott. *Cast* John Hubbard, Rita Quigley, Joan Blair, Charles Halton. 55 min.

A bank clerk's life becomes a nightmare because he fits the description of a maniac killer.

473. *Whistle Stop* (1946) United Artists. *Dir* Leonide Moguy. *Sc* Philip Yordan, from a story by Maritta M. Wolff. *Ph* Russell Metty. *Mus* Dimitri Tiomkin. *Cast* George Raft, Ava Gardner, Victor McLaglen, Tom Conway. 85 min.

When his girl dumps him for a nightclub owner, a gambler contemplates murder.

474. *White Heat* (1949) Warner Brothers. *Dir* Raoul Walsh. *Sc* Ivan Goff and Ben Roberts, suggested by a story by Virginia Kellogg. *Ph* Sid Hickox. *Mus* Max Steiner. *Cast* James Cagney, Edmond O'Brien, Virginia Mayo, Steven Cochran, Margaret Wycherly. 114 min.

A psychopathic gangster with a mother fixation fights an unrelenting battle with the law. The most famous noir gangster film, which leads the American crime picture to one of its most memorable extremes.

475. *Wicked Woman* (1954) United Artists. *Dir* Russell Rouse. *Sc* Clarence Greene and Rouse. *Ph* Edward Fitzgerald. *Mus* Buddy Baker. *Cast* Beverly Michaels, Richard Egan, Percy Helton, Evelyn Scott. 77 min.

Seedy B film about *femme fatale* who induces a bar owner to swindle his alcoholic wife and flee to Mexico.

476. *The Window* (1949) RKO. *Dir* Ted Tetzlaff. *Sc* Mel Dinelli, from the story "The Boy Cried Murder" by Cornell Woolrich. *Ph* William Steiner. *Mus* Roy Webb. *Cast* Barbara Hale, Bobby Driscoll, Arthur Kennedy, Paul Stewart, Ruth Roman. 73 min.

Boy witnesses a murder but no one will believe him. Film noir version of "The Boy Who Cried Wolf," set in New York City's tenement district.

477. *Without Honor* (1950) United Artists. *Dir* Irving Pichel. *Sc* James Poe. *Ph* Lionel Lindon. *Mus* Max Steiner. *Cast* Laraine Day, Dane Clark, Franchot Tone, Agnes Moorehead, Bruce Bennett. 69 min.

Shrill melodrama in which a woman thinks she has killed her illict lover.

478. *Without Warning* (1952) United Artists. *Dir* Arnold Laven. *Sc* Bill Raynor, from L.A. County Sheriff's Dept. files. *Ph* Joseph Biroc. *Mus* Herschel Burke Gilbert. *Cast* Adam Williams, Meg Randall, Edward Binns, Harlan Warde. 75 min.

Semidocumentary police film of search for crazed man who strangles blonde women.

479. *Witness to Murder* (1954) United Artists. *Dir* Roy Rowland. *Sc* Chester Erskine. *Ph* John Alton. *Mus* Herschel Burke Gilbert. *Cast* Barbara Stanwyck. George Sanders, Gary Merrill, Jesse White. 83 min.

A successful businesswoman who lives alone sees a murder in the apartment building across the street, but no one will believe her.

480. *Woman in Hiding* (1940) United Artists. *Dir* Michael Gordon. *Sc* Oscar Saul. *Ph* William Daniels. *Mus* Frank Skinner. *Cast* Ida Lupino, Howard Duff, Stephen McNally, John Litel, Peggy Dow, Taylor Holmes. 92 min.

Distraught woman flees her murderous husband, soon meeting a man who plans to take her back. Woman-in-distress thriller with some good details and an effective climate of noir paranoia.

481. *The Woman in the Window* (1944) RKO.

Married psychology professor's flirtation with a beautiful woman gets him into deep trouble. The first of a pair of important middle-class nightmares by Fritz Lang. See page 16.

482. The Woman in White (1948) Warner Brothers. *Dir* Peter Godfrey. *Sc* Stephen Morehouse Avery, from the novel by Wilkie Collins. *Ph* Carl Guthrie. *Mus* Max Steiner. *Cast* Eleanor Parker, Alexis Smith, Sydney Greenstreet, Gig Young, Agnes Moorehead, John Abbott, John Emery, Curt Bois. 109 min.

Ornate gothic thriller (adapted from a classic literary precursor to the modern suspense novel) in which a woman's mysterious double appears to warn her against the scheme of a villainous count.

483. The Woman on Pier 13 [also titled I **Married a Communist**] (1949) RKO. *Dir* Robert Stevenson. *Sc* Charles Grayson and Robert Hardy Andrews, from a story by George W. George and George Slavin. *Ph* Nicholas Musuraca. *Mus* Leigh Harline. *Cast* Laraine Day, Robert Ryan, John Agar, Thomas Gomez, Janis Carter, William Talman. 73 min.

Shipping executive is pressured by Communist infiltraters to take over a labor union. Waterfront noir; also the first of the "Red scare" melodramas.

484. The Woman on the Beach (1947) RKO. *Dir* Jean Renoir. *Sc* Renoir and Frank Davis, from the novel *None So Blind* by Mitchell Wilson. *Ph* Leo Tover, Harry Wild. *Mus* Hanns Eisler. *Cast* Joan Bennett, Robert Ryan, Charles Bickford, Nan Leslie, Walter Sande. 71 min.

Coast Guard officer recovering from war experiences becomes involved with the cynical wife of a tragically blinded painter. Strange, hypnotic mood piece that is Jean Renoir's only film noir.

485. Woman on the Run (1950) Universal. *Dir* Norman Foster. *Sc* Alan Campbell and Foster, from a story by Sylvia Tate. *Ph* Hal Mohr. *Mus* Emil Newman, Arthur Lange. *Cast* Ann Sheridan, Dennis O'Keefe, Robert Keith, Frank Jenks, John Qualen. 77 min.

Woman helps police search for her fearful husband, who is hiding out because he witnessed a murder.

486. A Woman's Face (1941) MGM. *Dir* George Cukor. *Sc* Donald Ogden Stewart, from the play by Francis de Croisset. *Ph* Robert Planck. *Mus* Bronislau Kaper. *Cast* Joan Crawford, Melvyn Douglas, Conrad Veidt, Osa Massen, Reginald Owen, Albert Basserman, Marjorie Main. 105 min.

Acerbic woman, hideously scarred in a childhood accident, runs a European blackmailing ring.

487. A Woman's Secret (1949) RKO. *Dir* Nicholas Ray. *Sc* Herman J. Mankiewicz, from the novel *Mortgage On Life* by Vicki Baum. *Ph* George E. Diskant. *Mus* Frederick Hollander. *Cast* Maureen O'Hara, Melvyn Douglas, Gloria Grahame, Bill Williams, Victor Jory. 85 min.

A woman shoots another whom she had built up to success; flashbacks relate why.

488. Women's Prison (1955) Columbia. *Dir* Lewis Seiler. *Sc* Crane Wilbur and Jack DeWitt. *Ph* Lester H. White. *Mus* Mischa Bakaleinikoff. *Cast* Ida Lupino, Jan Sterling, Cleo Moore, Audrey Totter, Phyllis Thaxter, Howard Duff, Warren Stevens. 80 min.

Ruthless superintendent makes life hell for female inmates.

489. World for Ransom (1954) Allied Artists. *Dir* Robert Aldrich. *Sc* Lindsay Hardy. *Ph* Joseph Biroc. *Mus* Frank DeVol. *Cast* Dan Duryea, Gene Lockhart, Patric Knowles, Reginald Denny, Nigel Bruce. 82 min.

World-weary private eye tries to prevent a nuclear scientist from being kidnapped. First of several late noirs which Robert Aldrich imbues with a magnified intensity of style and meaning.

490. The Wrong Man (1956) Warner Brothers. *Dir* Alfred Hitchcock. *Sc* Maxwell Anderson and Angus MacPhail, from a story by Anderson. *Ph* Robert Burks. *Mus* Bernard Herrmann. *Cast* Henry Fonda, Vera Miles, Anthony Quayle, Harold J. Stone, Nehemiah Persoff. 105 min.

New York musician's life is virtually destroyed because he resembles a holdup man. One of the best films ever made on the popular noir theme of a man falsely accused of criminal act.

Appendices

Appendix A
"Off-Genre" and Other Films Noirs

Since Borde and Chaumeton (1955), critics and scholars have frequently echoed the theme that film noir cannot be generically defined nor confined to crime films, and yet the only publication to deal with "off-genre" films noirs at any length has been Silver and Ward's *Film Noir* (1979). That book's discussion appears in a ten-page appendix covering four types of films: Westerns, Gangster, Comedy and Period films. The following list offers a somewhat different opinion, both in the case of those four generic headings (two of which should not even be considered "off-genre") and by its inclusion of ten other generic headings or film types.

OFF-GENRE FILMS NOIRS

Western
Pursued (Walsh, 1947)
Blood on the Moon (Wise, 1948)
The Gunfighter (Henry King, 1950)
The Furies (Mann, 1950)

Devil's Doorway (Mann, 1950)
The Outcasts of Poker Flat (Newman, 1952)
The Halliday Brand (Lewis, 1957)

Comedy
Lady on a Train (Charles David, 1945)
Monsieur Verdoux (Chaplin, 1947)
Unfaithfully Yours (Preston Sturges, 1948)

The Lucky Stiff (Foster, 1949)
Beat the Devil (Huston, 1954)

Problem Picture
The Lost Weekend (Wilder, 1945)
Smash-Up (Heisler, 1947)
The Snake Pit (Litvak, 1948)

An Act of Murder (Gordon, 1948)
The Lady Gambles (Gordon, 1949)

Romantic Melodrama
Love Letters (Dieterle, 1945)
Night Unto Night (Siegel, 1949)

Paid in Full (Dieterle, 1950)
Autumn Leaves (Aldrich, 1956)

Fantasy
Flesh and Fantasy (Julien Duvivier, 1943)
The Picture of Dorian Gray (Albert Lewin, 1945)
Repeat Performance (Werker, 1947)
The Spiritualist [The Amazing Mr. X] (Vorhaus, 1948)
Alias Nick Beal (Farrow, 1949)

Costume Drama
Reign of Terror [The Black Book] (Mann, 1949)
Black Magic (Ratoff, 1949)

Espionage Thriller
Confidential Agent (Herman Shumlin, 1945)
Cloak and Dagger (Lang, 1946)
Berlin Express (Tourneur, 1948)

War
The Steel Helmet (Fuller, 1951)
Attack! (Aldrich, 1956)

Science Fiction
Invasion of the Body Snatchers (Siegel, 1956)

Adventure
The Treasure of the Sierra Madre (Huston, 1948)
Lust for Gold (S. Simon, 1949)

Horror
The Beast with Five Fingers (Florey, 1946)
The Val Lewton Films 1942–46

Miscellaneous Dramas and Oddities
Keeper of the Flame (Cukor, 1942)
The Great Flamarion (Mann, 1945)
The Lost Moment (Martin Gable, 1947)
Macbeth (Welles, 1948)
The Great Sinner (Siodmak, 1949)
We Were Strangers (Huston, 1949)
Night Into Morning (F. Markle, 1951)
The Tall Target (Mann, 1951)
Death of a Salesman (Benedek, 1952)
Glory Alley (Walsh, 1952)
The Bad and the Beautiful (Minnelli, 1952)
Night of the Hunter (Charles Laughton, 1955)
The Bad Seed (Mervyn LeRoy, 1956)
A Hatful of Rain (Zinnemann, 1957)
Lonelyhearts (Vincent J. Donehue, 1958)

AMERICAN PRECURSORS

Two Seconds (Mervyn LeRoy, 1932)
I Am a Fugitive from a Chain Gang (LeRoy, 1932)
Payment Deferred (Lothar Mendes, 1932)
Crime Without Passion (Hecht and MacArthur, 1934)
The Scoundrel (Hecht and MacArthur, 1935)
Fury (Lang, 1936)
You Only Live Once (Lang, 1937)
Let Us Live (Brahm, 1939)
Rio (Brahm, 1939)
Blind Alley (Charles Vidor, 1939)

NOIR "B" FILM SERIES

"The Whistler" films 1944–1948

COLOR FILMS NOIRS

Leave Her to Heaven (John M. Stahl, 1945)
Rope (Hitchcock, 1948)
Niagara (Hathaway, 1953)
Hell's Island (Karlson, 1955)
I Died a Thousand Times (Heisler, 1955)

Slightly Scarlet (Allan Dwan, 1956)
A Kiss Before Dying (Oswald, 1956)
Accused of Murder (Kane, 1956)
Vertigo (Hitchcock, 1958)

BLACK AND WHITE POSTNOIRS

The Third Voice (Cornfield, 1960)
Underworld U.S.A. (Fuller, 1960)
Hoodlum Priest (Irvin Kershner, 1961)
Blast of Silence (Allen Baron, 1961)
Man-Trap (E. O'Brien, 1961)
Experiment in Terror (Blake Edwards, 1962)
Cape Fear (J. Lee Thompson, 1962)
The Manchurian Candidate (John Frankenheimer, 1962)
The Trial (Welles, 1962)
Shock Corridor (Fuller, 1963)

The Naked Kiss (Fuller, 1964)
Kitten with a Whip (Douglas Heyes, 1964)
Brainstorm (William Conrad, 1965)
Mirage (Dmytryk, 1965)
Mickey One (Arthur Penn, 1965)
The Money Trap (Burt Kennedy, 1966)
The Incident (Larry Peerce, 1967)
In Cold Blood (Richard Brooks, 1967)

Appendix B
Chronology of the Film Noir

The 490 films from the annotated filmography are listed in the order of their release, using the earliest verified American release date traceable. Each title is listed along with an abbreviation for company or studio and a number signifying the month of release.

1940 (5 films)
Rebecca UA (4)
They Drive by Night WB (8)
Stranger on the Third Floor RKO (8)

Angels Over Broadway Col (9)
The Letter WB (11)

1941 (11)
High Sierra WB (1)
Rage in Heaven MGM (3)
A Woman's Face MGM (5)
Out of the Fog WB (6)
Ladies in Retirement Col (9)
Among the Living Par (9)

The Maltese Falcon WB (10)
Suspicion RKO (11)
I Wake Up Screaming Fox (11)
Blues in the Night WB (11)
The Shanghai Gesture UA (12)

1942 (5)
This Gun for Hire Par (5)
Moontide Fox (5)
Crossroads MGM (7)

The Glass Key Par (10)
Street of Chance Par (11)

1943 (5)
Shadow of a Doubt U (1)
Journey into Fear RKO (2)
The Fallen Sparrow RKO (8)

The Seventh Victim RKO (8)
Whispering Footsteps Rep (12)

1944 (18)
The Lodger Fox (1)
Phantom Lady U (1)
Voice in the Wind UA (3)
Double Indemnity Par (5)
Gaslight MGM (5)

Christmas Holiday U (6)
The Mask of Dimitrios WB (7)
Strangers in the Night Rep (9)
The Woman in the Window RKO (10)
Laura Fox (10)

Ministry of Fear Par (10)
Dark Waters UA (11)
Bluebeard PRC (11)
When Strangers Marry Mon (11)

Guest in the House UA (12)
Murder My Sweet RKO (12)
Destiny U (12)
Experiment Perilous RKO (12)

1945 (22)

The Suspect U (1)
Hangover Square Fox (2)
Circumstantial Evidence Fox (3)
Strange Illusion PRC (3)
Escape in the Fog Col (4)
Two O'Clock Courage RKO (4)
The Unseen Par (5)
Conflict WB (6)
Jealousy Rep (7)
Bewitched MGM (7)
Strange Affair of Uncle Harry U (8)

Johnny Angel RKO (8)
The House on 92nd Street Fox (9)
Mildred Pierce WB (10)
Danger Signal WB (11)
My Name Is Julia Ross Col (11)
Detour PRC (11)
The Spider Fox (12)
Fallen Angel Fox (12)
Cornered RKO (12)
Scarlet Street U (12)
Spellbound UA (12)

1946 (42)

The Spiral Staircase RKO (1)
Whistle Stop UA (1)
Shock Fox (2)
Three Strangers WB (2)
Fear Mon (3)
The Mask of Diljon PRC (3)
Deadline at Dawn RKO (3)
Strange Impersonation Rep (3)
The Dark Corner Fox (4)
Night Editor Col (4)
The Blue Dahlia Par (4)
Gilda Col (4)
The Glass Alibi Rep (4)
The Postman Always Rings Twice
  MGM (5)
Her Kind of Man WB (5)
The Stranger RKO (5)
Somewhere in the Night Fox (6)
Suspense Mon (6)
Strange Triangle Fox (6)
Inside Job U (6)
Specter of the Rose Rep (7)

Black Angel U (8)
The Killers U (8)
The Big Sleep WB (8)
Notorious RKO (9)
Crack-Up RKO (9)
The Strange Love of Martha Ivers
  Par (9)
Shadow of a Woman WB (9)
Decoy Mon (9)
So Dark the Night Col (10)
Nobody Lives Forever WB (10)
The Dark Mirror U (10)
The Strange Woman UA (10)
Deception WB (10)
Nocturne RKO (10)
Two Smart People MGM (11)
The Chase UA (11)
The Verdict WB (11)
Undercurrent MGM (11)
The Locket RKO (12)
Temptation U (12)
The Man I Love WB (12)

1947 (53)

Dead Reckoning Col (1)
The Lady in the Lake MGM (1)
Humoresque WB (1)
Blind Spot Col (2)
The Brasher Doubloon Fox (2)
The Red House UA (2)
Boomerang Fox (2)
Nora Prentiss WB (2)

Fall Guy Mon (3)
Backlash Fox (3)
The Macomber Affair UA (3)
The Guilty Mon (3)
Johnny O'Clock Col (3)
Fear in the Night Par (4)
Framed Col (4)
Born to Kill RKO (5)

Desperate RKO (5)
Shoot to Kill SG (5)
The Two Mrs. Carrolls WB (5)
Calcutta Par (5)
The Woman on the Beach RKO (6)
Moss Rose Fox (6)
The Web U (6)
Ivy U (6)
The Unfaithful WB (7)
They Won't Believe Me RKO (7)
Possessed WB (7)
Brute Force U (8)
The Long Night RKO (8)
Crossfire RKO (8)
The Pretender Rep (8)
Cry Wolf WB (8)
Body and Soul UA (8)
Kiss of Death Fox (8)
Deep Valley WB (9)

Lured UA (9)
The Arnelo Affair MGM (9)
Singapore U (9)
Railroaded PRC (9)
Dark Passage WB (9)
The Unsuspected WB (10)
Ride the Pink Horse U (10)
Key Witness Col (10)
Nightmare Alley Fox (10)
High Tide Mon (10)
Bury Me Dead PRC (10)
Out of the Past RKO (11)
Whispering City EL (11)
Love from a Stranger EL (11)
The Gangster AA (11)
The Flame Rep (11)
The High Wall MGM (12)
The Paradine Case UA (12)

1948 (43)

For You I Die FC (1)
T-Men EL (1)
Sleep, My Love UA (1)
I Walk Alone Par (1)
Secret Beyond the Door U (2)
Call Northside 777 Fox (2)
A Double Life U (2)
To the Ends of the Earth Col (2)
The Naked City U (3)
Sign of the Ram Col (3)
The Hunted AA (4)
Ruthless EL (4)
The Big Clock Par (4)
All My Sons U (4)
The Woman in White WB (5)
The Lady from Shanghai Col (5)
I Wouldn't Be in Your Shoes Mon (5)
I, Jane Doe Rep (5)
Raw Deal EL (5)
The Street With No Name Fox (6)
Race Street RKO (6)
Canon City EL (7)

Shed No Tears EL (7)
Key Largo WB (7)
The Velvet Touch RKO (8)
Larceny U (8)
The Pitfall UA (8)
Hollow Triumph EL (8)
Bodyguard RKO (9)
Escape Fox (9)
Sorry, Wrong Number Par (9)
Moonrise Rep (10)
Cry of the City Fox (10)
Behind Locked Doors EL (10)
The Night Has a Thousand Eyes Par (10)
Kiss the Blood Off My Hands U (10)
Road House Fox (11)
He Walked By Night EL (11)
Parole, Inc. EL (12)
The Dark Past Col (12)
Force of Evil MGM (12)
Incident Mon (12)
Whiplash WB (12)

1949 (52)

Criss Cross U (1)
The Accused Par (1)
Shockproof Col (1)
Act of Violence MGM (1)
A Woman's Secret RKO (2)
Flaxy Martin WB (2)

Caught MGM (2)
Knock on Any Door Col (2)
Jigsaw UA (3)
The Bribe MGM (3)
The Clay Pigeon RKO (3)
Impact UA (4)

The Set-Up RKO (4)
City Across the River U (4)
The Undercover Man Col (4)
The Crooked Way UA (4)
Flamingo Road WB (4)
C-Man FC (5)
Champion UA (4)
Manhandled Par (6)
Illegal Entry U (6)
Take One False Step U (6)
House of Strangers Fox (7)
Follow Me Quietly RKO (7)
Too Late for Tears UA (7)
Johnny Stool Pigeon U (7)
So Evil My Love Par (8)
The Window RKO (8)
Scene of the Crime MGM (8)
White Heat WB (9)
Rope of Sand Par (9)
Thieves' Highway Fox (9)

Red Light UA (9)
The Hidden Room EL (10)
The Woman on Pier 13 RKO (10)
Trapped EL (10)
Beyond the Forest WB (10)
Abandoned U (10)
Border Incident MGM (10)
They Live by Night RKO (11)
Strange Bargain RKO (11)
Chicago Deadline Par (11)
The Reckless Moment Col (11)
All the King's Men Col (11)
Tension MGM (11)
The Threat RKO (11)
A Dangerous Profession RKO (11)
Port of New York EL (12)
Undertow U (12)
The File on Thelma Jordon Par (12)
Whirlpool Fox (12)
Woman in Hiding UA (12)

1950 (57)

Gun Crazy UA (1)
Guilty Bystander FC (1)
Storm Warning WB (2)
Backfire WB (2)
The Tattooed Stranger RKO (3)
The Black Hand MGM (3)
Outside the Wall U (3)
Quicksand UA (3)
House by the River Rep (3)
The Secret Fury RKO (3)
The Capture RKO (4)
Side Street MGM (4)
One Way Street U (4)
Stage Fright WB (4)
D.O.A. UA (4)
The Damned Don't Cry WB (5)
In a Lonely Place Col (5)
No Man of Her Own Par (5)
Shadow on the Wall MGM (5)
The Asphalt Jungle MGM (5)
Destination Murder RKO (6)
Armored Car Robbery RKO (6)
Night and the City Fox (6)
Caged WB (6)
This Side of the Law WB (6)
Where the Sidewalk Ends Fox (7)
Once a Thief UA (7)
Where Danger Lives RKO (7)
Born to Be Bad RKO (7)

711 Ocean Drive Col (7)
The Lawless Par (7)
Underworld Story UA (7)
Mystery Street MGM (7)
Panic in the Streets Fox (8)
Sunset Boulevard Par (8)
Convicted Col (8)
A Lady Without Passport MGM (8)
Kiss Tomorrow Goodbye WB (8)
The Sleeping City U (9)
Shakedown U (9)
Union Station Par (9)
Edge of Doom RKO (9)
The Breaking Point WB (9)
Between Midnight and Dawn Col (10)
No Way Out Fox (10)
Dark City Par (10)
Without Honor UA (10)
Woman on the Run U (10)
The Sun Sets at Dawn EL (11)
Dial 1119 MGM (11)
Walk Softly, Stranger RKO (11)
Southside 1-1000 AA (11)
Highway 301 WB (12)
Try and Get Me UA (12)
Hunt the Man Down RKO (12)
The Killer That Stalked New York
  Col (12)
Under the Gun U (12)

1951 (39)

Gambling House RKO (1)
The Man Who Cheated Himself Fox (1)
Cry Danger RKO (2)
The Thirteenth Letter Fox (2)
Cause for Alarm MGM (2)
The Enforcer WB (2)
Lightning Strikes Twice WB (3)
The Second Woman UA (3)
M Col (3)
The Scarf UA (4)
Fourteen Hours Fox (4)
I Was a Communist for the F.B.I. WB (5)
Appointment with Danger Par (5)
House on Telegraph Hill Fox (5)
The Prowler UA (5)
The Man with My Face UA (6)
Three Steps North UA (6)
No Questions Asked MGM (6)
Hollywood Story U (6)
Strangers on a Train WB (6)
Ace in the Hole Par (7)
He Ran All the Way UA (7)
Sirocco Col (7)
Two of a Kind Col (7)
Roadblock RKO (7)
The Hoodlum UA (7)
The Strip MGM (8)
Iron Man U (8)
His Kind of Woman RKO (8)
The People Against O'Hara MGM (9)
The Well UA (9)
A Place in the Sun Par (9)
Tomorrow Is Another Day WB (9)
The Mob Col (10)
Detective Story Par (11)
The Raging Tide U (11)
The Unknown Man MGM (11)
The Racket RKO (11)
The Big Night UA (12)

1952 (26)

Another Man's Poison UA (1)
On Dangerous Ground RKO (1)
This Woman Is Dangerous WB (2)
The Sellout MGM (2)
The Green Glove UA (2)
Scandal Sheet Col (3)
Captive City UA (4)
Hoodlum Empire Rep (4)
Talk About a Stranger MGM (4)
Macao RKO (5)
The Narrow Margin RKO (5)
Without Warning UA (5)
The Sniper Col (5)
Loan Shark L (5)
Clash by Night RKO (6)
Sudden Fear RKO (8)
Don't Bother to Knock Fox (8)
Beware, My Lovely RKO (9)
Affair in Trinidad Col (9)
The Thief UA (10)
Night Without Sleep Fox (11)
The Turning Point Par (11)
The Steel Trap Fox (11)
Kansas City Confidential UA (11)
Strange Fascination Col (12)
Ruby Gentry Fox (12)

1953 (21)

Angel Face RKO (2)
Jeopardy MGM (2)
I Confess WB (2)
The Hitch-Hiker RKO (2)
The Blue Gardenia WB (3)
The Glass Wall Col (4)
Man in the Dark Col (4)
The System WB (4)
City That Never Sleeps Rep (6)
Pickup on South Street Fox (6)
Dangerous Crossing Fox (7)
I, the Jury UA (8)
No Escape UA (9)
Vicki Fox (9)
A Blueprint for Murder Fox (9)
99 River Street UA (9)
The Big Heat Col (10)
Jennifer AA (10)
The Glass Web UA (11)
Stranger on the Prowl UA (11)
Man in the Attic Fox (12)

1954 (26)

Wicked Woman UA (1)
Forbidden U (1)
World for Ransom AA (1)
Highway Dragnet AA (2)
Riot in Cell Block 11 AA (2)
Crime Wave WB (3)
Loophole AA (3)
Witness to Murder UA (4)
Drive a Crooked Road Col (4)
Playgirl U (5)
The Long Wait UA (5)
Hell's Half Acre Rep (6)
Pushover Col (7)

Make Haste to Live Rep (8)
Human Desire Col (8)
Shield for Murder UA (8)
Private Hell 36 F (9)
Suddenly UA (9)
Rogue Cop MGM (9)
The Human Jungle AA (10)
The Sleeping Tiger A (10)
The Naked Alibi U (10)
Cry Vengeance AA (11)
Twist of Fate UA (11)
The Other Woman Fox (12)
Black Tuesday UA (12)

1955 (20)

The Big Combo AA (2)
Women's Prison Col (2)
Murder Is My Beat AA (2)
New York Confidential WB (3)
Crashout F (4)
Tight Spot Col (5)
Kiss Me Deadly UA (5)
The Big Bluff UA (6)
Mr. Arkadin Alex (8)
The Phenix City Story UA (8)

The Naked Street UA (8)
The Night Holds Terror Col (9)
Female on the Beach U (9)
Illegal WB (10)
The Big Knife UA (11)
The Desperate Hours Par (11)
Killer's Kiss UA (11)
Queen Bee Col (11)
The Crooked Web Col (12)
Sudden Danger AA (12)

1956 (19)

Storm Fear UA (1)
The Killer Is Loose UA (2)
Please Murder Me DCA (3)
The Steel Jungle WB (3)
The Harder They Fall Col (4)
Timetable UA (4)
The Come-On AA (4)
Terror at Midnight Rep (4)
Nightmare UA (5)
The Price of Fear U (5)

While the City Sleeps RKO (5)
Shadow of Fear UA (6)
The Killing UA (7)
Beyond a Reasonable Doubt RKO
   (9)
A Cry in the Night WB (9)
Death of a Scoundrel RKO (10)
The Man Is Armed Rep (10)
Julie MGM (11)
The Wrong Man WB (12)

1957 (12)

Nightfall Col (1)
Crime of Passion UA (2)
The Night Runner U (2)
Shadow on the Window Col (3)
Footsteps in the Night AA (3)
The Garment Jungle Col (5)

The Burglar Col (6)
Sweet Smell of Success UA (6)
Valerie UA (8)
Short Cut to Hell Par (9)
Affair in Havana AA (10)
Plunder Road Fox (12)

1958 (7)

Screaming Mimi Col (4)
Cry Terror MGM (4)
Touch of Evil U (5)
The Lineup Col (6)

Appointment with a Shadow U (11)
I Want to Live UA (11)
Murder By Contract Col (12)

1959 (7)

The Last Mile UA (1)
City of Fear Col (2)
Step Down to Terror U (3)
Man in the Net UA (4)

Cry Tough UA (8)
The Crimson Kimono Col (10)
Odds Against Tomorrow UA (10)

Appendix C
Totals by Studio or Releasing Company

Alexander	1
Allied Artists (AA)	17
Astor (A)	1
Columbia (Col)	55
Distributors Corporation of America (DCA)	1
Eagle Lion (EL)	15
Film Classics (FC)	3
Filmakers (F)	2
Lippert (L)	1
Metro-Goldwyn-Mayer (MGM)	36
Monogram (Mon)	9
Paramount (Par)	33
Producers Releasing Corporation (PRC)	6
RKO	64
Republic (Rep)	17
Screen Guild (SG)	1
20th Century–Fox (Fox)	46
United Artists (UA)	76
Universal (U)	48
Warner Brothers (WB)	58

Appendix D
Directors' Filmographies

All films from the annotated filmography are listed by director (alphabetically) and then year (chronologically by release date).

Adreon, Franklin: *Terror at Midnight* (1956), *The Man Is Armed* (1956)

Aldrich, Robert: *World for Ransom* (1954), *Kiss Me Deadly* (1955), *The Big Knife* (1955), *The Garment Jungle* (1957, uncredited co-dir)

Allen, Lewis: *The Unseen* (1945), *So Evil My Love* (1948), *Chicago Deadline* (1949), *Appointment with Danger* (1951), *Suddenly* (1954), *Illegal* (1955)

Archainbaud, George: *Hunt the Man Down* (1950)

Arnold, Jack: *The Glass Web* (1953)

Asher, William: *Shadow on the Window* (1957)

Auer, John H.: *The Flame* (1947), *I, Jane Doe* (1948), *City That Never Sleeps* (1953), *Hell's Half Acre* (1954)

Baker, Roy Ward: *Don't Bother to Knock* (1952), *Night Without Sleep* (1952)

Bare, Richard: *Flaxy Martin* (1949), *This Side of the Law* (1950)

Beaudine, William: *Incident* (1948)

Benedek, Laslo: *Port of New York* (1949), *Affair in Havana* (1957)

Bennett, Charles: *No Escape* (1953)

Berke, William: *Shoot to Kill* (1947)

Bernhard, Jack: *Decoy* (1948), *The Hunted* (1948)

Bernhardt, Curtis: *Conflict* (1945), *Possessed* (1947), *The High Wall* (1947), *Sirocco* (1951)

Berry, John: *Tension* (1949), *He Ran All the Way* (1951)

Biberman, Abner: *The Price of Fear* (1956), *The Night Runner* (1957)

Birdwell, Russell: *The Come-On* (1956)

Boetticher, Bud: *Escape in the Fog* (1945), *Behind Locked Doors* (1948), *The Killer Is Loose* (1956)

Borzage, Frank: *Moonrise* (1948)

Bradley, David: *Talk About a Stranger* (1952)

Brahm, John: *The Lodger* (1944), *Guest in the House* (1944), *Hangover Square* (1945), *The Locket* (1946), *The Brasher Doubloon* (1947), *Singapore* (1947)

Bretherton, Howard: *Whispering Footsteps* (1943)

Cagney, James: *Short Cut to Hell* (1957)

Cahn, Edward L.: *Destination Murder* (1950)

Carlson, Richard: *Appointment with a Shadow* (1958)

Castle, William: *When Strangers Marry* (1944), *Johnny Stool Pigeon* (1949), *Undertow* (1949), *Hollywood Story* (1951)

Clurman, Harold: *Deadline at Dawn* (1946)

Conway, Jack: *Crossroads* (1942)

Cornfield, Hubert: *Sudden Danger* (1955), *Plunder Road* (1957)

Cromwell, John: *Dead Reckoning* (1947), *Caged* (1950), *The Racket* (1951)

Cukor, George: *A Woman's Face* (1941), *Gaslight* (1944), *A Double Life* (1948)

Curtiz, Michael: *Mildred Pierce* (1945), *The Unsuspected* (1947), *Flamingo Road* (1949), *The Breaking Point* (1950), *Man in the Net* (1959)

Daniels, Harold: *Roadblock* (1951)

Dassin, Jules: *Two Smart People* (1946), *Brute Force* (1947), *The Naked City* (1948), *Thieves' Highway* (1949), *Night and the City* (1950)

Daves, Delmer: *The Red House* (1947), *Dark Passage* (1947)

de Cordova, Frederick: *Her Kind of Man* (1946), *Illegal Entry* (1949)

Del Ruth, Roy: *Red Light* (1949)

de Toth, André: *Dark Waters* (1944), *The Pitfall* (1948, *Crime Wave* (1954)

Dieterle, William: *The Accused* (1949), *Rope of Sand* (1949), *Dark City* (1950), *The Turning Point* (1952)

Dmytryk, Edward: *Murder My Sweet* (1944), *Cornered* (1945), *Crossfire* (1947), *The Hidden Room* (1949), *The Sniper* (1952)

Doniger, Walter: *The Steel Jungle* (1956)

Douglas, Gordon: *Kiss Tomorrow Goodbye* (1950), *Between Midnight and Dawn* (1950), *I Was a Communist for the F.B.I.* (1951)

Dupont, E.A.: *The Scarf* (1951)

Endfield, Cy: *Underworld Story* (1950), *Try and Get Me* (1950)

Erskine, Chester: *Take One False Step* (1949)

Essex, Harry: *I, the Jury* (1953)

Farrow, John: *Calcutta* (1947), *The Big Clock* (1948), *The Night Has a Thousand Eyes* (1948), *Where Danger Lives* (1950), *His Kind of Woman* (1951)

Feist, Felix: *The Threat* (1949), *The Man Who Cheated Himself* (1951), *Tomorrow Is Another Day* (1951), *This Woman Is Dangerous* (1952)

Ferrer, Mel: *The Secret Fury* (1950)

Fleischer, Richard: *Bodyguard* (1948), *The Clay Pigeon* (1949), *Follow Me Quietly* (1949), *Trapped* (1949), *Armored Car Robbery* (1950), *The Narrow Margin* (1952)

Florey, Robert: *Danger Signal* (1945), *The Crooked Way* (1949)

Forde, Eugene: *Backlash* (1947)

Foster, Lewis: *Manhandled* (1949), *Crashout* (1955)

Foster, Norman: *Journey Into Fear* (1943, co-dir), *Kiss the Blood Off My Hands* (1948), *Woman on the Run* (1950)

Fregonese, Hugo: *One Way Street* (1950), *Man in the Attic* (1953), *Black Tuesday* (1954)

Friedman, Seymour: *Loan Shark* (1952)

Fuller, Sam: *Pickup on South Street* (1953), *The Crimson Kimono* (1959)

Gage, John: *The Velvet Touch* (1948)

Garnett, Tay: *The Postman Always Rings Twice* (1946), *Cause for Alarm* (1951)

Godfrey, Peter: *The Two Mrs. Carrolls* (1947), *Cry Wolf* (1947), *The Woman in White* (1948), *Please Murder Me* (1956)

Gordon, Michael: *The Web* (1947), *Woman in Hiding* (1949)

Gordon, Robert: *Blind Spot* (1947)

Goulding, Edmund: *Nightmare Alley* (1947)

Haas, Hugo: *Strange Fascination* (1952), *The Other Woman* (1954)

Haskin, Byron: *I Walk Alone* (1948), *Too Late for Tears* (1949)

Hathaway, Henry: *The House on 92nd Street* (1945), *The Dark Corner* (1946), *Kiss of Death* (1947), *Call Northside 777* (1948), *Fourteen Hours* (1951)

Hawks, Howard: *The Big Sleep* (1946)

Hecht, Ben: *Angels Over Broadway* (1940), *Specter of the Rose* (1946)

Heisler, Stuart: *Among the Living* (1941), *The Glass Key* (1942), *Storm Warning* (1950)

Hitchcock, Alfred: *Rebecca* (1940), *Suspicion* (1941), *Shadow of a Doubt* (1943), *Spellbound* (1945), *Notorious* (1946), *The Paradine Case* (1947), *Stage Fright* (1950), *Strangers on a Train* (1951), *I Confess* (1953), *The Wrong Man* (1956)

Hively, Jack: *Street of Chance* (1942)

Hopper, Jerry: *The Naked Alibi* (1954)

Horner, Harry: *Beware, My Lovely* (1952), *Vicki* (1953)

Humberstone, H. Bruce: *I Wake Up Screaming* (1941)

Huston, John: *The Maltese Falcon* (1941), *Key Largo* (1948), *The Asphalt Jungle* (1950)

Ingster, Boris: *Stranger on the Third Floor* (1940), *Southside 1-1000* (1950)

Jackson, Pat: *Shadow on the Wall* (1950)

Juran, Nathan: *Highway Dragnet* (1954), *The Crooked Web* (1955)
Kane, Joseph: *Hoodlum Empire* (1952)
Kardos, Leslie: *The Strip* (1951)
Karlson, Phil: *Scandal Sheet* (1952), *Kansas City Confidential* (1952), *99 River Street* (1953), *Tight Spot* (1955), *The Phenix City Story* (1955)
Kazan, Elia: *Boomerang* (1947), *Panic in the Streets* (1950)
Keighley, William: *The Street with No Name* (1948)
Keller, Harry: *Step Down to Terror* (1958)
Kern, James V.: *The Second Woman* (1951)
Koch, Howard W.: *Shield for Murder* (1954, co-dir), *The Last Mile* (1959)
Korda, Zoltan: *The Macomber Affair* (1947)
Kress, Harold F.: *No Questions Asked* (1951)
Kubrick, Stanley: *Killer's Kiss* (1955), *The Killing* (1956)
Landers, Lew: *The Mask of Diljon* (1946), *Man in the Dark* (1953)
Lang, Fritz: *Ministry of Fear* (1944), *The Woman in the Window* (1944), *Scarlet Street* (1945), *Secret Beyond the Door* (1948), *House by the River* (1950), *Clash by Night* (1952), *The Blue Gardenia* (1953), *The Big Heat* (1953), *Human Desire* (1954), *While the City Sleeps* (1956), *Beyond a Reasonable Doubt* (1956)
Larkin, John: *Circumstantial Evidence* (1945)
Laven, Arnold: *Without Warning* (1952)
LeBorg, Reginald: *Destiny* (1944, co-dir), *Fall Guy* (1947)
Lederman, D. Ross: *Key Witness* (1947)
Leisen, Mitchell: *No Man of Her Own* (1950)
Leonard, Robert Z.: *The Bribe* (1949)
Lerner, Irving: *Murder by Contract* (1958), *City of Fear* (1959)
Lerner, Joseph: *C-Man* (1949), *Guilty Bystander* (1950)
Levin, Henry *Night Editor* (1946), *Convicted* (1950), *Two of a Kind* (1951)
Lewis, Joseph H.: *My Name Is Julia Ross* (1945), *So Dark the Night* (1946), *The Undercover Man* (1949), *Gun Crazy* (1950), *A Lady Without Passport* (1950), *The Big Combo* (1955)
Litvak, Anatole: *Out of the Fog* (1941), *Blues in the Night* (1941), *The Long Night* (1947), *Sorry, Wrong Number* (1948)
Losey, Joseph: *The Lawless* (1950), *M* (1951), *The Prowler* (1951), *The Big Night* (1951), *Stranger on the Prowl* (1953), *The Sleeping Tiger* (1954)
Lubin, Arthur: *Impact* (1949)
Lupino, Ida: *The Hitch-Hiker* (1953)
McCarey, Ray: *Strange Triangle* (1946)
MacDougall, Ranald: *Queen Bee* (1955)
McEvoy, Earl: *The Killer That Stalked New York* (1950)

Machaty, Gustav: *Jealousy* (1945)

Mackendrick, Alexander: *Sweet Smell of Success* (1957)

Mankiewicz, Joseph L.: *Somewhere in the Night* (1946), *Escape* (1948) *House of Strangers* (1949), *No Way Out* (1950)

Mann, Anthony: *Strangers in the Night* (1944), *Two O'Clock Courage* (1945), *Strange Impersonation* (1946), *Desperate* (1947), *Railroaded* (1947), *T-Men* (1948), *Raw Deal* (1948), *He Walked by Night* (1948, uncredited co-dir), *Border Incident* (1949), *Side Street* (1950)

Marin, Edwin L.: *Johnny Angel* (1945), *Nocturne* (1946), *Race Street* (1948)

Markle, Fletcher: *Jigsaw* (1949)

Marshall, George: *The Blue Dahlia* (1946)

Martin, Charles: *Death of a Scoundrel* (1956)

Maté, Rudolph: *The Dark Past* (1948), D.O.A. (1950), *Union Station* (1950), *The Green Glove* (1952), *Forbidden* (1954)

Mayer, Gerald: *Dial 1119* (1950), *The Sellout* (1952)

Mayo, Archie: *Moontide* (1942, co-dir)

Milestone, Lewis: *The Strange Love of Martha Ivers* (1946)

Miller, David: *Sudden Fear* (1952), *Twist of Fate* (1954)

Minnelli, Vincente: *Undercurrent* (1946)

Moguy, Leonide: *Whistle Stop* (1946)

Montagne, Edward: *The Tattooed Stranger* (1950), *The Man with My Face* (1951)

Montgomery, Robert: *Lady in the Lake* (1947), *Ride the Pink Horse* (1947)

Negulesco, Jean: *The Mask of Dimitrios* (1944), *Three Strangers* (1946), *Nobody Lives Forever* (1946), *Humoresque* (1947), *Deep Valley* (1947), *Road House* (1948)

Neill, Roy William: *Black Angel* (1946)

Newman, Joseph M.: *Abandoned* (1949), *711 Ocean Drive* (1950), *Dangerous Crossing* (1953), *The Human Jungle* (1954)

Newton, Joel: *Jennifer* (1953)

Nigh, William: *I Wouldn't Be in Your Shoes* (1948)

Nosseck, Max: *The Hoodlum* (1951)

Oboler, Arch: *Bewitched* (1945), *The Arnelo Affair* (1947)

O'Brien, Edmond: *Shield for Murder* (1954, co-dir)

Ophuls, Max: *Caught* (1949), *The Reckless Moment* (1949)

Oswald, Gerd: *Crime of Passion* (1957), *Valerie* (1957), *Screaming Mimi* (1958)

Ozep, Fedor: *Whispering City* (1947)

Parrish, Robert: *Cry Danger* (1951), *The Mob* (1951)

Pevney, Joseph: *Shakedown* (1950), *Iron Man* (1951), *Playgirl* (1954), *Female on the Beach* (1955)

Pichel, Irving: *Temptation* (1946), *They Won't Believe Me* (1947), *Quicksand* (1950), *Without Honor* (1950)

Polonsky, Abraham: *Force of Evil* (1948)

Preminger, Otto: *Laura* (1944), *Fallen Angel* (1945), *Whirlpool* (1949), *Where the Sidewalk Ends* (1950), *The Thirteenth Letter* (1951), *Angel Face* (1953)

Price, Will: *Strange Bargain* (1949)

Quine, Richard: *Drive a Crooked Road* (1954), *Pushover* (1954)

Rapper, Irving: *Deception* (1946), *Another Man's Poison* (1952)

Ratoff, Gregory: *Moss Rose* (1947)

Ray, Nicholas: *A Woman's Secret* (1949), *Knock on Any Door* (1949), *They Live by Night* (1949), *In a Lonely Place* (1950), *Born to Be Bad* (1950), *On Dangerous Ground* (1951), *Macao* (1952, uncredited co-dir)

Reinhardt, John: *The Guilty* (1947), *High Tide* (1947), *For You I Die* (1948)

Reis, Irving: *Crack-Up* (1946), *All My Sons* (1948)

Renoir, Jean: *The Woman on the Beach* (1947)

Ripley, Arthur: *Voice in the Wind* (1944), *The Chase* (1946)

Robson, Mark: *The Seventh Victim* (1943), *Champion* (1949), *Edge of Doom* (1950), *The Harder They Fall* (1956)

Rogell, Albert S.: *Shadow of Fear* (1956)

Rossen, Robert: *Johnny O'Clock* (1947), *Body and Soul* (1947), *All the King's Men* (1949)

Rouse, Russell: *The Well* (1951), *The Thief* (1952), *Wicked Woman* (1954) *New York Confidential* (1955)

Rowland, Roy: *Scene of the Crime* (1949), *Witness to Murder* (1954), *Rogue Cop* (1954)

Santley, Joseph: *Shadow of a Woman* (1946)

Saville, Victor: *The Long Wait* (1954)

Schuster, Harold D.: *Loophole* (1954)

Seiler, Lewis: *Whiplash* (1948), *The System* (1953), *Women's Prison* (1955)

Seiter, William A.: *Make Haste to Live* (1954)

Sekely, Steve: *Hollow Triumph* (1948)

Shane, Maxwell: *Fear in the Night* (1947), *City Across the River* (1949), *The Glass Wall* (1953), *The Naked Street* (1955), *Nightmare* (1956)

Sherman, George: *Larceny* (1948), *The Sleeping City* (1950), *The Raging Tide* (1951)

Sherman, Vincent: *Nora Prentiss* (1947), *The Unfaithful* (1947), *Backfire* (1950), *The Damned Don't Cry* (1950), *Affair in Trinidad* (1952), *The Garment Jungle* (1957, co-dir)

Siegel, Don: *The Verdict* (1946), *Private Hell 36* (1954), *Riot in Cell Block 11* (1954), *The Lineup* (1958)

Siodmak, Robert: *Phantom Lady* (1944), *Christmas Holiday* (1944), *The Suspect* (1945), *The Strange Affair of Uncle Harry* (1945), *The Spiral Staircase* (1946), *The Killers* (1946), *The Dark Mirror* (1946), *Cry of the City* (1948), *Criss Cross* (1949), *The File on Thelma Jordon* (1949)

Sirk, Douglas: *Lured* (1947), *Sleep, My Love* (1948), *Shockproof* (1949)

Sloane, Paul H.: *The Sun Sets at Dawn* (1950)

Stanley, Paul: *Cry Tough* (1959)

Stevens, George: *A Place in the Sun* (1951)

Stevens, Mark: *Cry Vengeance* (1954), *Timetable* (1956)

Stevenson, Robert: *To the Ends of the Earth* (1948), *The Woman on Pier 13* (1949), *Walk Softly, Stranger* (1950)

Stone, Andrew L.: *Highway 301* (1950), *The Steel Trap* (1952), *A Blueprint for Murder* (1953), *The Night Holds Terror* (1955), *Julie* (1956), *Cry Terror* (1958)

Sturges, John: *Sign of the Ram* (1948), *The Capture* (1950), *Mystery Street* (1950), *The People Against O'Hara* (1951), *Jeopardy* (1953)

Tetzlaff, Ted: *The Window* (1949), *A Dangerous Profession* (1949), *Under the Gun* (1950), *Gambling House* (1951)

Thorpe, Richard: *The Black Hand* (1950), *The Unknown Man* (1951)

Tourneur, Jacques: *Experiment Perilous* (1944), *Out of the Past* (1947), *Nightfall* (1957)

Tuttle, Frank: *This Gun for Hire* (1942), *Suspense* (1946), *A Cry in the Night* (1956)

Ulmer, Edgar G.: *Bluebeard* (1944), *Strange Illusion* (1945), *Detour* (1945), *The Strange Woman* (1946), *Ruthless* (1948), *Murder Is My Beat* (1955)

Van Dyke, W.S.: *Rage in Heaven* (1941)

von Sternberg, Josef: *The Shanghai Gesture* (1941), *Macao* (1952, co-dir)

Vidor, Charles: *Ladies in Retirement* (1941), *Gilda* (1946)

Vidor, King: *Beyond the Forest* (1949), *Lightning Strikes Twice* (1951), *Ruby Gentry* (1952)

Vorhaus, Bernard: *Bury Me Dead* (1947)

Wallace, Richard: *The Fallen Sparrow* (1943), *Framed* (1947)

Walsh, Raoul: *They Drive by Night* (1940), *High Sierra* (1941), *The Man I Love* (1946), *White Heat* (1949), *The Enforcer* (1951, uncredited co-dir)

Webb, Robert D.: *The Spider* (1945)

Welles, Orson: *Journey Into Fear* (1943, uncredited co-dir), *The Stranger* (1946), *The Lady from Shanghai* (1947), *Mr. Arkadin* (1955), *Touch of Evil* (1958)

Wendkos, Paul: *The Burglar* (1957)

Werker, Alfred L.: *Shock* (1946), *He Walked by Night* (1948, co-dir)

Whorf, Richard: *Love from a Stranger* (1947)

Wilbur, Crane: *Canon City* (1948), *Outside the Wall* (1950)

Wilde, Cornel: *Storm Fear* (1956)

Wilder, Billy: *Double Indemnity* (1944), *Sunset Boulevard* (1950), *Ace in the Hole* (1951)

Wilder, W. Lee: *The Glass Alibi* (1946), *The Pretender* (1947), *Once a Thief* (1950), *Three Steps North* (1951), *The Big Bluff* (1955)

Wiles, Gordon: *The Gangster* (1947)

Windust, Bretaigne: *The Enforcer* (1951, co-dir)

Wise, Robert: *Born to Kill* (1947), *The Set-Up* (1949), *House on Telegraph Hill* (1951), *Captive City* (1952), *I Want to Live* (1958), *Odds Against Tomorrow* (1959)

Wood, Sam: *Ivy* (1947)

Wyler, William: *The Letter* (1940), *Detective Story* (1951), *The Desperate Hours* (1955)

Yarbrough, Jean: *Inside Job* (1946), *Shed No Tears* (1948), *Footsteps in the Night* (1957)

Zeisler, Alfred: *Fear* (1946), *Parole, Inc.* (1948)

Zinnemann, Fred: *Act of Violence* (1949)

Appendix E
Bibliography of Works Cited

Borde, Raymond, and Chaumeton, Etienne. *Panorama du Film Noir Americain.* Éditions du Minuit, 1955.

Durgnat, Raymond. "Paint It Black: The Family Tree of the Film Noir." *Cinema* (U.K.), August, 1970.

Higham, Charles, and Greenberg, Joel. *Hollywood in the Forties.* A.S. Barnes, 1968.

Hirsch, Foster. *The Dark Side of the Screen: Film Noir.* A.S. Barnes, 1981.

Kaplan, E. Ann, ed. *Women in Film Noir.* BFI, 1978.

Karimi, Amir Massourd. *Toward a Definition of the American Film Noir.* Arno Press, 1970.

Ottoson, Robert. *A Reference Guide to the American Film Noir: 1940–1958.* Scarecrow Press, 1981.

Place, J.A., and Peterson, L.S. "Some Visual Motifs of Film Noir." *Film Comment*, January, 1974.

Porfirio, Robert G. "No Way Out: Existential Motifs in the Film Noir." *Sight and Sound*, Autumn, 1976.

Schrader, Paul. "Notes on Film Noir." *Film Comment*, Spring, 1972.

Silver, Alain, and Ward, Elizabeth, eds. *Film Noir: An Encyclopedic Reference to the American Style.* Overlook Press, 1979.

Index to Part 1

(Citations are to pages 1-122)

Index to Filmography

(Citations are to entry numbers)

Calhoun, Rory 330
Calker, Darrell 19, 174, 254, 363
Call Northside 777 57
Callahan, George 331
Calleia, Joseph 91, 106, 150, 241, 438
Calvert, Phyllis 14
Calvet, Corinne 337
Camden, Joan 59
Cameron, Owen 278
Campaneez, Jacques 241
Campbell, Alan 485
Cane, Charles 105
Canon City 58
Capell, Paul 52
Captive City 59
The Capture 60
Cardwell, James 130, 161
Carey, Harry 9
Carey, MacDonald 230, 352
Carey, Phil 191, 319, 344, 356, 429
Carleton, Marjorie 93
Carlson, Richard 13, 20, 440
Carmichael, Hoagy 205
Carné, Marcel 237
Carney, Alan 315
Carnovsky, Morris 76, 105, 157, 345, 425
Carpenter, Margaret 126
Carr, John Dickson 97
Carradine, John 39, 54, 128
Carroll, John 134, 186
Carroll, Leo G. 178, 301, 374, 379, 400, 411
Carson, Jack 41, 257
Carson, Kit 356
Carter, Ellis 181
Carter, Janis 143, 275, 483
Caruso, Anthony 197
Case, Kathleen 180
Caspary, Vera 38
Cassell, Wally 70, 73, 155, 169
Cassevetes, John 5, 277
Castelnuovo-Tedesco, Mario 238
Castle, Don 155, 166, 192
Castle, Peggie 187, 238, 283
Castle, William 173, 207, 450, 465
Caught 61
Caulfield, Joan 227
Cause for Alarm 62
Cavanagh, Paul 182, 346
Celli, Teresa 34
The Chair for Martin Rome (novel) 89
Challee, William 111
Chamberlain, George Agnew 330
Chamberlain, Howland 141
Chambers, Whitman 73, 254, 353
Champion 63
Chandler, George 392
Chandler, Jeff 1, 132, 199

Chandler, Raymond 32, 37, 48, 225, 266, 400, 455
Chaney, Lon, Jr. 294
Chanslor, Roy 33, 114
Charisse, Cyd 419
Charles, Zachary 144
Charney, Jack 311
Charteris, Leslie 446
The Chase 64
Chase, Borden 199
Chavance, Louis 426
Cheirel, Micheline 76, 373
Chekhov, Michael 378, 379
Chester, Hal E. 78
Chicago Deadline 65
La Chienne 342
Children of the Dark (novel) 91
Chodorov, Edward 334
Christians, Mady 7
Christie, Agatha 240
Christine, Virginia 281
Christmas Holiday 66
Ciannelli, Eduardo 256, 303
Circumstantial Evidence 67
Citizen Kane 339
City Across the River 68
City of Fear 69
City on a Hunt see No Escape
City That Never Sleeps 70
Clark, Alan R. 167
Clark, Dane 18, 110, 163, 251, 261, 469, 477
Clark, Fred 89, 173, 332, 408
Clarke, Charles 262, 406
Clash by Night 71
The Clay Pigeon 72
Clements, Stanley 58, 113
Clift, Montgomery 185, 308
Clothier, William 139, 294
Clouzot, Henri 426
Clurman, Harold 106
Cobb, Lee J. 44, 57, 103, 146, 206, 252, 368, 425
Coburn, Charles 195, 238, 241, 301
"Cocaine" (story) 127
Cochran, Steve 64, 95, 169, 317, 387, 436, 474
Cockrell, Frank 104
Cockrell, Marion 104
Codee, Ann 373
Coffee, Lenore 25, 232, 405
A Coffin for Dimitrios (novel) 256
Cohn, Art 194, 349, 436
Colbert, Claudette 347, 369
Cole, Lester 9, 167
Cole, Royal 302
Collier, Constance 470
Collier, John 108